the unheard

the unheard

a memoir of
deafness and africa

JOSH SWILLER

A HOLT PAPERBACK

HENRY HOLT AND COMPANY ■ NEW YORK

Holt Paperbacks
Henry Holt and Company, LLC
Publishers since 1866
175 Fifth Avenue
New York, New York 10010
www.henryholt.com

A Holt Paperback® and ® are registered trademarks of
Henry Holt and Company, LLC.

Library of Congress Cataloging-in-Publication Data

Swiller, Josh.
    The unheard : a memoir of deafness and Africa / Josh Swiller.
        p.   cm.
    "A Holt paperback."
    ISBN-13: 978-0-8050-8210-4
    ISBN-10: 0-8050-8210-7
    1. Swiller, Josh.   2. Americans—Zambia—Biography.   3. Peace Corps
(U.S.)—Biography.   4. Zambia—Description and travel.   5. Zambia—
Social conditions—21st century.   6. Deaf—Biography.   I. Title.
    CT275.S98725A3   2007
    968.94'042—dc22   2007012047

Henry Holt books are available for special promotions and
premiums. For details contact: Director, Special Markets.

First Holt Paperbacks Edition 2007

Designed by Kelly Too

Printed in the United States of America
1 2 3 4 5 6 7 8 9 10

For Augustine Jere

Before there can be a utopia in the world, there must be a utopia in every human heart.

—ANANDA MOYI MA

note to the reader

Every event depicted within this book took place, though some events were reordered for narrative clarity. Most of the details come from the extensive journals and photographic records I kept while in Africa. The names and physical characteristics of some characters have been changed.

Martin Meredith's *The Fate of Africa* provided much of the historical details, along with the quote from Frederick Chiluba. The works of the late Ryszard Kapuscinski were also a source of information.

A note on pronunciation: In Bemba, all syllables start on the consonant and end on the vowel. All vowels are long. Thus, Mununga is pronounced Moo-noo-nga and Chiluba is Chee-loo-ba (I is pronounced ee).

the unheard

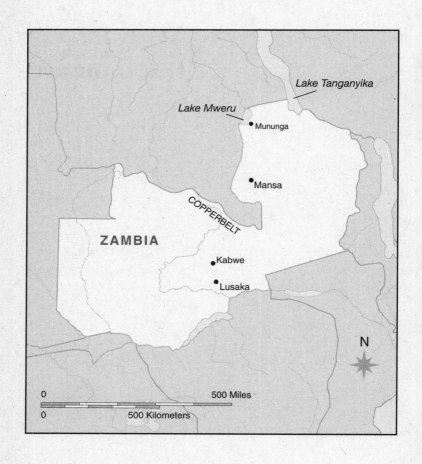

Prologue

We were sitting on Jere's living room floor in the dark, clutching our handmade weapons—two-by-fours with five-inch nails driven all the way through them, so that the business end of the nails emerged like fangs from the mouth of a poisonous snake. Whenever I shifted my grip, splinters from the rough, unfinished surface of the wood jabbed into my palm. It was almost ten o'clock, late for Mununga—late for any village deep in the Zambian bush. By this time on any other night, the village would have been asleep for hours. But not tonight.

Jere and I sat beneath the window, our legs touching. A half-gallon plastic jug of banana wine rested between his knees when we weren't drinking from it. The floor was smooth cool cement, covered in the middle by a single bamboo mat. Ordinarily, a couch made of varnished lumber and cheap scratchy foam surrounded the mat, but we'd stacked that up against the door, behind a tall dresser made from *mpanga* boards stained the color of dried blood.

"This way," said Jere, my friend, the best friend I'd ever had, "if they try to come in through the door, the furniture will stall them, and if they try to come in through the window, we'll hit them with these."

He rubbed his weapon against the floor as he spoke, trying to show confidence. But I could feel his fear. It had a smell to it, sour and rich. As for myself, I wondered what it would be like to hit someone with a club studded with nails. Would I hear his screams? Would the club get stuck if I swung too hard? I imagined wrestling the nails out of ragged, bloody flesh. I wondered how it would feel to be beaten to death, to grasp that things broken wouldn't be fixed. It seemed like it would hurt.

I was terrified; I was exhausted; but I had also reached a state where terror and exhaustion were subsumed by survival and life became the immediate moment and nothing else. Weapon. Wine. Door. The bruise on my face. My heartbeat—this was all my mind could focus on.

I had become way too familiar with this state.

Thing is: beyond the furniture, on the other side of that door, was a mob. The mob wanted to kill Jere and me. We knew this because they had said, "We're going to kill you."

This is what almost two years of Peace Corps service had come to.

Jere picked up his makeshift weapon, a rake for his maize fields in a previous incarnation, and swung it a few times.

"You were brave stepping in the middle of the argument," he said. "Boniface and his men were quite drunk. I've never seen him like that."

"I had my hearing aids off," I admitted. "Didn't hear him. Didn't hear anything."

"Ai, I always forget about those things."

Someone smashed loudly into the door, knocking the dresser back an inch. We jumped up.

"They're on now," I said. "I heard that."

Jere nervously eyed the door, then spoke. "I hate this place."

An hour earlier Jere had been in a shouting match, the culmination of six months of escalating enmity, with a village elder named Boniface. Shouting matches were rare in Mununga, where keeping face and allowing others to do the same was integral to the culture. A crowd flocked to the health clinic where we worked to observe the argument, the two men, one tall and well built, one short and pear-shaped, screaming and waving their hands at each other. When I tried to break it up, Boniface, the tall man, stormed out. He returned ten minutes later with a group of drunk men, threw open the door to Jere's office, pointed at Jere, and yelled— and I couldn't understand him because of the background noise and the language barrier, so I'm paraphrasing here—"I'm going to reach down your throat and rip out your fucking soul." Jere, the Mununga Rural Health Catchment Area's senior clinic officer and the bravest, wisest man I knew, cowered behind his desk. We had seen what drunken mobs could do in this town; it wasn't pretty. The last mob had left a half-mile-long bloodstain in the road.

I turned my hearing aids off, and stepped forward, smack between the two adversaries and tried to calm Boniface down. That's when I was hit in the face with a rock.

"Does your jaw hurt?" Jere asked.

"No," I said.

It hurt.

We pushed the door closed, jammed a half section of the couch underneath the doorknob, shoved the dresser behind that. Then we picked up our weapons again. I took a swallow from the jug of wine. There were more loud noises from outside.

"Is that them?" I asked Jere.

"That's the river."

"Are you sure? That sounded like shouts."

"It's the river," he repeated.

I wasn't convinced. I grabbed his forearm. "I'm not good with sounds from far away, Jere. I've explained this to you."

"Yes, I know."

I looked him in the eye. The loud noise outside continued. "Is that really the river?"

"No."

I'm deaf—that's why I couldn't make out the source of the noise. The hearing aids in my ears amplified sounds several thousand times but from behind a closed door it was still impossible to tell the difference between the rustle of a river and the shouts of a mob. If the fat lady was out there on the dirt lawn sharpening a machete and singing for the two of us, I couldn't tell. Deafness made our precarious situation more precarious. But deafness was the reason I was here in Mununga in the first place, and it was the reason I'd come to love this place and call it home.

Jere and I stood tensed by the door. I bent to look through the keyhole, then jerked back with the thought that someone could jam a stick through the hole into my eye. Ten minutes passed.

"It's late," said Jere. He took out his handkerchief and wiped his forehead, which was plastered with sweat. "It's very late. We've been here hours. I think they must have gone."

"I don't think so," I replied.

"No, I think it was just a drunken boast. I don't think Boniface would really kill us."

"Well, this is Mununga. It is Boniface. You saw what they did on Christmas."

"That's true," Jere agreed. "But I really think they've gone."

"You sure? Listen closely."

"Yes, I'm sure," he said, and as he spoke a rock shattered through the window, showering us with glass. It clattered across the room, disappeared in a dark corner. The smells of wood smoke, perspiration, and alcohol poured through the broken window in a sudden rush that made it hard to breathe. The noise from outside, unobstructed, grew louder—at least now I could be sure it wasn't the river.

Pressing my back flat against the wall, I curled my hand tightly around my weapon. Another rock came through the window, flying neatly through the hole the first one had made, cracking against the far wall.

"They're throwing rocks!" Jere hissed.

"Really?"

We drew back, watched the door, and waited.

part
one

Akashi ushilala, bakakumbwa insonshi ne mitenge.

The village in which you do not sleep is admired for its roofing.

First Day

A month after arriving in Zambia, about halfway through my Peace Corps training, I visited Mununga for the first time. I traveled north for two days from the city of Kabwe, the training site, to where the pavement ended at a lake town called Kashikishi; there, I caught a pickup that made its way up a dirt road, wracked and cratered like it had been cleared by dinosaurs. Villages, forests, marshes, and more villages passed by, giving way to glimpses of Lake Mweru, a giant kidney bean of water stretching to the western horizon. After three hours of this, at the crest of a large hill, a thick log rested in the road—a military checkpoint. A couple of soldiers got up from beneath a mango tree, collected a toll from the driver, and kicked the log out of the way. The road descended into the broad Mununga River valley, crossed a one-lane bridge, and suddenly we came upon the town. There was nothing to prepare you for it: after forty miles of scattered villages and blasted road, the valley was full of activity.

A market spread out in all directions from the bus stop. It thronged with merchants, fish sellers, dealers of various sundries and vegetables, and toutboys—rambunctious, ropy-muscled young toughs who bullied travelers on and off of vehicles for tips. People were everywhere, walking, running, laughing, flirting, staggering, hauling packages on their heads, toting fish, birds, children. Children played kung fu tag. Teenage cigarette vendors sat in the sun without a drop of shade and sold one cig and one match at a time. Goats scavenged as men drove them along with sticks. When I hopped off the truck, all the commotion instantly stopped. A thousand pairs of eyes simultaneously turned and stared.

"Remember," Administration had said to us Peace Corps volunteers as we prepared for this inaugural visit to our villages, "most of these people, the vast majority, have never seen a non-Zambian before. Many have never even met someone from another tribe. You're going to be the first look they'll have at an American. You're going to be ambassadors. You're going to influence how a lot of people see the United States and the world."

Cool, an ambassador. On the trip north, I had daydreams of heroic rescues and grateful young maidens. Donning a black cowboy hat, I would oversee Great Works of Development while learning Great Lessons about Humanity. "We are all one people," I would write back home, "black or white, hearing or deaf. One family." But the looks on the faces in the vast market crowd read less like gratefulness and camaraderie and more like abject shock; it was like a pterodactyl had just landed in their midst and they were trying to decide whether to back away slowly or run like mad.

I stood in the road for fifteen minutes. Then I caught the next pickup out of town.

A MONTH AFTER THAT I CAME BACK TO MUNUNGA FOR GOOD. Administration dropped me off in front of a blue and yellow shack with my clothes, a new mattress, a two-year supply of hearing aid batteries, and a loaf of fresh bread. Instantly, like they had been waiting all week just for my arrival, dozens of children ran to watch me unload. It was a beautiful day, the sky a gauzy, cloudless blue.

"This is it," Administration said to me, peering at the kids and shack from behind the steering wheel of his Land Cruiser.

"Now, promise me you'll watch out for river snails. They live in freshwater, even clean-looking water like this river. You can't see their larvae and once they get in your skin, they burrow through your bladder and then you pee blood for the rest of your life."

"Ok. I'll look out for them," I said.

"Schistosomiasis."

"Shit so what?"

"Schistosomiasis. That's what the snail is called. The one that messes up your bladder."

"So don't go in the river?"

"No, I'm not saying that," Administration said, holding up his hands in a gesture of innocence. "I'm not allowed to tell you what to do. This is a free country. You might not get it."

On an earlier expedition, Administration had chosen Mununga as a site for a volunteer solely because of the river—it was that beautiful. In retrospect, he probably could have done more research. He was from Cincinnati and didn't know any of the history of the area, didn't know about its reputation for violence, didn't know that urban Zambians, even the ones embracing the global economy and technological age head-on, feared Mununga. "Oooh, Mr. Joshua," the city folk had said when I had told them during training about my placement. "You are brave to go there."

"Why is it brave?" I asked them, but they shook their heads in that floppy, figure-eight way that could mean anything, and wouldn't say.

After Administration drove off I faced the village children. They stared at me from a safe distance. We watched each other like that for a good five minutes before I broke the ice by chucking pebbles at them. They laughed and threw them back. A long, tin-roofed building, easily the biggest building as far as I could see, was built into the hill behind them, so with nothing better to do, after making friends I put my bags away and headed over for a look around. The boys trailed along. The first room I looked into was a small office with a large desk in the middle. The walls were white, faded, with cobwebs shading the corners. A chubby round-faced man who looked to be in his early thirties sat in a shaft of sunlight, gazing at a chessboard on the desk. He held a beer in his right hand, a handkerchief in his left, wore a wrinkle-free T-shirt that read BOB's STORES. With the handkerchief hand, he jabbed the air over the board, perhaps planning his next move.

He jumped up when I stuck my head in. "Hey! You are the white man who will dig us wells," he exclaimed.

"Yes," I said. "How'd you guess?"

He laughed, throwing back his head. Then just as suddenly he turned serious. "But you are alone? They only sent one?"

"Only one."

"Why only one? Mununga needs more than one."

I didn't know how to answer that. I introduced myself. He told me his name, Augustine Jere and that he was the clinic officer, and shook my hand in both of his.

I motioned to the board. "Who are you playing?"

"I'm playing with myself," Jere said. "Do you play?"

"No. But I could learn to."

He nodded, wiped his face with his handkerchief. It was an open face with thoughtful eyes, a swollen nose, and a ready smile— a trustworthy face. "You could," he said. "White men are very smart."

"No more than anyone else."

"But you invented penicillin. And automobiles. And airplanes."

"Well, don't forget nuclear weapons. And acid rain. And Pet Rocks."

He gave a thumbs-up. "Yes. Those, too. Very impressive. Maybe that's why they only send one. Yes, I think one is enough. Even for Mununga."

Enough for what, I wondered, but before I could ask, Jere leaned over the side of the desk and took two beers out of a small cooler, handing me one, gesturing for me to sit down. The cooler was for vaccinations, he said with a nod, but as they were out of those and had been out for a week, might as well use it to keep the beer cold. It has always been my way to plunge into new situations headfirst, and after a little more small talk, I started telling Jere about wells. As he had declared, wells were what I was there for, but, I explained, when they were dug, it wouldn't be by me— the villagers would do the digging and the villagers would be in charge of everything. That was the Peace Corps' philosophy— they called it sustainable development.

Jere wasn't very impressed. "Can't you just drill a borehole?" he asked. "Those take two, three days. And they go very deep."

"We could," I said, "but no one learns anything when you dig a borehole. A truck comes, drills, leaves. What is the community going to do if the borehole breaks? Or if they need another well? Wait around for another volunteer to show up? No, the goal is to teach the community how to take care of itself."

This all sounded good and was based on decades of trial and error, but I had little idea how to go about putting it into practice. I did get some well construction experience during training, but that was just a single day digging a hole in a dirt field and mixing cement in a wheelbarrow. Then, to learn the community organization skills we'd need, the other volunteers and I practiced splitting up hypothetical jobs while eating vanilla wafers. *You dig. I'll mix. He'll cook lunch.* What that had to do with organizing communities wasn't really clear to any of us. But I didn't know the depths of my ignorance yet, and could never have imagined the consequences of going in blind. Community empowerment, sustainability, and personal responsibility—that, I told Mr. Jere, was all we needed to dig the wells.

"Sounds good," he said with a smile, but I wasn't sure if he believed it. He seemed eager to get off the subject.

We finished our beers, put back another round, then Jere called out and a skinny boy with an overbite appeared, took some kwacha—the Zambian currency—and ran off to get more. We drank those as well. Evening came and filled the sky with such reds and oranges it was like the valley had been slipped inside a sliced papaya. The smells of the day—sweat, cocoa butter, kerosene, and fish lying in the sun—were swept away by the evening breeze. I was getting buzzed.

"Let me show you the clinic," Jere said. He stood up and whacked his kneecap on the desk. He groaned. "That hurt."

Jere's office, another office, three treatment rooms, and a storeroom opened off the clinic's long outdoor hallway. A couple of yards away were two ramshackle buildings: one was a ward for infectious diseases and one was for AIDS. A film of dust coated every floor of the facility despite the efforts of a cheerful elderly volunteer, bent over and sweeping with a handful of reeds. Jere introduced me to Mr. Mulwanda, the inpatient clinician, a bald and sleepy man in his forties who spoke very slowly. Whenever Mulwanda smiled, frowned, thought, or talked, his eyes crinkled up and disappeared.

There were four things I remember most clearly about that first tour of the clinic. First: the pregnant women who lay on the hallway floor waiting for their water to break. Clutching sleeping infants and beset by flies, they timidly shrank away as we approached. They were children, most of these mothers, much younger than I was (I was twenty-three), but they seemed already worn down by their lives.

The second thing: a poster on a door highlighting a newspaper article that claimed AIDS originated from top-secret malaria tests carried out by the United States in the early eighties in Haiti, East Africa, and North America's homosexual population.

"You don't really believe that, do you?" I asked Jere.

"Of course I do," he responded. "Everyone knows about this."

Third thing: the bats. They nested on the ceiling beams of every room, dark gray blobs like dead lanterns covered with hair.

"Should those be there?" I asked.

"Yes, they eat mosquitoes," Jere said.

"But what about rabies?"

"Oh, that's always fatal."

The fourth thing: Jere and I exited the last treatment room to find a barrel-chested man in his mid-fifties standing in the hallway, his chin tilted so high in the air that at first I thought he was a patient with a sprained neck. This was Boniface.

"Ba Jere," he said, in a remarkably loud and deep voice.

"Mr. Boniface," Jere replied, eyes lowered, at once deferential. "This is our Peace Corps volunteer, Mr. Josh. He has finally arrived."

"Welcome," Boniface said to me, in English.

"Pleased to meet you," I said.

He stared at me from over his wide cheekbones. "You are from America. Come with me." And before I knew what was happening, this Mr. Boniface was leading me by the hand down the stairs and down the hill toward the river, around huts and banana groves, past scores of startled villagers—quite a few of whom ran into their huts when they saw me—to a large hut distinguished by a rusty sheet-metal roof; every other hut we passed had a thatch roof made of straw and mud.

Boniface opened the door, motioned for me to enter, sat me on a chair, and a young woman brought a glass of water that tasted like sand. It was dark; when my eyes adjusted, I saw that the room was large and well furnished—chairs, bamboo mats, a couch, a table, and three young faces peering at me from behind a doorway. Boniface took a seat, sped through—in English—a long list of greetings and salutations and blessings on our health and ancestors, and then told me, again in English, without prompting or pause, the story of his life.

He was born in Mununga way back before there was even a bridge over the river and you had to cross by canoe, or, in the dry season, by hopping from rock to rock. Then he had gone to school in Lusaka, learned English, served in the army, swung a pickax in a copper mine. Twenty years later he had returned to the village with only his clothes and his smarts and now he owned two shops at the market, both with tin roofs, and had three wives.

I missed a lot of what he said and was stunned by the speed of this introduction, but I grew excited as it dawned on me that I'd fulfilled one of the Peace Corps' basic goals. "Find the village leaders," they had instructed us in community development class—and here I'd found one, no looking.

"Congratulations on your successes, Mr. Boniface," I said when he finished his story. He had talked for forty-five minutes straight, his chin pointed at the top of my head the entire time like the bow of an aircraft carrier.

"Thank you," he replied. "Now tell me, you have come to my village to dig wells?"

"Yes, exactly. To dig wells."

He nodded. "Mr. Joshua, there is no chief in our village. Our chief died and we are waiting for our next chief. With no chief the people look to me for leadership. I give them leadership. The people listen to me and do what I tell them. If I tell them to work, they work. If I tell them to dig, they dig. If I tell them not to dig, they do not dig. So, what do you want me to tell them?"

Was this a trick question? "To dig?" I asked.

"No. It is not so simple. You will be digging very deep for water right? You won't be working alone?"

"No," I said.

"Yes." He smiled as if he had just settled an obvious point.

"Yes?"

"No."

"What?" I wasn't fazed; I often had conversations like this. It was a common effect of trying to follow rapid speech with lipreading and hearing aids. Basically, with aids you're constantly translating every line of language into itself—a concept that always makes me think of the interpreters in glass-walled and soundproofed rooms at the UN, the long rows of them with their dark suits and earpieces. What power these interpreters have! They could start a war with a few words here and there. But what if they miss a phrase? Maybe they just pretend they heard and make something up. That's what I usually did.

Boniface leaned forward, gazing intensely in my eyes. "Mr. Joshua, you need workers, good workers. I have them. I think you and I are vital to each other. So if I organize your workers, what will you do for me? How will we work together?" He sat back, letting his words sink in. When I didn't say anything he added, "Everyone knows white men have money and my roof is old, my wife is sick, and my children are hungry. We can work together."

I realized then what he wanted, and felt foolish for not catching on earlier. Boniface just gave off that vibe like he had an agenda and he'd already figured out your place in it.

"Mr. Boniface, I can't do anything for you except bring you clean water," I said. "That's how community development works. There's no money involved. But clean water's important. It will save many lives. People will work for free."

"Are you sure?"

"No. Yes. What are you asking me for?"

"An agreement."

"An agreement?" I repeated, and then I went further—too far. I often did; I couldn't help myself—especially when dealing with someone who had, knowingly or not, taken advantage of my inability to hear. "You mean like a bribe? You want a bribe. I can't believe it."

"No, I do not."

He looked uncomfortable. I couldn't stop myself.

"Yes, you do. Unbelievable. I just got here."

Boniface stood up from his chair and walked toward the door. "It was nice to meet you, Mr. Joshua," he said. "I think you should leave."

JERE HAD INVITED ME OVER FOR DINNER THAT EVENING, FOR WHICH·
I was deeply grateful because I had no idea where to eat and I was
drained from an entire day of being a space alien, all the villagers
staring and pointing, freezing to the spot or scrambling off the
path when I passed. Jere never did that. He treated me warmly
from the first moment and made no assumptions.

Now it was night and we were sitting in his *insaka*, a kind of
thatch gazebo. The only light came from a kerosene lantern and
the distant stars. While his wife cleared up the bowls from the
meal Jere produced a bottle of banana wine, and I peppered him
with questions.

"Who is Boniface?" I asked.

"He's a very powerful man," Jere said.

"Like a chief?" I offered. "He kept saying that."

"Not exactly." He swallowed a glass of wine. "When you were
at his house you didn't say anything that might upset him, did
you?" he asked.

"No," I lied. "Of course not."

"Good."

"I wouldn't do that."

"Good."

"But supposing I did, why would it matter?"

Jere looked around to make sure we were alone. He was, I
learned later, from a different tribe, the Nyanja, who lived mainly
in southeastern Zambia. Mununga, up near Zaire, was Bemba
tribe. Because this wasn't Jere's home area, he had to be careful
with what he said.

Then he told me a story that chilled my bones, one that in my
nineteen months in the village was never far from my mind. The
most powerful *ndoshi*—witch doctors—in the entire country lived
in Mununga, he said. Shopkeepers traveled here from as far away
as Zimbabwe, a three-day bus journey each way, to obtain an

infallible talisman for the success of their stores. They came because—and here Jere chuckled uncomfortably—the talisman they needed was the dried heart of a teenage boy.

"A dried heart?" I interrupted. "No way."

It was true, Jere insisted. Mununga ndoshi had the ability to reach right into a chest and pull out business success, still beating. The heart-deprived teenagers were buried or abandoned out in the bush. The ndoshi dried the hearts in the sun with special herbs found in the forests and the businessmen took them back to the cities and placed them in altars above the front entrances to their stores, where, supposedly, they attracted customers like tropical ulcers attract flies.

It was a striking story and yet I couldn't tell if I was supposed to believe it or not. It sounded too much like Indiana Jones.

"Things like that, Ba Josh," Jere continued, "is why they call this place Gomorrah. That's why you have to be careful with what you say."

I didn't hear him right. "This place is going to rah?"

"It's Gomorrah."

"Gomorrah?"

"You don't like Gomorrah? Fine, it's Sodom."

I felt like I was still missing something. "So wait, you're saying Boniface is ndoshi? He's going to freeze-dry my heart if I hurt his feelings?"

Jere shook his head. "I'm pretty sure witchcraft doesn't work on white people. I just want you to be aware."

"Of what? Aware of what? He seemed kind of like a jerk, to be honest."

"He can make things difficult. He can stop people from helping you."

I thought about this. Those early days in the village I wanted to get as much done as possible, save as many lives as I could and make a difference and heal the world and so on, so I mostly had wells on my mind; and also, beyond bringing help to others, I was focused on a personal quest to find some help of my own. So I didn't really consider that Jere meant my own life could be in danger. But maybe he didn't either.

"So how do I get people to dig?" I asked.

Jere closed his eyes for a minute, rubbed his stomach.

"Carefully," he said.

Deaf Not Deaf

I'd come to the village to find a place past deafness. I know that seems strange to say, I mean, do you eat burritos to find out what chocolate tastes like? Maybe you do if you've reached the end of your options, and I'd already looked everywhere else.

That first day in Mununga, Jere was the only person to ask me about my hearing aids and when I told him what they were, he responded with total disbelief. No one else in the village had noticed them or, if they had, they hadn't said anything. Maybe they thought the aids were large earrings all white guys wore.

"Are those radios?" Jere had asked, pointing.

"Not radios. I'm deaf," I answered.

He laughed. "You're deaf? Come on, you're not deaf."

I could see how he might think that. We'd talked for hours, in quiet surroundings with little background noise and I'd been able to catch almost all of what he said and guess the rest. Jere spoke in a loud and clear voice and that was the key. In the States, I had pursued relationships with women for their speaking voices alone. Clear speech beat a pretty face any day in my book. In quiet places, with a loud talker and my aids, I could actually hear close to 80 percent—well enough that people didn't believe I was deaf.

"Check this out," I said to Jere and took off an aid, wiped it with a shirttail, and put it in his ear. When I turned it on, his eyes shot open and he jerked his head away. The aid fell on his desk and bounced. They were pretty hardy. Jere looked at me, rubbed the side of his face, looked at the hearing aid now beeping like mad. Smiling back at his stunned expression, I waited for his questions, mentally preparing the speech I had written for just such an occasion: *These are hearing aids. They take all the sounds of the world and turn them up louder. I can't hear without them, not a thing. You will need to talk loudly and face me when you talk, and I'll still miss some things, but I'll make up for it.*

Instead Jere said, "You ever read *The Odessa File*?"

"What?" I replied, startled.

"I have it at home. It's a great book. About the CIA. I will get it for you."

He left the room. I put the aid back on and considered that this might be the place I'd been looking for.

I got my first hearing aids when I was four years old. To that point, I was slow to pick up language, slow to show an interest in the world at large. I wasn't very social or curious. I mostly sat under a table in the front room of my family's big apartment on Manhattan's Upper West Side and stared at the corner.

"That boy is slow," my grandfather decided.

Underneath the table were shadows and dead spiders, the ridges where baseboards fit together, the pattern of the wood floor, cities of floating dust. It had not yet occurred to me that the silence of things was an absence. Then my mother figured out I couldn't hear. There was no exact moment of recognition—it was more of a slow dawning. She took me to pediatrician after pediatrician, all of whom told her she was being neurotic and that I was just a delayed learner. Finally, one tested my hearing, and said, "Well, what do you know." We went downtown to the League of Hard of Hearing and I got fitted with hearing aids and was born for a second time, into a noisy new world that expected things from me.

"I knew it the whole time," my grandfather said when we got home.

What the world now expected of me was no small thing. With hearing aids, I was supposed to hear. Briefly, my parents considered forgoing aids and sending me to a school for the deaf, but back in the mid-seventies, schools for the deaf were notoriously poor at teaching their students the English they needed to live independently in the hearing world. Rejecting that route, my mother instead found an audiologist on the Upper East Side, Adele Markwitz, who immediately set out a regimen to maximize my hearing. Adele had developed an intense and unconventional program for training hearing-impaired children. She did not believe in limits, excuses, or self-pity. I would wear hearing aids every waking moment, she decreed, attend regular schools, and three or four afternoons a week I would come to her office to learn how to lipread and to speak.

At home, my mother supplemented Adele's lessons with constant practice while my dad, a psychiatrist, was away at the hospital. Ma was a gifted painter who had dreams of pursuing her art, but with the birth of four sons in six years, two of them deaf, she gave up those dreams so we could pursue ours. Later, my youngest brother, Sam, who was born with less hearing than me (but I lost the rest of mine by the time I was four or five so we were pretty much even), would work with Adele as well. Sign language wasn't part of our educational program, nor was learning about the deaf community. Sam, born four years after me, and my cousin Ben, born four years after him, were the only deaf people I knew until after I finished college.

Learning to function in the hearing world was hard work. Lipreading was the key to understanding the speech of others; after much practice I learned to recognize the difference in the shape of a mouth saying "please" and "thank you"; saying "peas" as opposed to "cheese." I became quite good at it and could lipread from all sorts of angles: "The peas please, please pass the peas"— sure, no problem. Learning language this way made for an eclectic vocabulary—while only 20 percent of English syllables are recognizable on the lips, nearly 100 percent of all televised basketball coach profanities are. I learned many interesting words from Bobby Knight.

Lipreading was the warm-up; the real focus of my sessions with Adele was on improving my speech. Day after day, week after week, year after year, Sam and I labored to enunciate everyday words by reading from Babar, the Berenstain Bears, and Dr. Seuss. S's were particularly difficult for me to say correctly—"The Grinch sssstole Christmasss"—I whistled them, hissing like a snake. S is the highest-pitched sound in English and even with my hearing aids turned up full blast, I couldn't hear it, and it is difficult to say a sound you can't hear.

Which points to one of the intractable problems I faced: hearing aids helped a great deal—they were invaluable actually—but they were as sensitive as two microphones shoved into my ears.

Flesh-colored, comma-shaped, aids wrap around the back of the ear then connect via a little plastic tube to a mold that fits snugly in the ear canal. Sound enters the aids, is amplified and sent into the tube, through the mold, and into the ear past the eardrum. A little way past the eardrum are cochlea, seashell-shaped tubes the circumference of quarters, in which fifteen thousand tiny hair cells wave and shudder with the incoming sound. These waving motions are conveyed via the hearing nerve to the brain, which then interprets them as downshifting trucks or growling dogs, clattering dishes or beeping timers, or often, if the sound came through hearing aids, just loud white noise. Hearing aids amplify every single sound they encounter, including the ones you'd rather they didn't—your own voice, the vacuum cleaner, the bus brakes and baby cries, your mother calling you to do chores.

All that noise is difficult to decipher, so hearing is not quite the right word for what hearing aids bring forth. Amplified 90 decibels, voices aren't saying words so much as the idea of words. With lipreading and guesswork, your brain has to turn the ideas into words—and while I did fine in quiet places, in noisy surroundings I was lucky to get a tenth of what was said.

We worked hard at hearing. My mother spent hours every day laboriously repeating words and phrases that gave Sam and me difficulty. It's not that easy to say "the snakes slid through the sand," a hundred times before dinner, but she never once complained or gave up. On weekends, my father read entire novels to us. I was extremely grateful to my parents for their dedication though I have to point out one confusing aspect of their approach: despite all their work, they never wanted to talk about deafness. I don't think they were ashamed of it so much as they worried that mentioning it too often would damage my self-confidence, but I wasn't able to grasp that distinction at a young age. I was certain something was so wrong with me that it couldn't even be mentioned. If everyone avoids something it has to be a bad thing, no?

It's actually not so hard to pretend deafness isn't there. It doesn't announce itself when it enters a room like a spastic limb or a Seeing Eye dog does. Looking at a picture, you can't pick out a deaf person unless you search for the hearing aids, and these can always be hidden under long hair or slipped into a pocket before the photographer says cheese. Then, if you believe that the quality of the person's image in the picture, his attractiveness and wrinkleless-ness and so forth, has a direct correlation on the quality of his life, you can easily convince yourself that the un-disabled, untroubled-seeming person in the photograph really is those things. *He's no different from us, he just says "what?" a lot.*

This is obviously mistaken. Imagining your underwear is gold doesn't make it so. But here's the rub: Adele's lessons worked so well that they reinforced the seeming legitimacy of downplaying my disability. Many people never realized that I was deaf. I could speak almost perfectly. You only picked up the faintest deaf accent if you were really listening for it, if I was tired, or if you were a highway patrolman and I was exaggeratingly slurring my words in a play for sympathy to get out of a speeding ticket. Like the high school sophomore at the college bar with a great fake ID, I could fool everyone into believing I was who I pretended to be—which enabled me to go places (Mununga, for one) I wouldn't have otherwise.

Great, yes, but it gnawed on me that this way of navigating the world was based on a fundamentally untenable position, a two-sided lie. To others: I can hear you; to myself: it doesn't matter how much I miss or how alone I feel so long as others think I can hear.

It drove me crazy. I kept doing it, it was all I knew. It drove me to Africa.

Varieties of the Deaf Experience, Part I

Growing up, the best release valve I had for frustration, deafness-related or otherwise, was fighting with my brother Zev. I have three brothers. Ari, the oldest, was always tall and well spoken, cut a good figure in adult company, kept his bed neat, and did his homework without being told. I was the second born, Sam was last. Zev, the third, nineteen months younger than I, was the only one of the four of us who didn't grow over six feet, but he offset any disadvantages his size caused with a gift for battle. On demand, he could tap into that pure energy mothers use to flip cars off their trapped children.

The two of us together were like gas and fire. Upset about a world that was always just this side of incomprehensible, I would push his buttons until a fight started. Usually we'd just brawl to a standstill and inside an hour we'd be calmed down and in front of the TV, chugging sodas and watching sitcoms. Picking fights was probably an unfair way for me to blow off steam, and to his credit, Zev always got his revenge, either physically or in more subtle ways, by twisting my perceptions of the things I couldn't quite hear.

"Why can't they just set a bonfire and attract planes?" I asked him of *Gilligan's Island*, having missed all the dialogue between Skipper and Gilligan and the rest—TV back before closed captions being less a boob tube and more a string of inexplicable mysteries.

"Because they live in the future," Zev replied.

"They live in the future?"

"Yes, everyone in the world is dead."

"Everyone in the world is dead?"

"Yes. Are you going to keep repeating everything I say?"

"But I thought this was supposed to be a funny show."

Zev shook his head. "No. Everybody dies."

Take that and put it under your eight-year-old's pillow at night.

"I'm not going to school," I told Ma when she woke me the morning after Zev had explained the *Gilligan's Island* apocalypse. "Everybody's dead."

"Don't do this to me," she said.

"I'm not doing it to you."

But pretty quickly I got bored of lying in bed so I got up and watched her try to wake up Zev. Every morning, he clung to sleep with the tenacity of a pit bull in a death match. Ma'd strip the bed of blankets, sheets, and pillows, strip his body of all its clothes, and still he'd cling to the fringe of the mattress in a convincing paroxysm of a boy in deep sleep.

When she gave up, I ran to the kitchen, got a glass of water, and threw it in his face.

"I'll kill you!" He jumped up screaming. "I swear to God! You're dead!"

"You both missed the school bus." Ma popped her head in the room. "You'll have to take the crosstown." She gave us each two quarters.

On the way to the bus stop, Zev ducked in a bodega and bought two Twix bars with his money, then he boarded the bus without paying a penny. Who was going to stop him? He was six and looked about three and a half: short and thin, with small features and big round eyes. He gave me one of the candy bars and we ate together as we rode through the park.

So Zev and I battled. We broke knuckles; we chucked rocks through windows, Atari consoles through drywall; we swore to never forgive, forgave, fought again. Ari and Sam joined in on occasion, and every three days the four of us ate through eight bags of groceries, every month two or more of us would have concerned teachers requesting a parent-teacher conference. When I was eight, Mom ran the New York City marathon, twenty-six miles through five boroughs, and when she got home, silver body-temperature cape still wrapped around her, she had to cook us dinner—Dad simply saying to her when she walked in the door, "It's your turn," and locking himself in the bathroom with the Sunday *Times*. Babysitting trumped marathon running—Mom didn't argue.

Maybe this was why my parents largely ignored my deafness. Not because they were scared of damaging my self-esteem but because the collective energy of the four of us banging off the walls drowned out a quiet thing like the inability to hear. And maybe that's not so bad. I learned to adjust, think on my feet, forget what I couldn't do, and focus on what I could. As a kid learns to swim by being thrown into the deep end of the pool, so I learned to get by in the hearing world. In a way, as much as it frustrated me, I learned to love being in the midst of incomprehensible chaos. I could pretend to listen as well as any politician could, which turned out to be an invaluable skill in Mununga. What was I but a politician those first few months?

Of course, there were plenty of moments when the devices and stratagems all failed, such as in sixth grade when I gave a long report in social studies class on a mythological hero named Herakools. I had spent a week researching the report, writing it in cursive letters, drawing illustrations of half-clothed Greek immortals for the cover, and tying the whole thing together with a spine of red yarn. Then I stood before the class and read the report with the solemnity of the bearded men I had seen davening over their books in temple. Herakools—it was a word I'd read plenty of times, but never heard. No one understood what the heck I was talking about. The last five minutes of class were reserved for my report, but so sure was I in my research that I went on long past the bell—which I didn't hear anyway. Herakools went to Hates, after all. He was the son of Zoos. He wrestled with Care-boos. The teacher, a kindly man named Mr. Johnson, didn't know what to say and let me talk into the lunch hour.

I was in tears after I found out why everyone in the class looked so confused. When Ma picked up Zev, Sam, and me from elementary school I was still in tears.

"What's the matter?" said Ma.

I told her.

"Get over it," she said. She wasn't big on emotional displays.

"Herakools! Herakools! Oh that's funny!" said Zev, sparking another brawl.

Pretty early on I developed a strategy of not trusting others with my feelings and trying to figure things out on my own. I read books voraciously, TV and radio being pretty much out of the question, but nothing I read had the answers I was seeking. *Portnoy's Complaint* when I was nine, a series of biographies of Lou Gehrig (the greatest, no question) when I was ten, and *On the Road* when I was eleven: sex, cruel death, and drugs—an early introduction, but they didn't seem applicable to my particular situation. People complained, died pitifully, and ended up in New Jersey; I knew that already. That's where my mother's parents were buried. But where was the wisdom on being deaf?

My parents, seeking to get my mind off my mind, encouraged me to find regular hobbies. I learned to ski, went to basketball camps, played on every Little League team, tied half-hitch knots out in the woods with the Boy Scouts. That still left some free time, so to give me something else to do besides harass Zev, my parents even had me take piano lessons. The teacher secured for this purpose came with impeccable credentials. She played in a professional orchestra and taught Bach to legions of children on the Upper West Side. Every week, she arrived at our apartment exactly on time and sat on the piano bench in the living room with perfect posture, in a white blouse and black heels, looking like she had just walked off the Lincoln Center stage.

"My students win awards," she liked to say.

After four years of weekly lessons all I'd learned was how to smash my brother's fingers in the key guard and to play a passable "Heart and Soul"—a major feat in retrospect, as it never sounded like anything but rhythmic door slamming to me. In time, I did grow to appreciate music, slow jazz and Van Morrison in particular, but not in time for my piano teacher.

"I don't think piano is Josh's instrument," she told my folks.

When we moved to the suburbs, the junior high school required all students without exception to take choir or band so my parents bought me a saxophone. For three years, into freshman year of high school, I sat in the orchestra pit through practices and concerts and pretended to blow my horn while the conductor, a preoccupied man with bad skin and a beard, did those conductor things with his stick. No one knew what to do with the deaf saxophonist—there'd never been one in the band before—but I talked clearly enough and did well in classes, so why, everyone figured, couldn't I play a little Beethoven? He had been deaf after all. But in the cacophony of a full orchestra rehearsal, I couldn't tell the difference between a good note and a bad one, a long one and a fat one, a short or a tall one. I might as well have been sitting in a washing machine.

So twice a week, I slumped in my seat, the sax in my lap, and daydreamed of being anyplace else, in a forest somewhere, in a battle, a desert, a tank, on a spaceship in a galaxy far away. The school finally released me from its musical requirements when I repeatedly (and not unintentionally) interrupted the spring concert my freshman year with wayward notes. It boggles my mind now that they had ever insisted I sit in a room with a hundred instruments, every last one blaring. I mean, how was I graded on it?

When I was older and finally did begin to come across people who seemed genuinely concerned for me, who wanted to know what deafness was like, I didn't know what to do with their sympathy. They were mostly female. They had soft hands, serious faces, and steady eye contact. "How much can you hear with your hearing aids?" these sensitive women asked.

I spread my hands about two feet apart. "That much," I said.

"Really?"

"Well, maybe this much," I said and closed my hands until they nearly touched.

"Oh. I'm sorry. That must be hard."

When I kissed them, they smelled of baby powder. But it was best not to abuse such kindness. It felt like a sellout as well: trading the great and relentless mentor I'd been given in deafness for cheap pity. And afterward, the sensitive women never called, as I had explained to them I couldn't talk on the phone.

In the end, after all the piano lessons and episodes of *Gilligan's Island* and great works of literature, the only coping strategies that really took when I was young were starting fights and daydreaming. Causing trouble was the one guaranteed way to catapult myself through a world that didn't really seem to care if I drifted off or not.

In my defense, I may have picked up this particular coping strategy of channeling instead of deflecting aggression from watching my father. "I can't understand anything," I would say to him, as we sat on his bed with Zev watching *Cheers*. "Why? What is the point of that? Why can Zev hear?" Dad would shake his head and pat my leg through the commercial break. As soon as the show was over he'd bark at Ma.

One time he shut off the television set and turned to me. "It's just a television show," he said. "You're not missing much. We all have our burdens. Everyone does."

"Really?" I responded. "What's your burden? What's Zev's burden?"

Dad didn't answer, though he'd seen and been through plenty in his life. Zev just rolled his eyes and pointed at me.

I think back to being ten years old. My parents threw a lot of dinner parties, noisy affairs with many courses and loud adults talking over each other and eating with gusto, and I knew that if I was lost in the din and couldn't follow what was being said, neither could Sam. I would turn off my hearing aids, look to him, and lip-read hourlong conversations in complete silence. Having a brother to share this huge and unspoken experience with was invaluable, but after a while we'd get bored.

"This is dull," I'd mouth to him.

"It sucks hairy balls of shit," he mouthed back. He was six—Ari, Zev, and I had taught him much of his vocabulary by sitting on him and saying curse words until he repeated them back to us. "What the fuck are we going to do?" he asked.

"We could gross out Grandpa," I suggested. My father's father, the retired cardiologist with strong opinions, was moody and tight with a buck, a much better talker than listener, and liked word-play, dirty limericks, and long jokes in which he could talk in a cockney accent or an Irish brogue. He was also an easy mark—grossing him out was a snatch, and furthermore, it threw him off for the rest of the evening—he'd become too upset to talk and just stare at his plate, seething at the decline of civility. Sam went to the kitchen and got a handful of grapes, passed some to me, and we shoved as many as we could up our mouths and noses. Zev, also bored by now of the adult conversation, caught on and grabbed a few grapes from my hand.

"You ask," I mouthed to Sam.

He nodded, his head just above the table, grape-stuffed nostrils straining like the cocoons of giant insects.

He tapped Grandpa's arm. "Grandpa, tell me a story," he asked.

"Certainly." Barely looking at Sam, Grandpa took a prescription pad out of the breast pocket of his jacket and read something he'd written: "There once was a man named Begin and a man named Sadat. They sat down for dinner and the man named Begin said, 'Let's begin' but the man named Sadat said, 'Who sadat?' 'I sadat,' said Begin. 'No, I Sadat,' said Sadat."

Grandpa cracked himself up and took off his glasses to rub the tears from his eyes.

"Wahh-choo!" I blew a grape across the table into Sam's lap.

"Wahh-choo!" Sam blew two grapes right into his water glass.

"That is disgusting." Grandpa thrust his pad back in his jacket. "You children. What terrible manners. Disgusting."

"WAHH-CHOO!" This was Zev. He held his face in horror. "Mom! Call Dr. Liebowitz! A grape flew out of my brain!"

"Enough!" growled my father.

We quieted down for a few minutes. But as the adult conversation continued, a steady unintelligible garble, and, as none of the adults relayed what was being said to Sam and me, it wasn't long until I caused trouble again. I couldn't help myself. I needed the charge. And on those rare nights when I didn't start up something, it was only because I'd sunk into daydreams of the things I'd do when I got older, of the people I'd meet, and of a world where deafness didn't make a difference.

Phone Call

I had never heard of Zambia before I got the phone call from the National Peace Corps headquarters in D.C. telling me I would be living there for two years. In fact, I couldn't make out the name of the country that the woman on the other end of the line was saying so I had to grab the nearest person to relay the call for me. I was in southern Georgia at the time, where a girl I was dating was building houses with Jimmy Carter and the nearest person turned out to be a young man with a beard and a deep southern accent.

"Zambeeyah?" he said. I could barely understand him.

"Could you spell that for me?"

"Z. A. M. B. I. A. Y'all gon Africa?" He was from Columbus, Georgia. We'd been tacking up roof shingles together for a couple of days, but we hadn't spoken much because it was too hard for me to read lips, hold a conversation, and keep my balance while standing on a roof.

"Yeah," I said. "I guess."

"They speak African there?"

"I don't know. Probably."

He looked me up and down and shook his head. "How you gon heah that, if you ca heah t' phone?" He pointed at my ears.

"What?" I said.

"I said, 'How you gon heah that, if you ca heah t' phone?'"

"What?" I repeated.

"Zackly."

I researched the country in the local library. Zambia was good-sized, a little bigger than Texas, landlocked in the middle of the cone of Africa. It rested high on the Central African plateau, much of it more than a mile above sea level. To the south was Victoria Falls. To the north, the tail of Zaire (the once and future Congo) tried to cut the country in two. Zambia was shaped like a fetus, with Lake Mweru (where Mununga is) nestled into the soft part of the head, and the land between the head and the curled-up body, Zaire. The country's borders, drawn up in a meeting of colonial powers in Germany in the 1950s, paid no regard whatsoever to tribal boundaries. Seventy-two different tribes were shoehorned inside and told to get along.

For a long time, because of its location, Zambia—or, more accurately, the tribes that lived where it came to be—avoided the worst of European colonialism. Slave traders found it easier to pillage Africa's coastal areas than the sparsely populated central plateau, and Portuguese missionaries visited only every once in a long while. Then in the 1870s, the famous and somewhat befuddled explorer Dr. David Livingstone crossed through the area looking for the source of the Nile. He was nearly a thousand miles off course, but nevertheless searched the Zambian river basins for years. Cecil Rhodes, diamond miner and white supremacist (and originator of the famous scholarships bearing his name), became the territory's de facto dictator in 1888, when he obtained the mining rights. He mostly used the territory as a source of cheap (i.e., slave) labor for his mining operations in South Africa and ruled until his sudden death in 1902. The British government took over from the mining interests in 1924 and the territory was named Northern Rhodesia. In 1964, it became the independent nation of Zambia and Kenneth Kaunda was elected president.

On taking office, Kaunda declared himself an African humanist. Kaunda wrote two books describing his humanist philosophy and preached nonviolence at home while sending troops abroad to help support violent independence movements in Zimbabwe, South Africa, Namibia, and other places. An emotional man, he was prone to weeping in public and carried a white hankie everywhere to wipe away his tears. In portrait photos, he gazes forlornly at the camera like he has just lost a child. He spoke often and eloquently of the patience, humility, friendliness, forgiveness, and all-around easygoingness of his people, but nevertheless was not against detaining them without trial.

In 1972 Kaunda declared a state of emergency, outlawing opposition parties. Over the course of the remaining nineteen years of his twenty-seven-year regime, he drove the national economy, once one of Africa's finest, right into the ground. After he left office, miles of secret tunnels were found, along with massive underground bunkers, one of which descended six elevator flights beneath a hidden entrance in a shantytown in Lusaka, the nation's capital. Yugoslavian engineers had built the bunker in the seventies and it was full of secret passageways, bookshelves that swung open when a hidden switch was touched, huge conference rooms walled in foot-thick steel. Kaunda claimed they were for security; his opponents claimed they were for torture.

Zambia was the third-largest producer of copper in the world after the United States and the Soviet Union, and when the market was strong, it kept Kaunda's state running smoothly. But when the world copper market collapsed in 1975 the country entered a long decline, culminating in a series of violent riots in 1991. These led to the first-ever free election, which Kaunda lost by a three-to-one margin to a five-foot-tall, bespectacled former trade unionist with a humongous forehead named Frederick Chiluba.

Kaunda accepted his defeat with grace, stepping down from power without a fuss, without the expected declaration of martial law. He gave Chiluba a tour of the imperial palace and then, weeping forcefully into his white hankie, climbed into his limo, and was driven away to a creative post-presidency career that included, among other things, a reputed coup attempt, a spell as a visiting professor at Boston University, and a televised appearance in the audience of *Dancing with the Stars*.

Chiluba had won 76 percent of the vote despite the fact that Kaunda had refused to update voter registration lists and had the army keep people away from the polls. That Chiluba and his party had won despite these and other shenanigans was a remarkable achievement, almost as remarkable was the fact that Kaunda had accepted the results. It should have been a time of hope, a brand-new leader after years and years of state corruption, but Zambia was in a bad way. In his first presidential address, in November 1991, Chiluba told his countrymen:

When our first president stood up to address you twenty-seven years ago, he was addressing a country full of hope and glory. A country fresh with the power of youth, and a full and rich dowry. Now the coffers are empty. The people are poor. The misery endless.

Chiluba visited Washington, D.C., two months after his election. There, as a gesture of American approval of Zambia's movement toward democracy, he was offered the service of the United States Peace Corps. He accepted. He shook Bush Sr.'s hand and smiled for the cameras, a photo op that was replayed nightly on Zambia's only TV station. The country was thrilled. Kaunda had pursued friendships with leaders like chairman Mao and Saddam Hussein, and that hadn't worked out well. Now, America, Big and Tall, winners of wars hot and cold, would help bring progress to Zambia for sure.

Flashbulbs popped. Plans were made for a first group of twelve volunteers. My application was pulled off a pile, and a call went out to southern Georgia. It was relayed through a roofer who sounded to me as though his tongue was shot through with Novocain.

"Zambeeyah," he said.

"Yeah," I replied.

"Well, mebbe tha don ha phon dere," he said.

"What?" I said.

"I said: 'Mebbe tha don ha phon dere.' Sheesh."

I took a guess. "Maybe."

"Zackly. Man, why you goin' dere?"

I didn't answer that, not because I couldn't hear, but because it was a little too complicated to get into.

Varieties of the Deaf Experience, Part II

I was introduced to an entirely different experience of deafness my first week in Zambia.

Peace Corps training took place in Kabwe on Zambia's central plateau. Kabwe was the fourth-largest city after Lusaka, the capital, and two cities in the copper-mining region. It was a planned city, laid out in orderly rows, with a large number of schools and Indian-owned stores all selling the same goods, and tree-lined avenues lifted right from some Englishman's dream of home. There were also large shantytowns, but these were tucked out of sight. You couldn't see them unless you went looking for them, and you couldn't smell them—a musky mix of sour mangoes and human waste—unless the wind stopped. Kabwe had been the headquarters of Zambia's railroad industry for thirty years but the rail system collapsed in 1993, leaving much of the city unemployed. When we started training the following January, the railmen, used to steady work and checks from the state, more or less lived at the bus station and the bars, waiting aimlessly for new lives.

Walking down the central thoroughfare on one of my first days in the city, I passed a large school with long open hallways sprawled across a dirt field. It looked like a Roman palace gone to seed. Large black letters were painted on a wall facing the road: BROADWAY DEAF UNIT. Curious, I went inside.

The deaf unit was at the end of the most remote hallway, in two classrooms underneath a mango tree, thirty students in all, split in two classes by age. One teacher, Mr. Mwelva, taught both classes at the same time. Mwelva was about forty, had a face bearded by razor burn. He was the only hearing adult in Kabwe who knew sign language and was paid extra for working with the deaf children. At first I thought his ability to teach two classes at once was a commendable feat of organization and discipline; my admiration was quickly tempered when I saw that by ten o'clock each morning he was drunk on *chibuku*, cheap maize wine served in a box. Instead of giving lessons, he glared at the students for a while, then rested his forehead dead center on his desk and slept. When he woke up, he sent the pupils to sweep the halls and wipe the walls with wet rags—that was the extent of his instruction. At least half his students couldn't count past their toes.

"Deaf children," he explained to me, not long after we met, "are meant to keep to themselves, to do what is told. They need more time and attention than we have available to give. Sacrifices must be made."

"Sacrifices?" I asked, making sure I heard him right.

"Yes, sacrifices."

"Who sacrifices?"

He nodded at the children. "They do."

I was new to the country then, not sure what my place was, still nervous about contracting incurable diseases from touching things. I didn't understand yet just how profound that sacrifice was, how little they were getting in return. So I didn't punch Mwelva in the eye.

Within a week, I was teaching at the Broadway School every morning on my way to Peace Corps training. I knew nothing about teaching, less about the Zambian curriculum, but for an hour every morning I was in charge of fifteen deaf teenagers. I had learned a little sign language the summer before when I lived at Gallaudet University, the national university for the deaf in Washington,

D.C. I wasn't fluent at it, but knew enough to converse, and American Sign Language and Zambian Sign were surprisingly similar. It helped also that the kids only knew a couple hundred words.

There were some telling differences: in ASL, for example, the sign for America was "great big melting pot," but the Zambian sign for America was of a soldier holding his rifle to his chest as he marched off to war—much more appropriate, if you ask me.

"America is so strong," a kid named Kennedy signed. "So strong. You can do anything. You beat everyone. Rambo."

"You're right," I said.

I tried to teach Kennedy and his classmates current events and geography, but these subjects were so distant from their daily lives as to be completely useless abstractions. So I taught them math, addition, and subtraction mostly. They took forever to do the problems I wrote out on the board because they had just a couple of pencils, which they had to pass back and forth. Also, Maba, a hearing student who was in the unit because he was dim-witted, restless, and drooled constantly, would get upset when the others were writing, which he couldn't do, and would grab at any pencil he saw being used. The students had to always keep one eye on him.

When Maba successfully seized a pencil he would hold it high in the air. "Teacha!" he'd yell, like he'd prevented a crime. "Teacha!"

His jaw always hung open and you watched saliva pooling in it like water in a sink. He didn't walk so much as stagger. He'd give me the pencil, now slimy with drool, I'd give it back to whomever it came from, Maba would grab it again, and the problems on the board would take forever to get done.

Elsewhere in the school, hearing students studied English and geometry and the history of their country. Sitting in ruler-straight rows, in ironed white shirts and blue pants and ties, they copied out line after line of polite conversations from the blackboards— *Sir, where is the bus station? Will you join me for lunch?*—raised their hands, and were called upon. Every morning at eight o'clock they all stood up and sang. On one of my first days, the sound of their morning song, filling the school to the rafters and spilling out the windows and doors, stopped me in my tracks. To my ears, of course, it could have been a windstorm or crying hostages, but it was striking nonetheless.

"What is that?" I asked Mr. Mwelva. We were standing in the hallway.

"That's our national anthem," he said.

"It's beautiful," I said, though I couldn't really tell. "Have you taught the deaf unit the anthem?"

"Of course not," he said. "They can't speak."

"I *know* they can't speak. But they could sign it."

Mwelva thought about that. "Good idea, Mr. Josh," he said. "They can sign it. We can teach the students to sign the anthem."

Our students played tag in the yard, oblivious to the singing that was happening all around them. "Mr. Mwelva, all these years it never occurred to you to teach them the anthem?" I asked.

"It's not on the curriculum."

"Well, what the hell is on the curriculum?"

"I don't know." He didn't seem too concerned.

My hands unconsciously balled into fists. I struggled to maintain my composure. I tend to curse a lot when angry, which tends to escalate situations, so I tried not to go there. "Well, have you looked?" I asked. "Have you asked around to find out what's on it?"

Mwelva shook his head. "That's not my job."

THERE WAS NOTHING IN PEACE CORPS TRAINING ON DEAF EDUCATION or on navigating an educational system based, apparently, on the principles of unlimited recess. Most of training was given over to learning how to dig wells, how to speak Bemba, and how not to get sick and die. Classes were in *insakas* in a grass field in a whitewashed campus on the edge of the city that may have aspired to be a college at some point. There were twelve of us volunteers, thirteen if you count Jake, a long-haired Virginian who showed up a couple weeks after we started, having transferred over from Mali to be our volunteer leader. He had a wealth of well experience from working water projects in the middle of the Sahara, but he spoke too quickly for me to ever understand much of what he said.

We were a motley group of Americans and couldn't have been more diverse if we had been cast for a television sitcom: there was a New York City go-getter, a nerd from Boston, a black guy from rural Illinois, a lesbian from Oklahoma, a farm girl from Wisconsin, a white Rastafarian from Kentucky, and a middle-aged alcoholic from rural Michigan who told us to call him Uncle Steve. The same strapping housing contractor played the roles of both ladies' man and aging hippie. And then there was me, the deaf guy.

To my surprise, I did well in language class. Bemba is a languorous, sliding-water language, all bwah, mbah, and mwah sounds, no *r*'s, *q*'s, *v*'s, *x*'s, or *z*'s. It has more than twenty different verb tenses, but not a single word for love. There are three reasons why I did well: first, I was used to paying attention when people spoke; second, I was used to asking people to repeat themselves; and third, I had experience with losing the topic of a conversation, saying something completely inappropriate, embarrassing myself and/or others, and then moving on.

The other volunteers weren't as accomplished in these skills. They struggled through the language lessons like stutterers in a speech contest. It felt like rightful karmic payoff.

"This is impossible," said Chris, the young long-haired Rastafarian from Kentucky. "Learning a new language is like learning to walk on your hands."

"I can walk on my hands," I said.

"You don't have to be smug about it."

"I'm not being smug. And if I am, I earned it."

He scoffed. Tall and sleepy-eyed, he looked sort of like an Aztec warrior waking up from a nap. "Smug."

We became friends. His approach to training was the total opposite of mine. While I arrived on campus in a rush each morning, breathless after an hour with the deaf unit, stomach tied in a knot of idealism or heartburn, Chris would stroll in late, laconic, completely at ease. It appeared that he had come to Africa, not to find himself or to lose himself or test himself—it just happened one afternoon to be the exit he took off the interstate. A honey-colored seventeen-year-old bombshell from his host family walked him to class each morning. When they parted, her fingers lightly raked his long arm.

"Are you a Rasta?" I asked him, gesturing toward the rainbow-colored skullcap he always wore.

"Ja, Rastafari, in the name of the mother and the father, world without end," he replied. "Remember that. That'll help you to keep perspective. Rastafarianism isn't just about smoke. It's about love and communion."

"I know that," I said. I pointed to the girl who had walked him to class. "Is she your girlfriend?"

"No. She is my sister."

"Your sister?"

"My sister"—he tapped his chest over his heart—"here."

I thought about that. "You're screwing her," I decided.

"Smug," he said.

Still, love. Communion. You could feel them in the air even though they might not have been in the language. The air hummed with potential and opportunity. We were witnesses to the dawn of a new democracy. Hordes of students, great rolling tides of them, washed over Kabwe's sunlit boulevards, carrying their books in straps over their shoulders, intent on acing their yearly exams and moving on to the next grade, the next school, to better lives. President

Chiluba himself had been born the son of a lowly miner and had worked as an office clerk and now he was shaking hands with George Bush at the White House. Anything was possible.

The deaf students were outside of all that. They weren't going to pass any tests. When I left Broadway School at nine-thirty each morning for Peace Corps training, they were done with lessons for the day. They cleaned the halls, then ran around the yard. They became great soccer players, the best in the city, but their minds were starving.

The first half-dozen years of life are the most crucial in education. The child's brain is hungry and flexible—it can learn dozens of words a day in several different languages just through overheard conversation, but deaf children, unless there is timely diagnosis and coordinated support, barely learn any language during that time. Such support is almost unheard of in Africa. Too late, the parent stares at the child and thinks, Why won't he say anything? By then, the fertile years for learning have passed, the mind has hardened around the absence of language, and the child, without ever knowing otherwise, is remaindered to a lesser kind of life. He can't understand everyone talking around him and only by demeaning and undignified gesticulations can he convey even the simplest ideas to people, who then assume that he's retarded. They give him a hoe and send him to the fields or they give him a broom and send him to the corner. At night, they give him a glass of banana wine, and he sits quietly against the wall and watches lips soundlessly move.

Mwelva called this their sacrifice. I didn't know what to call it. It made God seem sloppy and cruel.

Every morning when I arrived at the school my students greeted me like I was a triumphant soccer hero even though I couldn't coherently explain long division. None of the hearing students in the school had white teachers—that at least gave them pride.

"I love how you teach math," signed Kennedy with a big

Cheshire smile. The smartest kid in the class, he knew nothing of the man he was named for. "I love copying out problems. And then you explain what I did wrong! No one ever did that before. I love that. I love your shirt."

"Same here," I signed back. "Did you do your homework?"

"No. I didn't have a pencil."

"I don't believe you," I said, but just then Maba staggered over and handed me ten.

I started meeting up with Kennedy after training each day. He waited for me in the road outside the Peace Corps campus for two hours, the guard having deemed all four-foot-something of him too great a security threat to come inside; then I bought roasted groundnuts from a corner vendor and we ate them as we walked across town to where I was staying. It was an hourlong walk through the central shopping district with those Indian stores, through a wealthy residential neighborhood with houses peeking out from behind cement walls topped with razor wire, and finally across a lovely field of seven-foot elephant grass hiding an abandoned railroad line. By the time we reached the railroad, it was late afternoon, and a low sun lit up each strand of grass and washed out the blue in the sky. I asked Kennedy about his deafness: he told me how once two audiologists from somewhere in Europe, prim women with tight hair and lips, had shown up at Broadway School and tested ears and distributed used hearing aids. They'd picked an aid for Kennedy and made an earmold for him, but they were rushed and the mold was a poor fit. He could never wear it for more than ten minutes before it hurt and couldn't afford batteries besides; it was now locked away in Mwelva's office.

"I remember the sound though," Kennedy signed, his face lighting up. "I could hear cars! I could hear clapping! I could hear Mr. Mwelva speaking!"

He probably could have—I'd seen his hearing chart, his hearing was actually better than mine, he just hadn't gotten to learn language when he needed to.

"What did Mwelva sound like?" I asked.

"Wabba-wabba-wabba-wabba!" Kennedy shouted, his voice like he was under a foot of water.

"That's him," I said.

"I want to hear," he continued. "I want to go to America. I want to talk like you."

"You want to be like me? Start by doing your homework."

"I will, I promise," he said. But he didn't do it.

I WAS LIVING WITH A LOCAL FAMILY, A THIN COUPLE WITH A HALF-dozen relatives crashing in their living room, all of them devout Jehovah's Witnesses. The mother had ballerina posture and a baby on each hip. By some magic I could never figure out, she could breast-feed both of them and cook dinner for ten at the same time. The family was supposed to help me learn the customs of the Bemba tribe, the dominant tribe in Luapula Province where all of us volunteers would be stationed, but mostly they tried to get me to join their daily Bible classes.

"Will you come read *The Watchtower* with us?" Joseph, the rail-thin husband, asked.

"Sorry. I need to study," I replied.

He shook *The Watchtower* in his fist. "But what can be more important than this?"

I looked through the magazine. It offered predictions based on World War I for the dates of the apocalypse and God's coming return. World War I was the beginning of the end of the world. Or not. Or sort of. It seemed that they kept changing their mind as the world disobediently refused to end.

"It says here that the apocalypse will be any day now," I pointed out to Joseph.

He nodded cheerfully. "Yes."

"That's good?"

"Yes. Come to Kingdom Hall with us."

So I went to church with them, but just one time. I couldn't understand a single word that was said in the service, as has always been the case for me in big airy houses of worship that swallow up noise. The distance and high ceilings turn voices into flat hiccups of sound and the preacher might as well be a sheep bleating. Bored, I flipped through *Awake;* there were articles adding up the mathematical value of Hebrew letters in certain biblical passages, holy proof of the coming reckoning that thus far hadn't come when they reckoned. The room was full of people who seemed eager for the world to end, which kind of made me uncomfortable.

I turned to my homestay father and stood to leave. "Thank you, Joseph, but I have to go," I whispered.

Smiling, he said, "Go on, tell them."

"What?"

"Thank them."

He loudly clapped his hands and before I knew it, two hundred people dressed in their Sunday best had turned to stare at the lone white man in their midst. I turned bright red.

"Thank you," I said. I sat back down for the rest of the service.

After that, I declined all of Joseph's entreaties for Bible study, ducking into my room as soon as I got home and locking the door. Joseph knocked each day to invite me to join them, but pretty quickly I figured out his schedule and took off my hearing aids when he came around. In my room, I conjugated Bemba verbs, did push-ups, read Russian novels, and chewed sticks of Bazooka Joe. A goat outside the window ate the gum wrappers I floated down to him. He was gray colored and built solid, and his perfectly spherical testicle sac hung like a disco ball. He made serious eye contact and kept trying to tell me something with his long insistent baaing, maybe that he was a prince trapped by a spell, but I didn't speak goat. Then he turned around and rammed his head against a tree. When he crapped it was like quarters spilling out of a slot machine.

Behind the house, all the land was owned by the mining company, and I learned later that this particular lead mine, the largest in Africa, was the most polluted in the world. Actually I read that it was the most polluted in Africa, but I'm betting that gives it the world prize. A higher percentage of children in Kabwe was born brain damaged than in any other place on the continent. But the children didn't know that, and neither did their parents, and they waved to me as they frolicked on the rock pile behind the house until the sun went down.

After our walks through town, Kennedy often kept me company in my room until dinner.

"What are they reading?" he asked of the men and women in the living room.

"*The Watchtower*," I answered.

"What's in *The Watchtower*?"

"Math problems," I said, thinking of the numerical formulas for deciphering the Bible, and knowing that that answer would keep Kennedy from asking follow-up questions. We had nightly competitions to see who could do more sit-ups and blow bigger bubbles. His lips curled up when he exercised or chewed gum so he always looked like he was smiling, but he was actually a pretty subdued kid, prone to running over in his mind the worst things he could imagine. You would too, I suppose, if you spent all day, every day, with your face pressed against the glass of a club you couldn't join.

"Hey," he said. "What happens to us when you leave?"

"I don't know," I admitted.

"That's no good."

He was right. The Broadway students needed more stimulation than washing the halls. A month and a half into training, trying to figure out a way to leave them with a lasting sense of how they were worth more than their world allowed for and bored to tears of long division, I came up with the idea of having a group discussion of feelings. Feelings!—the students had never talked about them; could only name a half-dozen. Such a discussion would give them an opportunity to share coping techniques as well as new terms—or so I hoped.

We started with happiness. I listed happy activities like playing soccer and eating candy, and asked the students to add to the list and to explain their choices as they did so.

"Talking to hearing people would make me happy," Kennedy said.

"Understanding movies," said his friend Mutende.

"Those are good," I responded. "But I'm looking more for things you can do now. Not things you'd like to do."

"I want to wake wovies"—this was Miriam, a beautiful Indian girl whose father owned several shops and who lived in a house hidden completely by a twelve-foot fence. She talked out loud as she signed, her voice molassesed by a thick deaf tone. "I wook wike an actress."

"I want to hear music," said Margaret, Miriam's friend.

"Teacha!" Maba shouted, holding up Margaret's pencil.

"Why is he in cwass with us?" Miriam asked. "I want him in a different cwass."

"I want hearing aids same as yours," Kennedy said.

"Me too, me too," the rest of the class chimed in.

"I want to be tall," Kennedy added.

"Me too." The rest of the class agreed again.

They went on, out of my control, with a whole long list of things that *would* make them happy, not things that did: "I want to learn math. . . . I want to meet Rambo. . . . I want to drive a car. . . . I want to hear my mother. . . . I want a girlfriend. . . . I want to sing. . . . I want shoes. . . . I want to buy a goat."

I had no idea what to do with all that they wanted. "Good work," I said. "You know what you want."

"And?" asked Kennedy.

"And what?"

He grinned at me like he knew I was playing dumb and the gig was up. "How do we get these things?"

It hit me right then that working with these students might have been a mistake. Instead of inspiring Kennedy and the others, I was taunting them with an alternate reality so completely out of reach that they had never imagined it, never thought to express it until I showed up. I could speak, I could read books and lips; Kennedy was thirteen and couldn't write a sentence. He would never be able to talk. What hope could I give him?

"I don't know," I said. The class fell silent.

Kennedy's smile disappeared. "You don't know how we can get them?" he said. "Then why did you ask us?"

I checked my watch. There were twenty minutes to get through. I wrote some math problems on the board.

SIX WEEKS INTO TRAINING, OUR GROUP OF TWELVE VOLUNTEERS wore down to ten. Gerald, the quiet African American from Illinois, who nodded and grunted "Uhh-hmm, uhh-hmm, uhh-hmm," as he listened to lectures, and had brought one contact lens to Africa, which he switched from eye to eye each day, left after two weeks. Quick-talking Susie from L.A., energetic and idealistic in her sports bra, developed a puzzling and painful illness that was eventually diagnosed as an infection of her diaphragm muscle lining. None of us had ever heard of such a thing. Later, four or five months after we moved to our villages, two other volunteers, Stacey and Dave, would leave Africa and marry and move to Arizona. He was memorable for never once, in that time, wearing anything other than a flannel shirt or a blue tank top; she towered over him like a power forward over a point guard.

But seven weeks into training, there were still ten of us. We gathered early one morning at the Kabwe bus station to travel north to visit our villages. The point of the trip was to preview the feature presentation: to see the houses we'd live in, meet the people we'd be living with for the next two years. We packed overnight bags and eagerly waited at the station for the bus Administration reserved to take us to Luapula Province. Only the bus never showed. It was an important lesson: never buy bus tickets the day before traveling. Might as well just give the money away. *Travel rule number one*, I wrote in my shiny new journal. *Only buy ticket if you see bus there.*

We passed the whole day sitting at the station, waiting for the bus, eating roasted corn and fending off child beggars—not so difficult, except for the deformed ones. I had no defense against the boy whose left leg was swollen up like a parade float. As he circled us, it galumphed after him like a pet tree. I gave him half of my travel money.

"You're just going to encourage him," said Chris. "He'll just keep doing it. Won't get it fixed."

"Fuck off," I said.

The station was a festering mix of travelers, peddlers, beggars, punks, and disturbing smells you try not to imagine the source of. A man offered balls of ganja wrapped in newspaper, each one cheaper than a stick of gum. At some point, I had to take a shit, and what I saw in the latrine should never be described.

The next day Administration tried again to rent a bus for us, but there were no buses to rent in Zambia. Every vehicle in the country that could move, and many that couldn't, was on the road, carrying a full load—there were cars literally held together by string. If you popped their hoods, what you saw made you believe in miracles. There might be ten little elves in there. Administration eventually located a decrepit Chinese bus with an engine that sat in the aisle in a metal closet next to the driver. The exhaust was at the top of this metal closet. Despite the presence of a man sitting in the first row pouring water into said engine, when the bus started, smoke blew out the exhaust like a brush fire, right into our faces.

I was coughing black phlegm before we left the city limits. "I don't think this is healthy," I yelled to Chris, who shrugged. He was wearing sunglasses, leaning way back, watching the sun-wracked plateau, where the trees cowered from the glare like whipped stepchildren. I followed his lead and looked out the window but there was nothing interesting out there. The engine roared like it was blaming us for something terrible. We didn't move fast at all.

The bus lurched up the north road then broke down in the early dusk, only a hundred miles outside of Kabwe. We passed the night by the roadside. It was a cloudless, kaleidoscopic night of a million stars, more stars than the sky could hold practically, all of them hard lit, none of them familiar. The dark forest was full of sounds and energy that weren't there during the day, an energy that made me feel really, really small. The bus driver and the engine water-pourer smoked a joint and tended to a small fire. The entire night neither one spoke a single word, not that I could hear anyway. It was not an auspicious beginning to my African journeys, but an appropriate one—wherever you're going in Africa, there's no telling when you'll get there. *Travel rule number two*, I wrote. *Bring a sweater.*

That first trip to Mununga, I was on the ground for less than fifteen minutes. I hopped off the pickup and the villagers didn't know what to make of me (a feeling, truthfully, that was mutual), and after I left I couldn't help but think of the deep connection I had made with Kennedy and the other Broadway students. Our lives were so different but what we shared was real and powerful. They looked at me and saw my hearing aids, saw how they sometimes had to wave and point if Mwelva or some hearing teacher asked for me at the door, saw that I stared at people's lips when they spoke with an intensity that made many of them nervous. And when Kennedy and I walked across the city each evening, I'd put my aids in my pocket, so we could be together in the silence.

There was something to that, to being able to walk in peaceful silence whenever you wished, and I tried to tell Kennedy that, to help him appreciate that it was special. And he *was* appreciative, but said what he really wanted was to hear like I did.

Three more weeks and training drew to a close. I arranged for a meeting with Mr. Mwelva and the headmaster of Broadway School to ensure that instruction would continue after I left. Earlier, I had tried teaching sign language to other teachers at the school, ones who didn't appear to come to work drunk or planning to get that way, and at first a few of them were excited to learn, but then they felt foolish for fumbling repeatedly through the same basic signs and for knowing less than the filthiest students at school, and stopped trying to learn. Mwelva and the headmaster were unfortunately my only hope.

The Broadway headmaster was a small man with gigantic eyeglasses who favored brown sports jackets with padded shoulders and sleeves that seemed to end near his elbows—I didn't understand his sartorial style. His office was dominated by a jet-black desk, on top of which rested a ceramic blue elephant with its trunk raised, a clock embedded in its side. When he sat in his chair behind the desk, you had to constantly crane your neck around the elephant to see him.

Politely and then aggressively, I asked the headmaster why he and Mwelva hadn't put together a curriculum for the deaf students, why the deaf unit didn't have yearly goals or weekly lesson plans. After all, I pointed out, it was late March, the school year had started in early January, and the hearing students had already completed several months of lessons toward their yearly examinations, while the deaf students still waited for their first lesson. The headmaster's explanations varied—he didn't have test results, he didn't have enough teachers, he didn't have classrooms, there was a letter he was waiting for—but in his cheery, untroubled smile, the answer was simply: Really, Josh, who gives a shit.

"No!" I banged my fist hard on his desk. The elephant didn't move. "Open the class! Just teach them anything."

"We need authorization," said the headmaster.

"Whose authorization?"

"Mine."

"Then authorize it!"

He shook his head and smiled. From behind his chair he produced a bottle of Mosi and three glasses. "Mr. Josh, I can't just authorize it," he said, looking for a bottle opener in his desk drawers. "I need the test results from last year. Then I need the provincial office to approve the test results and send me a letter with their official approval. These things take time."

I grabbed his hand and held it the way all Zambian men held hands when they had something important to say, clasped.

"Forget the provincial office," I said. "Teach the class anyway. You can do it."

He extracted his hands from my grip and poured out three glasses of beer. He handed one glass to Mwelva, placed another underneath the elephant trunk for me. I switched gears and made a play for pity. "Think of how happy the children will be if they have lessons," I told him.

"I'm sorry, I just don't have authorization," the headmaster said, tilting his head back for a long swallow.

I lost it right then. I slammed my beer down on the desk. "This is fucking bullshit! Do your fucking job!"

The headmaster froze. Mwelva, silent until now, startled from the noise, gathered his bearings, and pushed himself to his feet. He nearly fell and clutched the armrest to stay upright.

"Mr. Joshua," he said, "we are not in America. We follow the rules here. People can't just go taking initiative whenever they feel like it. It makes problems. Patience is important. There is a saying: The anxious person fights with the door. Do you see what I mean? These children, there is no need to teach them really, they can only learn very little. They are deaf."

"I'm deaf," I said—out loud, and felt a huge surge of pride with those words, for maybe the first time in my life.

Mwelva laughed and the headmaster laughed with him. "No, you're not."

"But I am."

"No." He stared me in the eye. "You are not."

He sank back into the couch. The elephant on the desk, now shiny with spilt beer, seemed to say, You are not who you say you are, so how can you speak for others? You're just a door-wrestler.

"Cheer up," the headmaster said, having recovered from his shock. "The boys won't mind waiting for the results. They like running around."

"Can we at least put Maba in another classroom?" I asked him.

"No," he said.

Back at the classroom, Maba staggered around annoying the students while they waited eagerly for my report on the meeting.

"Well?" Kennedy asked when I walked in the door, but he guessed right away. His head dropped down and he stared at his hands. Then he shrugged. I apologized but he shook off the apology and told me not to worry. He was used to this, to doing nothing all day. I wasn't and he knew that and tried to help me see that it was okay. His friends followed his lead and soon the whole class was consoling me when they were the ones who had just been doomed to another year of not much.

"We'll be fine," they said. "It's no big deal. . . . Someone will come. . . . I like movies without words. . . . I can still be an actress." I sat on the edge of the teacher's desk in the front of the room and they gathered in a circle around me and thanked me for teaching them. "Smile, smile," Miriam repeated over and over, showing me what she wanted.

How could they be so grateful? I felt like I had failed them— me, and many others.

"Are you upset?" Kennedy asked. "Are you crying?"

Before I could answer, there was a clatter in the back of the room.

"Teacha!" Maba yelled. I looked up; he held every pencil in the class in his fist. They shone with his drool. He rushed forward to show them to me, stumbling, elbowing other students out of the way, splashing saliva on everyone. I took a step to meet him, grabbed his wrist, and twisted until he yelped in pain, dropped the pencils, and collapsed on the floor, bawling loudly.

Kennedy and the other students stepped back and stared at me, and I could see them recalibrating everything they knew about me. What had just happened? I was about to reach down and lift Maba to his feet and brush him off and apologize, then I thought, better to let them all think the worst. I left a few minutes later and didn't come back for almost two years.

Well Projects

A month after my arrival in Mununga, I moved from the small blue and yellow shack near the clinic to a large thatch-roofed hut a quarter mile farther into the village. I figured there I'd get some distance from the market's drunks, toutboys, and roving packs of staring children. My new landlord was jovial and prosperous; a tall man who wore a blue beret tilted low over one eye, he had two wives and three dugout canoes and a laugh like firecrackers. Then he drowned on the lake. Witchcraft was suspected, possibly tracing back to a scorned girlfriend at a fishing camp on the lakeshore. His two wives came to the hut with their young children one morning and asked me to move out—that day. They had no place else to go. Their children clung to them like bark to trees. I gave them all the kwacha I could spare and moved into another hut nearby, bought an old dirt-brown couch, and troweled out a concrete floor. There was a big mango tree in the yard, and while I smoothed out my new floor, the tree branches filled with children. "How are you? How are you?" they sang over and over, staring like owls.

The vast majority of villagers welcomed me to Mununga with open arms. Unlike Boniface on that first day, they seemed to have no agenda other than carrying out their chores and food-gathering and occasionally asking for a beer. Old men waved and called out greetings as they walked past; women carrying fifty pounds of groundnuts on their heads stopped and curtsied low. One man walked from a village hours upriver to bring me a gift of crocodile meat and bottom-feeding river fish. He asked for nothing in return and I never saw him again—perhaps best, as crocodile turns out to be a foul-tasting meat. Even one of the village lunatics got in a greeting: as I ate a snack on my porch, he patted my shoulders and showed me his dick.

"*Natotela*," I said. Thank you.

"*Awe, umusungu, natotela*," he replied. No, white man, *thank you.*

Across the path behind the mango tree that the boys gathered in was a small hut, and a lean muscular young woman with large eyes, high wide cheekbones, and a tiny snub nose—the kind of features actresses pay fortunes for—lived there. I started to notice that she stared at me quite a bit. Her staring was unusual because it was without any trepidation. A smile always flickered on her lips. She had perfect posture from a lifetime of balancing water jugs on her head, and thrust her figure forward with a hand behind her hip so that she seemed much closer than she was. For weeks she stared like this, never saying a word, but she didn't need words to get her point across. This made her especially alluring for a guy who couldn't hear.

"Who's that?" I asked Malama, the boy who had fetched Jere and me beers that first day at the clinic. The leader of the mango-tree gang, he had become my right-hand man. After I bought the couch he had taken to sleeping there every night.

"She Alice," he said.

"Alice?"

"Yes."

"Why does she stare like that?"

He smiled nervously, his face all overbite and ovals. "I don't know. You will marry her?" He often made jumps in logic like this.

"No, I'm not going to marry her."

He relaxed. "Good."

"Good? Why is that good?"

It took him a while to get out the answer. Malama's English was poor and while I could speak Bemba okay after two months of language training, I was much worse at understanding what was said. So we talked to each other in each other's language, which wasn't easy.

"She bad girl," he said.

I looked at Alice again. She didn't seem old enough to deserve such a label. "What's wrong with her?"

"She bad," was all Malama could say.

Malama had quickly become indispensable but most of our conversations those first months were like this, unsatisfying and mysterious. Crucial points were lost in translation. For example, one night, some traveling entrepreneurs hooked up a TV and VCR to a gasoline generator and I gave Malama kwacha to watch the movie. It was *Rambo,* the one where he's bonding with Taliban fighters in Afghanistan by blowing up hapless Soviet army draftees—the kind of movie you didn't need to understand the dialogue to follow, and Malama watched it in a trance. It unhinged his vision of the world.

"He kill so many," he said afterward. "Great man."

"It's just a movie," I told him.

"Is Rambo the president of America?"

"No. Bill Clinton is."

"So Rambo, vice president?"

"No, Malama. It's just a movie. It's not real. There's someone with a camera, taking snaps. Click. Click. Click. Like my camera. Like a dream. Sleep, dream, you know?"

He didn't believe me. At the market there were Rambo plastic bags, Rambo T-shirts, Rambo hand creams, Rambo traveling luggage, and Rambo cocoa butter for "lightening overly black skin." Every Rambo was in the same pose—mouth open in a twisted snarl, legs spread wide, machine gun low and to the right, long sweaty hair splaying with the effort of slaughtering people. Sylvester Stallone was the face of America in the remote African bush and Malama worshipped him and was sure he ruled the world. So if he said the beautiful girl across the way was a bad girl, how could I believe him?

Alice didn't stop staring. She grew bolder. At dusk, when the paths had emptied save for a few stragglers rushing home, she would come and sit right on the corner of my porch, watching me from there. This made me nervous.

In training, Maria, the Peace Corps nurse, had lectured often about rampant STDs and the skyrocketing rate of HIV infection. The numbers she shared made you worry for the future of the country; you could see that a bomb was about to go off, and when it did a generation would be dead and another would be parentless. Sometimes Malama and I came across AIDS victims while walking to the river—they lay motionless on bamboo mats in the shade of low banana trees, following us only with their eyes, alive, but only just. Forget sex, I had decided, back in training, I would be celibate as a monk in a cave for the two years of service. But in her lectures Maria hadn't mentioned flirting village girls, or explained what I should do when, after an evening of drinking in Jere's insaka, Alice appeared at my door, sweating and breathing hard. Her skin glowed. Some of the buttons of her blouse were undone.

"What do you want?" I asked her in Bemba.

She didn't know English. She tilted her head past the couch and Malama lying awake on it, toward the bedroom.

"No, we can't," I protested.

She nodded toward the bedroom again, widening her eyes, touching my arm.

"Please," I said. I backed away from her, went inside, ignored Malama's startled look, and pulled off my hearing aids.

"She Boniface family," Malama said the next morning.

"Right. Figures," I said.

"Would not make good wife. Bad girl."

"I said I wasn't going to marry her."

"Okay."

But the hooks were in.

IN MUNUNGA, MY MAIN JOB WAS TO TEACH VILLAGERS HOW TO DIG wells, and I thought at first, as many volunteers do, that working for the Peace Corps was about the job. Why would they put us in the middle of such naked, obvious need if they didn't want us to get cracking? Just about everyone in Mununga got their drinking water from the river and not coincidentally about a third of the children under five years old died from diarrhea and other waterborne disease. After settling in, I set right to work. I put up posters at the market announcing informational meetings and traveled to neighboring villages on foot and on motorbike to spread the word. But the turnout for meetings was always poor. Not many people were able to read the posters and fewer could spare the time to come. And then Jere was usually too busy working to translate for me, even though the meetings were right on the clinic porch, so they quickly devolved into games of charades—though, happily, deaf people are great at charades. *Dig, dig like this . . . and you will be happy! New well, clean water, mmm good! No, poop, poop, poop!*

The half-dozen villagers in attendance would smile politely.

"So when will you give us a well?" they'd ask, in Bemba.

"I'm not giving you one. You have to build one. All of us build it. Together."

"Yes, when will you build it?"

This wasn't anybody's fault. You can't just plop an idea like community ownership in people's laps like air-dropped food and expect them to know what to make of it especially if they've been scuffling their whole lives. After the meetings, I ate lunch on my porch with Malama, then hopped on my Peace Corps–issued motorcycle, a red scooter with just enough horsepower to get up the big hills, and rode out to the surrounding villages to spread the gospel of wells.

I had a surge of hope that a project would take shape when Mr. Bule and Mr. Kasonda, Mununga's two elected politicians, stopped by my hut one afternoon to introduce themselves and talk development. Bule, the older one, represented the villages on the far side of the river. His cheeks were covered in spittle and bristly white hairs in odd places and he had one eye. He wore a pair of eyeglasses missing one lens so that his empty eye socket was behind a corrective lens and his good eye peered through an empty frame. This made no sense. Malama brought him a stool.

"My other eye fell out in the middle of the night," Bule said, unprompted, in English, after taking a seat. "Not tonight, a different one. Clop! Like that. Rolled right under my chair." He nodded. "I got it in a jar."

I wasn't sure how to respond. "That's nice," I said.

Mr. Kasonda, who represented the clinic side of the river, was about fifty, talkative and fidgety, with a better command of English than Bule. He had grand plans for developing Mununga, involving asphalt, telephone poles, buses, a new market space, electricity even. His energy filled me with optimism: I could see water-filled wells dotting the valley like sunflowers. But a month later, in an unexpected move, Kasonda stole two hundred thousand kwacha from a government road project, snuck off to the Copperbelt, blew the money on whores, and then got beaten to death trying to steal a beer truck. So much for the politicians.

"Are they like that everywhere?" I asked Jere, my friend and guide.

"Well, Mununga is Mununga," he replied.

"Right. Gomorrah. Boniface and the witch doctors. So the politicians are in the same boat?"

"Ignore them," Jere counseled. "They don't have any real power. Go out to the villages, the headmen. Get to know the town."

FIFTY YEARS EARLIER, MUNUNGA HAD BEEN A SMALL RIVER VILLAGE, the hippos, crocs, elephants, and hyenas in the surrounding forest easily outnumbering people. The land was as fertile as the Nile Crescent, and in the river all sizes and shapes of fish swam. Travelers found it a blessed place. If you threw a stick in the ground, in a year's time it bore fruit. If you dipped your hand in the water, it came up holding dinner. A mile west of the village, the river emptied into Lake Mweru, a vast and shallow body of water. During the day, mist shrouded the hills of southern Zaire on the far side of the lake, so that they appeared to exchange places and vary their distances. Only at night, when the stars filled the sky, did the hills become solid. You knew Zaire by its darkness.

The village had stayed the same for generations. People hunted, fished, ate, slept, made love, raised children, sang songs, planted, grew old, didn't grow old, died. While the rest of the world had its hot wars and cold wars and space races and booms and busts, in Mununga the only really important measure of a life was how full your stomach was at sundown.

In the early seventies, Chinese engineers invited by President Kaunda built a one-lane bridge over the river. Shortly thereafter, a market formed nearby. Word got around that Mununga was a fine place to live, with good soil and a river full of fish. In the eighties, refugees began crossing Lake Mweru en masse from Zaire. Zaire was a continual mess, a country in name only. Shaba Province, on the other side of Lake Mweru, had been racked with wars for decades. The mines in Shaba regularly coughed up diamonds worth as much as nuclear secrets, and government officials, including Mobutu Sese Seke, the Zairian Godfather, fought to control the riches. They needed them to finance their wars. Tough luck for any villagers who got in their way. So while government agents, army generals, and diamond merchants flew in and out of Shaba on their private jets, village families piled their stoves, clay pots, bamboo mats, and children into dugout canoes and pushed off into Lake Mweru, paddling all day for Mununga, and a chance to start again.

I became friendly with a solidly built, tireless refugee named Mwansa who told me stories about his country and the journey across the lake. He had been a scout in the Zairian army before he came over, knew the potions for invisibility and invincibility, and had names for over a hundred stars.

"What did you do in the army?" I asked him once.

"Killed people," Mwansa said. He became a very good friend.

On maps of central Africa, Mununga was still a small, faint-typed name among other faint-typed names, but in reality it was a sprawling mega-community that dominated the surrounding area, more than fifty thousand people packed in, hut after hut after hut in every direction for miles. There was no rhythm or order to the organization, no category—town, village, refugee camp?—that fit it. Diseases spread like wildfire in the cramped conditions and where there had once been no end of food, hunger was now a problem. One net was no longer enough for a fisherman to make a living; he needed three, then four, then ten. The elephants, hyenas, and lions in the nearby forests were killed off or chased away and of all the once plentiful wild game, only a handful of hippos and crocodiles remained. These last animals the villagers left alone, the crocs especially, because it was understood that they were the nighttime bodies of ndoshi, and if bothered in any way would crawl out of the river and into the village for their revenge. They could eat a roomful of children if the situation required.

AFTER A FEW MORE WEEKS, KASEKE VILLAGE SHAPED UP TO BE THE ideal place for the first well project. A little more than a mile up the road from the clinic, it was also half a mile from the river, which meant that for the women of Kaseke fetching water was a thirty-minute round-trip—so a well would save time in addition to lives. And we wouldn't even need to dig that much. An old dried-out well sat in a clearing in the center of the village, with a crank and a bucket and everything. All we needed to do was deepen it. Finally, a Kaseke villager named Jefferson knew English and could translate for me. The project seemed like a slam dunk, a sure way to get my Peace Corps mission in gear.

Through Jefferson, I scheduled a meeting with the entire village. The villagers all sat in the central clearing when I arrived on my motorcycle at the appointed time, but I could tell immediately that something was off. The men sat on one side of the clearing and the women on the other, the men casting their eyes down, the women taking turns to get up and wail around a small fire. No one else stirred.

Jefferson took me aside. "My friend, the headman's mother has died," he said. "Let us have the meeting next Monday."

"Of course," I quickly agreed. "My condolences."

Next Monday came, and I rode up. Everyone still huddled in the clearing, barely moving or speaking except to wail.

"The headman's mother has died," Jefferson reported.

"I thought she died last week," I said.

He shook his head. He had recently moved to Kaseke from the Copperbelt to care for his mother who had forgotten how to dress herself. He still retained some of the city affects of a young man-about-town, mainly he was self-conscious about his receding hairline.

"This is a different mother," Jefferson said. "But do not worry, we are eager to hear you speak of wells."

In Bemba culture, the sister of a man's mother is also called mother. My right-hand man, Malama, for example, stayed with his aunt when he wasn't at my place and called her Mother—he could have conceivably had more than a dozen of them.

"No problem," I said to Jefferson. "My condolences. Take the time you need."

We rescheduled the meeting for the next day. But the next day not a single able-bodied man was in the village. I walked through the courtyards and banana groves looking for Jefferson, for any man, but they had all vanished. Women, children, chicken, ducks, goats, and a handful of cripples were all that remained. In my crude Bemba, I tried to question the women, but they eyed me fearfully and spoke quickly, and no one gave me an answer I could understand. It was baffling and also annoying—where had the men all gone and why couldn't they have told me beforehand? It seemed irresponsible to just take off like that.

Jefferson greeted me cheerfully that evening as I played cards with Malama on my porch.

"My friend!" he said. "So sorry! We spent so much time at funerals no food is left. Our people are hungry. Today, myself and all of the men we were fishing on the lake. We caught many fish."

"Oh," I said. "Well, that's good."

I felt chastened for having doubted him—what good was clean water without food, after all—but was beginning to wonder if we'd ever have the meeting. Jefferson was adamant, however, and insisted we reschedule it for the following afternoon.

"Fourteen hundred hours," he promised. "Come then. We will all be there."

At two in the afternoon the next day I rode up to Kaseke and it was empty again. I found Jefferson sleeping on a bamboo mat under a mango tree and kicked his bare foot with my boot, kind of hard.

He cracked open an eye. "My dear friend!" he exclaimed. "Why have you come to visit?" I stood over him, blocking the sun. He sat up, coughed, and struggled to his feet. "Guess what!" he said.

"We brewed maize spirits to celebrate our fishing. We caught many fish. Why don't you drink with us?"

"No." I felt like grabbing and shaking him. He was obviously drunk off his ass. "We were going to have a meeting. Remember?"

"Yes, a drink will be good for you," Jefferson insisted. "The men in Kaseke will think you are a good man if you drink. A man to trust. A man like them. Look, I will show you."

He disappeared behind a nearby hut, reappearing a minute later holding a glass half-full of maize spirits. Four men followed him, swaying and holding each other up. Jefferson handed me the glass and the men cheered when I put it to my lips and hugged me when it was empty. The liquid was almost pure alcohol, tasted like bleach smells, and burned my throat so I croaked like a chain-smoker for days.

"It will be okay, you see," Jefferson said. "Why do you look so upset? I promise you we will start our well soon."

But it would be almost a year.

It was deep into the dry season and all around us, bone-dry maize fields were being set on fire in preparation for the planting season. The crop fires spread raggedly and barefoot children slalomed through the burning stalks like Austrian gold medalists. The harvest had been months ago, and villagers didn't have that much to do as they waited for the rains to come—it was the perfect time to dig a well. But no one wanted to.

Jere shook his head when I told him about Kaseke at his insaka that evening. I went there most every night to have a drink and talk about life.

"Kaseke village is a tough one," he said. "It's a shame. The head-man there is real old and unhelpful. When I first came eight years ago, he wouldn't even let me vaccinate the children because he thought I was poisoning them. Then he fought against me when I tried to get everyone to dig latrines. We had to get the chief to order them to dig."

"You could have told me that three weeks ago," I said. "Saved me a lot of time."

"I thought a white man would have better luck."

That was reasonable. "Well, why didn't he?"

Jere thought about it, looked out over the field. The horizon glowed red from crop fires as if new worlds were being forged out there—worlds, I couldn't help thinking, that would need wells.

"I don't know why," Jere said. "You sound like an old man today."

The next village on the list was Museka, a large one up the river from the clinic. It stretched out along the riverbank and had several beautiful grass fields. These were unusual; grass was usually pulled up so it would be easier to see snakes. Jere came along to translate at my first meeting with Museka's headman and leaders, which gave me hope. He could set anyone at ease. And although here for once I had a meeting that was on schedule and well attended, it, too, quickly fell apart. The Museka village headman, eyes burned a dazzling red by sun and ganja, so that it looked like lit matches were stuck where his corneas should be, was adamant that any well be dug *for* the people of Museka—not *by* them.

"No one will pay my men for digging!" he shouted in Bemba— he always shouted—"and no one will get to own it. So, umusungu, why should we dig? Clean water? What's wrong with the water from the river? Our ancestors drank that water! I drank the water for thirty years. I'm fine!"

The headman's villagers murmured their agreement. Exasperated by his speech, and just fed up in general, I gave him and his men a lecture on children and waterborne disease, full of sarcasm, cold statistics, and borderline insults. After a while, Jere refused to translate. Instead, he told the crowd a parable: *If I give you a goat to watch*, he said, pointing at a large black one passing by, *and I say that the goat is yours for good, for life, if you just watch it carefully and prove that you are a responsible goat watcher, would you go and try to put trousers on the goat? Would you now?*

The villagers squatting in the dirt studied the goat and looked at each other and said, "*Eyy.*" The headman sucked on a joint and squinted thoughtfully at a banana tree, then turned to Jere with an approving smile.

"We've planted the seed," said Jere that night after we'd finished dinner and he'd translated the parable for me. We were in his insaka again—how many evenings I spent there—and were watching the sun set in seventy spectacular shades of red. "We'll go back in one month and it will have taken root."

I didn't believe him; I'd been running in place for too long.

"Your parable doesn't even make any sense," I said. "It has nothing to do with the situation."

"So what? People here just want to be told what to do in a way they can understand. They don't want perfectly logical explanations. You have to be very slippery—it is considered insulting if you are too direct. We say, 'Like a snake approaching its prey.'"

This was the first time I'd had this central tenet of Bemba culture spelled out for me. "Like a snake approaching its prey?" I repeated.

"Yes. That's how things get done," said Jere.

"But what gets done? Nothing gets done."

"Nothing? How many wells have you started?"

"None."

"Do you have any meetings lined up?"

"Nope."

"You've been in Mununga about four weeks?"

"Four months."

Jere nodded, reached up to rub the tip of his nose, studied the dust on the insaka's cement floor. Then he held his face in his hands and his body started to shake.

"Hey! How can you laugh?" I shouted. "I'm serious." But he

couldn't stop. I punched him hard on the shoulder. He just put his head facedown between his elbows and snorted. After a while he stopped and looked up, tears in his eyes.

Jere took pity on me and led me to the bar at the market and bought me Mosis for the next few hours. The bar was a single dingy room under a low tin roof, with benches along the walls, two wooden tables, and a noisy diesel generator powering a boom box and an icebox. Drunk men were sprawled about; they talked drunken gibberish, fell down a lot, and begged for drinks. The proprietor occasionally came out from behind the bar and beat one out the door with a sanded-down stick he kept for that purpose. I couldn't relax. I pestered Jere about the wisdom of crawling around blindly like a snake while people drank dirty water—why not just ask straight questions and insist on straight answers?—but Jere was in a frolicsome mood and shrugged off most of my queries; we drank and got steadily drunker.

"Buy him a beer," Jere said suddenly, pointing at one of the men.

"Talk louder," I said. "Radio."

"Buy him a beer!"

The man he pointed toward listed like a banana leaf with a snapped stem. "He's had enough," I said.

"That's the headman Museka."

Sure enough, ol' ganja eyes from that morning tottered to the bar, stood next to me, and, with his hands and eyes, asked for a round. I put the money down on the counter and the bartender brought the beer out of the icebox. The headman took it up in two hands, then put it down and grabbed my cheeks. He held my face close, red eyes staring deeply into mine. Then he kissed me full on the lips.

"Jesus Christ!" I rubbed off my mouth.

"You see?" Jere laughed. "You see how it's done? You made a friend!"

"Great." I kept rubbing. "So should I kiss every man in town to get a well started?"

"You could try meeting the chief," Jere suggested.

Headman Museka now drank from the bottle with one hand while the other one rested on my shoulders. He may have been talking into my ear also; I wasn't sure with all the noise. "You told me the chief died just before I got here," I said to Jere.

"They say there will be a new one soon."

"Should I kiss him too?"

"No."

The diesel in the bar's generator ran out and Jere gave the barkeep money for another liter and had him turn the radio up. The blasting rumba curtailed my attempts at further conversation. The music sounded to me like a lot of gearshifts grinding, but Jere stood up and danced. He sweated a lot but moved well for a man with a potbelly; he claimed to have been quite a soccer player back in the day. Headman Museka took his hand from my shoulder and pulled me to my feet and we joined Jere in the dark center of the room.

Jere

About five months after I arrived in Mununga, a new chief was inaugurated. He was small and wiry, an ex-boxer who liked to drink and start fights. According to Jere, he had been a shovel operator underground in a Copperbelt mine when someone tapped him on the shoulder and said, You're up, your people need you. He resisted at first because Mununga chiefs had a habit of dying sudden deaths in suspicious circumstances. One died while visiting another chief on an island in Lake Mweru, the next died in a Land Cruiser crossing Zaire, and the most recent one, a schoolteacher, had proclaimed, immediately after taking office, that one bottle out of every batch of banana wine brewed in Mununga be tithed to him. He drank himself to death within the year.

"That's not the brightest rule," I said to Jere.

"No," he agreed. "And now a shovel operator? They must really be running out of options."

The shovel operator didn't really have a choice—the Mununga chieftainship was passed down a matrilineal line and if you were called to serve that was it. So he left his job and his life in the Copperbelt and moved his family into the chief's palace. "Palace" was a stretch, but it was the largest home in Mununga, with six rooms, a tin roof, glass windows, and wooden doors. Set on a big grass field, it looked like a lost adobe cottage from the Arizona desert. Most every other dwelling in the village had a single room, tiny glass-less windows, and a thatch roof.

An inauguration ceremony was held on a long soccer field near the village school featuring incredibly sensual and athletic displays of rumba dancing by prepubescent girls, followed by inebriated men firing rifles in the air. Crowds lurched drunkenly in all directions; whenever gunshot sounded, a thousand people instinctively ducked. The new chief rode above the chaos on a litter made from an old armchair, carried by ten men. This was the first time we'd seen him: he wore a three-piece suit, had a bewildered smile, and was much smaller than we'd expected.

Caught up in the festivities, my optimism grew. This new chief, maybe he and I could become good friends and work together to actually finish something. Five months in the bush and I'd gotten crap done—but adding the chief's authority to my plans had to get the ball rolling. I worked out what I would say to this man, who from what I'd seen of his slightly shy, amiable demeanor, seemed like he'd be receptive to someone with concrete suggestions for how to get on governing.

A week after the inauguration, the chief held his first official meeting. Important government officials came from as far away as Mansa, the provincial capital, to pay their respects, among them the head of the provincial fisheries ministry (fishing was the area's most important business), and the heads of police and education, along with about a hundred village headmen and the area's Peace Corps volunteer.

Before the meeting was called to order, I spotted Boniface in the crowd and walked over to exchange greetings. He was standing in his inimitable way, chin up to the sky, a warship cruising through the waves. We had had an odd relationship since that first day when I'd accused him of seeking a bribe. I couldn't tell if we were pretending that the incident hadn't happened or if I was getting the cold shoulder.

"Are you enjoying my village?" Boniface asked me after the inquiries on each other's health. He spread out an arm to take in the crowd. "Here, you see, we are all friends and talk as friends."

"I'm glad we're friends," I said. "I was hoping we could be friends."

"Yes," he agreed. "And how is your well digging going? Many projects, I am sure. There is so much to do."

I still couldn't figure his angle. "It's going great," I lied.

Boniface nodded. "Yes, that's what Headman Museka tells me."

Was he mocking me, setting me up for something, or just playing it straight?—but before I could unleash a curt comment in reply, the chief walked out of his palace, across the lawn, and into the insaka where we all were gathered. He wore a brown suit and a brass crown shaped exactly like the paper hats they used to give out at Burger King and an expression pitched halfway between excitement and embarrassment. After making his way to a throne in the back of the insaka—the same armchair from his inauguration ceremony, removed from its litter and covered with a tan animal hide—he sat down and accepted greetings and gifts (chicken, beer, cash) from the government officials and headmen. Luckily, I had a five-hundred-kwacha bill in my pocket and I gave him that when it was my turn on the receiving line. Then, when the last man had presented his gift, bowed, and walked back to his seat, and we all wondered what would happen next and considered that not even the chief knew, the chief cleared his throat and started yelling at the top of his lungs.

"My people are crying!" he bellowed in English, loud enough for me to hear. "There is no development in my area! No roads, no electricity. My people are crying. They are crying because they have no electricity. I want development! *Eh, ba mwinemwishi?*"

"*Eh, mukwai!*" A hundred headmen amened.

"I have power! I have a lot of power!" the chief continued, turning to the government officials. "You will see my power. You with all your nicey-nicey talk! Where is my electricity? *Eh, ba mwinemwishi?*"

"*Eh, mukwai!*"

"I want my road! Where is my new road? My paved road? My people are crying for my new road. I will not be ignored. *Eh, ba mwinemwishi?*"

"*Eh, mukwai!*"

The call and response between the chief and the headmen went on for fifteen, twenty minutes, the government officials from Mansa displaying pained smiles throughout, adjusting and read-justing their ties. This tirade was for them. In front of everyone, they were being blasted for neglecting Mununga. These kinds of head-on attacks just weren't done. The air was charged with pride and awe, the cries of the headmen gained fervor and volume: Mununga had its chief.

"It was a great performance," I told Jere afterward, as we sat in his insaka waiting for his wife to bring out dinner. "Unreal. He let the government officials have it with both barrels."

"Well, he was a boxer back in the day," Jere said.

"Really? That's awesome." I was excited. "I am sure once we get a chance to talk he'll help me out with wells."

"You think so?" Jere asked cagily.

"Yeah, I do, why?"

"No reason." He was hiding something.

"No really, why?"

Jere smirked. "You know what his first ruling is? You remember I told you the last chief's rule about brewing wine? How everyone had to donate one bottle of every batch?"

"No. Not that."

"Yes."

I cursed under my breath. Wells still weren't going to get dug anytime soon.

MONDAYS AND THURSDAYS, I HELPED JERE WITH BABY WEIGHING AT the clinic to ensure that the growth of the infants of Mununga fell within healthy parameters. Weighing a single baby was fairly straightforward—you just placed it in a sling hanging from a produce scale. The problem was that at each weighing there were more than three hundred mothers and just the two of us to do the work along with Patrick, a young junior clinic worker who was inexperienced and high-strung. Crowds made Patrick jittery and he always excused himself within a half hour, claiming a fever or sore throat.

"He's sick a lot," I said to Jere. Jere just shrugged.

Mothers descended on the clinic from every direction for the weighings, the line of them stretching out for a hundred yards. Some were dressed in their Sunday best and stood straight-shouldered, clean, and proud; others, dazed by hunger and covered in dust, could barely stand. The youngest were thirteen and fourteen and held their infants like they were surprising things they had found by the road, and then the ones who looked too old to be mothers, who'd had a dozen kids and lost a dozen teeth and had breasts like pie crusts, were often only thirty-two, thirty-three.

The women placed their children, screaming hysterically at the sight of my white skin, in the green cloth sling and I wrote down the number the needle pointed to. If the number was low, mother and child were sent back to Jere who gave them a stern lecture, protein powder, and whatever vitamins he had in stock. If the number was really low, and it often was, then Jere sent someone to fetch me back to the office.

"Look at this," Jere said during one of my first sessions, holding up two children, one in each hand, high in the air like glasses in a toast. "Two-year-old twins, two kilograms each."

I looked: they had stick-figure limbs, the shrunken faces of very old men, bellies swollen like balloons. Jere laughed and held them out to me. "They weigh less than papaya. Here! Try for yourself."

I didn't move to take them. I couldn't understand why he was laughing.

"*Bamayo!*" he yelled. He turned to the twins' mother and gave her a tongue-lashing. She assumed an apologetic but defiant expression. But Jere kept on lecturing her until all the defiance left her face.

"Will they live?" I asked, after the mother had taken them away.

Jere scowled. "Not if they're lucky. Why didn't she come here earlier? Now they're retarded. Their brains have been starved."

Among the women at baby weighing, quite a few had given birth to a dozen children, and in these mothers, eyes gaunt from the experience, bodies hollowed out like gutted fish, there seemed sometimes to be an attitude that sick children were disposable. You sensed it in the way they presented a sick child for the scale—they'd already made their break. The flesh-and-bone infant in their hands, the fruit of their loins, might as well have been a turnip. We knew that at home, their other kids were getting the sick child's share of food—and was that wrong? Someone needed to grow strong and work the fields; the mothers might as well hedge their bets.

Right or wrong, that distance was a painful thing to see. Sometimes, in the middle of baby weighing, I tried to grab a little distance of my own. Stealthily reaching up, I turned off my hearing aids and continued working in silence. It was a coping strategy I had often used back in the States in noisy unintelligible places like dinner parties and restaurants; instantly, I was transported from commotion to a hushed and peaceful place. However, turning my hearing aids off while weighing babies made everything more confused. What was peaceful about a five-pound child slung limply in my hands like an overstretched rubber band?

"I'm not doing enough," I said to Jere, that night after the twins came to the clinic, thoughts of undug wells and malnourished children weighing on my conscience. "I feel like I need to do more."

"How's your chess these days?" he asked.

"Not very good."

"I will teach you."

I was bewildered. "That will help?"

"Oh yes," said Jere. "I haven't had a good game in seven years."

Other days at the clinic, I often ended up in the office of Mr. Mulwanda, Mununga's sleepy inpatient clinician. He counseled patients, handed out pills, cleaned infections, stitched wounds, and delivered babies. I liked that he let me help him do these things; he even taught me to clean and dress tropical sores on my own. But Mulwanda's main prescription for the various illnesses and injuries he saw at the clinic was to tell people to go home and rest. The Mununga clinic, most likely the busiest rural health clinic in all of Zambia, had no blood supply, no IVs, no X-ray machine, no other diagnostic tools, and an inconsistent supply of the most basic drugs. The only thing the clinic never ran out of was aspirin. By necessity, Mulwanda had learned to tell people to take it easy.

The first time that I really gathered what Jere, Mulwanda, and Patrick were up against in their effort to treat illness in the town was when I had an injury of my own. While riding my motorcycle through a flash storm one evening, I hit a pothole and soared headfirst over the handlebars. When I went to the clinic to get my wounds cleaned up, Mulwanda pried a pebble out of my elbow, exposing a deep bloodless hole. We peered inside.

"What's that gray thing?" I asked him.

"That is a vein," he said.

"Should it be hanging out like that?"

Smiling, he batted it back and forth with his finger, like a cat playing with a string. He always smiled. "Sure, why not?"

Luckily, this was on a day when there were some medicines and Mulwanda prepared an injection of antibiotics to ward off the tropical bacteria that could turn a paper cut into flesh-eating soup in just a couple of days. Another patient, a young man, was led into the room just as Mulwanda was about to stick me, and he handed me the needle.

"Do this yourself," he said, and went to the new patient.

His calmness was comforting. I cradled the needle, flashing back to my father's dream that I follow in his footsteps and become a doctor—Mununga College of Medicine, Class of '94—then I stuck it in my butt. Mulwanda called me over to his desk and put my fingers on the patient's wrist.

"Feel this," Mulwanda said.

"Feel what?" I only felt cool skin. Then suddenly something beneath the surface jumped and buzzed in all directions like an angry trapped bee.

I ripped my fingers away. "Jesus! What the hell is that?"

Mulwanda chuckled. "Irregular heartbeat."

The young man looked up at me quickly and then back at the floor. He had shoulders as broad as a market stall. He had put on nice clothes to come to the clinic, a spotless T-shirt and jeans ironed to a crease, and he looked too clean and healthy for such an erratic heartbeat.

"How are you going to treat him?" I asked Mulwanda.

"A Valium and an aspirin," he said.

"That can't be right. That can't be enough. Give him something else. Give him some of these antibiotics."

Mulwanda stood up from his desk. "Come look." He took me by the hand to the clinic pharmacy, a small, windowless room no bigger than a hot tub. I'd never been inside before. There were three long shelves of drugs and vitamins, mostly aspirin, and a crate of condoms covered in dust—this was the total pharmaceutical supply for about fifty thousand people.

"You see?" he asked.

"That can't be enough medicine."

"It's not."

"What's a Valium and an aspirin going to do for irregular heartbeat?"

Mulwanda's eyes crinkled as he chuckled again. "He will sleep without a headache."

"Ba Mulwanda, this is not a joking matter."

"You are right," he agreed. "Maybe you have some medicine?"

I didn't have any medicine. A Valium and an aspirin would be all the young man would get. Mulwanda walked back over to him and told him to go home and rest.

Thing is, I started joining in the laughter about such things. Jere, Mulwanda, and I—even high-strung Patrick at times—you had to find the humor, otherwise you just drove yourself nuts. You laughed about the babies who looked like pineapples, the kids who'd ignored their skin sores until they were the size of steaks, the men with cases of the clap so painful they walked like pigeons, the treatments made up out of the blue. Once a child who had not stopped hiccupping in two days was brought to the clinic, and I told Jere and Mulwanda that in America people frightened hiccups away. They had me run screaming into the room. The poor boy kept right on hiccupping while he pissed his shorts.

JERE WAS MARRIED AND HAD TWO CHILDREN, A BOY AND A GIRL, THREE and four. I didn't talk to his wife much because in the village a man was not supposed to talk to another man's wife. Also she looked fierce, didn't know English, was hugely pregnant, and men and women ate separately—there was scant opportunity for conversation. Jere's son, Palije, on the other hand, I got to know quite well. He was attached to Malama, who pretty much lived in my hut, and so he spent most of his days there. Occasionally I woke up in the morning to find Palije lying under my bed, narrating a conflict between my hiking boots and my running shoes. I'd put in my hearing aids and say good morning, but he'd pretty much ignore me. He liked to carry things in his mouth—matches, money, a length of string tied to a book and dragged around the yard—so he often couldn't speak anyway.

Beauty, Jere's four-year-old daughter, was a different story. She was quiet and solemn and had that innate dignity such kids have. She was attached to her father in a way that was rare in the village, always minding him, making sure he was okay. She ran for Jere when he came home from the clinic, tackling his leg around the knee, and he limped her around the dirt lawn of his house, groaning like a wounded bull. She pressed her face into his thigh, laughing uncontrollably. I didn't see other village men doing this. They did not play with their children; it just wasn't done. But I guess I might be like that if there were a one-in-three chance my child would die.

"She's special. Smart. I like her better than the other one," Jere said of Beauty one evening in his insaka. "Palije's strange."

As we talked, Palije was crawling around on the floor with an empty cigarette pack in his mouth, and seemed to be having a conversation through the pack with his left hand.

"He seems all right to me," I said.

"But he's got a cigarette pack in his mouth," Jere said. "Palije! Take that out!" He reached down and ripped the pack from his son's mouth. The boy stared at his father, as stunned as if he had just landed there from another world.

Jere crumpled the pack into his pocket. "Do you have any children?" he asked.

"No," I said.

"Do you want any?"

"Some day."

"I can help you find someone, if you want."

"That's okay."

We drank a lot together, Jere and I. If we weren't quaffing his home-brewed wine, I usually insisted on buying the drinks because I felt sheepish for all the food, company, and guidance he freely provided me. I tried to give him money, thick glinting stacks of orange five-hundred-kwacha bills (the highest Zambian denomination, worth less than a buck), but he declined these. So I bought us beers and told him about the places I'd been, about redwood trees, pale Ivy League girls walking to class in snow boots, Swedish fish, fall in New England, the view of the Great Plains from an airplane—anything that seemed to spark his interest. But usually I was the one asking the questions. Jere's insaka was the switchboard of the community and every evening men materialized out of the night to pass by and discuss the latest gossip. Jere always translated what they said, repeating himself if I asked.

One time during those early months I said to him, "You know, you must be the only person in the village who hasn't asked me for anything. Everyone else wants clothes, a motorcycle, a ticket to America. How is it you don't need anything?"

"I wish you'd study your chess," he answered. "You never think your moves through."

"Why are you so hung up on chess?" I asked, but he didn't answer, and so it was a while yet before I understood how he needed me.

Cultural Exchange

There was a saying in the Peace Corps around the time of my service: Volunteers who go to South America come back to the States politically active, volunteers who go to Southeast Asia return spiritually aware and curious, and volunteers who go to Africa?—they come back drunk and laughing.

I learned this saying during the first in-service volunteer conference. The eleven of us remaining volunteers had gathered in Mansa, site of Peace Corps regional headquarters, to discuss adjustment and development issues, get rabies booster shots from Maria the nurse, compare how much weight we'd lost, and set off a few firecrackers for the Fourth of July. Mansa was a small city with broad dirt streets, a flat, tired sky, and haggard-looking men sitting on weatherbeaten porches, staring as you passed. It felt time-warped, like the Wild West; tumbleweeds, posses, and John Wayne on his horse would not have been out of place there. The one anomaly was the bank, which, with its gleaming steel walls and Kevlar-ed guards, resembled a fortress on Mars.

I soon found out I wasn't alone in getting nothing done. The other volunteers complained of the same kinds of setbacks that I faced in Mununga, how powerful men blocked their efforts and villagers viewed them with suspicion and fear.

"Relax," Administration said. "You guys are trying too hard. You're the first Peace Corps volunteers ever in this country. Your villages are way out there—President Chiluba wanted you in this province, about the most remote place there is in Zambia—so it's going to be pretty impossible to complete your projects. Don't worry about them. Have fun. You are taking the first step in a long journey. The first step is the most important; we don't expect you to get to the end. Cultural exchange is what your job is really about. Cultural exchange."

This was news to me. I had come halfway around the world expecting to make a difference and in training they had made digging wells seem as straightforward as changing lightbulbs. But it was obvious by now that we lacked the crucial enzyme of development: money. We had none, were never going to get much. A painful thing to realize when you considered the difference just one borehole well could make.

"Cultural exchange?" I asked Administration to make sure.

"Yes, cultural exchange," he repeated. "Your real job is to stay alive."

"Stay alive?"

"Yes, stay alive. But I'll tell you what. Beers are on me tonight."

I stopped listening to Administration after that and spent the rest of the conference talking to Maria. She was older, in her late thirties, thin and gracious, with enormous soft brown eyes that made her look more timid than she was. In her prior life, she'd been an emergency room nurse in Missoula. She told me about that job, about other countries she'd visited and people she'd met; and I told her about Mununga, which means I alternately complained about or made light of how little I had accomplished.

"Sounds to me like you're doing great," she said.

"It does?"

"You do what you can," she said. "Sometimes it isn't meant to be."

"What's not meant to be?"

"My supervisor at the hospital used to say that all the time. It was supposed to make us feel better if we lost someone on the table. But I left all that to come to Africa, so maybe it didn't work."

She often ended up contradicting herself like that. I liked her honesty. When we kissed that night, I felt so grateful. It was after the holiday fireworks—little blips of light on a dark field that set the wild dogs howling.

"Why are you here?" I asked her when we got to her room.

"Here in Africa or with you?"

"Either one."

She explained: a marriage that drifted apart, a lover promising everything and then leaving, a feeling of dissatisfaction that daily life couldn't reach. She had applied to work for the Peace Corps to get away from Montana and think things over, and soon after being hired, at a conference in Kenya for the Eastern Africa medical staff, she went to bed with a tall, sad country doctor. He cried thank you thank you when he came, then wept about his wife in Illinois. Maria started to wonder then if a life following your heart was also, by definition, a lonely life.

"I'm here because I keep choosing the wrong men," she concluded. "I keep settling for less than I want. The difference between what I want and what I get is so big."

"What do you want?"

"Really not that much," she said. "Someone who can appreciate a sunset and then screw my brains out."

I bit my tongue. "I'll keep an eye out," I promised.

"Cultural exchange?" Jere asked, when I returned to Mununga. "What's that?"

"I'm not sure," I admitted. "I sort of stopped paying attention."

"Is that like where you bring a Bible and tell us what God to believe in?"

"No," I said. "Well, maybe. Jere, please don't make this harder than it needs to be."

"Cultural exchange," he thought out loud. "I have an idea." He went to his house and came back with two books on chess openings. I wasn't too surprised. He handed them to me. "Check out the Sicilian defense. It's from Italy."

Cultural exchange: the free interchange of the languages, traditions, customs, and beliefs of cultures. My new focus. I walked around the village trying to figure out how to go about it. That may sound naive but when I wasn't helping out at the clinic I had all kinds of time.

I was reminded of an experience I had during training in Kabwe. I had become friends with Rave and Walter, two basketball junkies studying at the Teachers' College. In Africa, unlike America, basketball is the game of the rich. You need good shoes and a ball, which aren't cheap, and a slab of flat concrete and a straight metal pole—very hard to find. Soccer, on the other hand, which in the States is the sport of the well-manicured suburbs, is the sport of the poor in Africa. Everywhere in the village barefoot children kicked around homemade balls of plastic scraps wrapped in reeds. But Rave and Walter, despite not having too much money, were crazy about hoops. They each had shirts with Michael Jordan's name and number, and pestered me about his recent decision to retire and play American cricket, like I had some influence in the matter. A couple of afternoons a week the three of us played twenty-one and when their college had a game against the Zambian National Air Force, they invited me to play.

Since I was eleven and watched Bernard King drag the Knicks to the play-offs on gimpy hamstrings and fractured fingers taped together into Vulcan greetings, basketball was the sport I loved most. All through junior high, my afternoons and evenings were spent in the driveway practicing my jump shot and I became a decent player. The first half of the game against the Zambian National Air Force was one of those times when the basket is as wide as the Sahara and the ball is an extension of your own nerves. There was a crowd of a couple hundred students surrounding the potholed court and they were into it, chanting, I was told later, "*Umusungu, umusungu, umusungu*"—"White man, white man, white man."

"All you white people are just better at basketball, huh?" Walter said to me when I put my hearing aids on at halftime (I had to take them out to play).

"Yeah, we are," I said.

The second half was more of the same. It was a tight game, but we pulled away. My defender became frustrated and shoved me to the ground, drawing a bloody gash on my knee. In response, I threw a half-court bounce pass between his legs. Rave called a time-out and pulled me aside.

"Cut it out," he hissed.

"Cut what out?"

"This is the air force. They will bomb you in your village."

What? I thought, with their Popsicle-stick planes? But I saw then just how furious the pilots looked. Rave and Walter started deliberately turning the ball over until we fell behind. I didn't want to throw the game so I stopped passing to them and tried to win single-handedly—which didn't work.

"We should have won," I told Rave and Walter afterward.

"We did win," Rave said. "Nobody's going to die."

So was that cultural exchange?

Or was it this: When I wandered around the village asking people to wash their hands before eating, with ashes if they couldn't afford soap, they asked me for shoes. When they rubbed their stomachs and complained of hunger, I offered them aspirins and mangoes. Was that it?

Have fun, Administration had said. Have fun? How?

The answer was obvious when it finally arrived. Watching the girls and boys flirt with each other at the market it hit me: what's the one thing that cuts through all cultures, that every person in the world knows about?

Sex, of course. So one night, I introduced Malama to the *Sports Illustrated* swimsuit issue. With great ceremony, I lit the kerosene lamp and a couple of mosquito coils in the front room, took the magazine from its special place underneath my mattress, and set it down on the floor in front of the couch. I called Malama over.

"What is this?" he asked, catching sight of the cover.

I put my arm over his shoulder. "My friend," I said, "this is my culture. This is America."

I opened the magazine past the sports recaps to a photograph of a woman wearing little but fine white sand.

Malama gaped. "America?" he pointed.

"Yes," I said. "Or she might be Australian."

He stared at her; she smiled back. Slowly, reverently, Malama began to turn the pages, running his fingers over the models, smiling back at their smiles.

"Why she different?" he asked of one.

"She's Chinese. From China."

"Not America? China? Everyone like this in China?"

"No, I don't think so. But I've never been there."

He touched the Chinese woman's thigh, artfully half-covered by a shallow wave. "I want to go to China," he said. "America first, China second."

Breasts didn't interest Malama so much—women in the village breast-fed a dozen children one right after the other, so breasts were not considered sexual. But a grown woman's thighs, these he had never seen. In the cities, women could be stoned to death for wearing short skirts; in the villages, they never even tried to wear them. The swimsuit issue had photos of blacks, whites, blondes, and brunettes, of a woman on a horse, a woman by a pool, a woman running in the sand dunes, another one hugging her shoulders in a field of tropical flowers—all of them with thighs. Malama's eyes nearly fell out of his head.

"Enjoy. Just don't get the pages stuck together," I told him, making a motion with my wrist.

"Oh, I never do that," he said.

"I'm kidding, it's okay."

He dropped the magazine. "I don't do it!" he stammered and left the hut. I had to run after him and apologize to get him to come back. I had to tread lightly with this kind of cultural exchange.

The swimsuit issue quickly became legendary among a certain population. Nearly every afternoon, I came home from the clinic to find Malama and a half-dozen of his friends crouched on my floor, peering down at the magazine, debating each picture like Talmudic scholars discussing Shabbat rituals. They argued their favorites, acted out poses, moved each other's arms and legs into the right positions, and stretched the skin around their eyes to look Chinese. When they reached some kind of consensus, only Malama, I noticed, was allowed to turn the page.

Mission accomplished, I guess, but I was soon bored again. The magazine became involved in another, less successful endeavor to expand sexual horizons. This involved Chiluba, the woman who came daily to cook, draw water, wash my clothes, and keep my house in order.

Back on my first evening in the village, Jere had asked me if I wanted a woman. I hadn't understood him at first. "I can have you one for three thousand kwacha a month," he had said. That was five bucks. "But one who talks English will be a little bit more."

"No, thank you, Mr. Jere," I had responded.

"No, I will arrange," he insisted. "I know where to find one. Are looks important? You're tall. She should be big, no? I have someone in mind."

"Mr. Jere, I don't need you to find me a woman."

"But she will take care of everything."

"I am sure she will. But it's not necessary," I said.

It took me a couple of days to figure out what he meant and a few days after that I took up the offer. It was impossible to cook meals and keep the hut free of dust while helping out at the clinic.

Chiluba had the same name as Zambia's president—something Jere always liked to point out: "Look, the president is cooking your dinner!"—but she was a lot taller and bigger than he was, with traps and deltoids like river stones. She had been living in the Copperbelt with her father, a government minister who had long ago divorced her mother, and was attending a missionary school there, when her father suffered a heart attack while on top of a prostitute. Chiluba was sixteen. Just like that, she had to go live with her mother in the bush and her education was over for good.

Every morning, she showed up at my hut at the crack of dawn, grabbed a reed broom, bent over, and swept the place out. Then while I was at the clinic or off canvassing villages she took the previous day's dirty plates and clothes down to the river to wash, did the food shopping, and cooked lunch. Afternoons were slower and were often passed sitting on my porch with her two sisters, arguing and braiding hair. Her English was pretty good, better than Malama's at least, because of her years at the missionary school.

She had an endearing way of asking for things. "Why don't you want to buy a new broom?" she'd ask. Or "Why can't we have goat meat?" "Why don't you want to give me a thousand kwacha for a new shirt?"

"Don't ask—just say what you want and we'll buy it," I'd tell her, but she never would.

But here's the thing about Chiluba, and why I tried to share the swimsuit issue with her. Of everyone I met in Mununga, she more than anyone seemed trapped in the wrong world. Twenty-two and a virgin, ancient by village standards, she had no interest in men. She never flirted with young men at the market, barely waved when they called out greetings as they passed the hut. There was an abruptness in her interactions with them, a distaste even. One afternoon, after a few glasses of banana wine, we talked about her marriage prospects and she surprised me with a story of lying next to her girlfriends back at the missionary school, of how they shared small cots in cramped dorm rooms, of how they held each other, and of how, after lights out, they had kissed.

"Very nice," she said. "Lips very soft."

"Nothing wrong with that," I said.

"I miss."

She became flushed and shy and we talked of something else. Why did she even mention such things to me? Maybe because no one had ever asked her. And I was so different, so strange; she had no concept for how to talk to me, no evasive techniques if I was out of line.

In Zambia, homosexuality was against the law. It wasn't taught in the classrooms or mentioned in the newspaper or on the radio. The official national rate was zero percent. Maybe the percentage was lower than in the developed world because it was so important to have as many children as possible to work the fields; still, looking at Chiluba, watching her interact with men, listening to her stories of school, it seemed totally bogus. At some point she would be purchased and married and then would spend her days keeping house for some man she hadn't chosen, lying under him whenever he felt like it. A perfectly ordinary, respectable village life. But I wanted her to experience more than this. It could be a cultural exchange.

We drank another cup each of banana wine. I gathered my nerve. "Do you know what an orgasm is?" I asked her.

"A what?" Chiluba said. "What's that?"

I went into the house and brought out *Ulysses* and read her the last page, letting my voice rise with Molly Bloom's as she steamed yes toward climax yes.

"That was an orgasm," I said, when I was done.

Chiluba's eyes went wide. "Yes."

"She's alone in bed, see? With her hands here. Or maybe here too. You see what she's doing?"

"Very nice!" Chiluba shook like a leaf and refilled her glass. She looked kind of frightened.

I thought that went well. The next step was the magazine. Chiluba was leaving that night to spend a weekend at her mother's hut up the lake, so I grabbed the swimsuit issue from the pile of Malama's things and ran after her as she left.

"Take this with you," I said. "Read it when you're alone. Pretend you are back in the dorm room, lying in bed with your friends. Pretend you are holding them like you used to."

Chiluba rolled the magazine up and tucked it under her arm so no one would see it. "I understand," she said.

"You can even pretend they are touching you. You know, everywhere. Like the woman in the book?"

She blushed. "Okay."

"But bring the magazine back or Malama will be upset."

"Okay."

In retrospect, I was way too vague. Also by village standards this conversation was inappropriate and disrespectful, but in my defense, in a just world, maybe it wouldn't be.

"Did you like the magazine?" I asked Chiluba when she returned.

"Yes," she said. "*Sana!* Very much! I did it with my mother."

"Excuse me?"

"The magazine. Together." Chiluba made the motion of turning pages. "We did it together."

So I had mixed success with my masturbation proselytization. But there was one cultural exchange project that had success written all over it. Late one night while I sat on the couch reading by candlelight, Malama twitching in his dreams next to me, and the rest of the village long gone to bed, there was, for several long minutes, a rhythmic clunking noise I couldn't place. Then I realized someone was knocking on the door. It was Alice, the girl from across the way. She stood in my doorway, a stiff breeze rustling her blouse. She'd licked her full lips until they were wet.

"What do you want?" I asked her in Bemba.

But I knew exactly what she wanted.

She ran her tongue over her lips, making them shine further and smiled her conspiratorial smile.

"Go home, Alice," I said. "Please go."

DESPITE HIS DECISION, STRICTLY ENFORCED, TO EXTEND THE PREVI-ous chief's tax on home-brewed wine, I did not give up my dream that the new chief and I would unite into a powerful force for wells and wellness and so a month or so after he arrived, I put on my nicest shirt, a pink Izod that I'd bought for fifty cents at the market, and paid him an unannounced visit. The palace by then had a brand-new eight-foot-high thatch fence around it and a line of supplicants waiting outside. The *kapasos*, the chief's private police, led me right to the front of the line and ushered me through the palace gate. The chief sat on his throne in his insaka, wearing his usual brown suit and brass Burger King crown. He greeted me warmly and listened attentively as I spoke of community development principles. When I finished, he inquired in his decent English if, for my first project, I could install piped water in the palace.

"Piped water?" I responded. "Where would the water be coming from?"

"Underground," he said.

"No, Chief, I mean, where would the pipes connect to? What would be the water source?"

"The water would come from the pipes, Mr. Joshua. You white men can build anything."

Inwardly I sighed. A dozen men filled the insaka, along with a couple of chickens and a mean-eyed guard cradling a rifle. Not understanding English, they stared fixedly at me like I was juggling burning things. I gathered that it wouldn't be a good idea to decline the chief's request in front of everyone.

"I'll look into it," I said.

"Wonderful," the chief said. "Do you want a drink?"

Accepting a drink meant drinking until I couldn't anymore, and that meant nothing further would be accomplished that day other than drunkenly riding my motorcycle home and passing out on the couch.

"Sure."

"Good." The chief motioned a kapaso to bring me a glass. "Together, Mr. Joshua, our work will give my people hope," he said. "When they see the piped water in my palace they will know that change has come." He drained a whole glass of banana wine in one long swallow and refilled it from a jug at his feet. He pointed at a majestic mango tree about fifty feet away. "You see that tree?" he asked.

"Yes."

"That's where I hung my brother-in-law last night."

"What? You killed your brother-in-law?"

The chief laughed deeply and patted my arm in a soothing gesture as if I were a child. He translated what I had said to the audience—they guffawed as well. "No, Mr. Joshua, I didn't kill him. I hung him by his arm. I had to do it, as chief. He tried to punch me."

A woman and a young girl came out of his house and walked toward us, carrying steaming pots of food. They uncovered them, revealing boiled Mweru fish and *ubwali*, maize porridge, the village staple. It smelled delicious.

"I am glad you are in my village," the chief said.

And it struck me then, smelling that food, exchanging warm greetings with the other hungry men in the insaka, and looking at the mango tree and trying to picture hanging there from an arm all night, that I was glad too. So I wasn't that busy save for my work at the clinic, but I was welcomed here, celebrated even, plied with food and drink. But it was more than that—I realized all of a sudden that I had found a place where my deafness didn't matter—I hadn't thought about it in ages. It didn't get in the way of anything. It didn't bother the chief. It didn't hamper cultural exchange. At gatherings large and small, everyone directed their words to me because they all wanted the umusungu to hear what they had to say, so I could read their lips easily, and if I had trouble understanding them even then, they blamed themselves, their poor English, and repeated themselves, louder and slower, and again still. No one talked over each other, no one spoke out of the side of their mouths, nor did anyone comment on my slight deaf accent because how could they know I spoke English strangely? And always in the flat open village spaces there was a bare minimum of background noise, which for me has always been the hardest hurdle toward understanding speech.

For the first time in my life, deafness was gone. Or not gone—I still couldn't tell whether that noise was a man calling or a dog barking, or if this one was a child crying or a bird song and I still, of course, missed all conversation that wasn't said directly at me—I mean that for the first time deafness did not close off a single possibility. That was a lovely feeling. I ate lunch with the chief. I didn't have to talk on the phone. The wine was free. People were glad to see me.

Yes, there was rawness and brokenness, the daily parade of the wounded and the ill at the clinic, but I was doing what I could and felt in small ways useful.

"So what did the chief say?" Jere asked me the next morning. "Is he going to help with the wells?"

"Define help," I said.

Jere laughed. "How much did he make you drink?"

Varieties of the Deaf Experience, Part III

I'd tried to find that place beyond deafness and hearing before.

In junior high and high school, I had tuned out most lessons, reading Nietzsche, Ayn Rand, *The Happy Hooker Goes to Washington*, or whatever book currently had my interest during class. My teachers, ill at ease with my disability and my skill at asking difficult questions when they forced me to pay attention, usually let me be. And while my spoken English still had a lot of rough spots—I thought that zealots were zeeelots, racists were rahsis, and for the longest time had been tricked by my father into believing that the bridge to Jersey was named after George Washingmachine (Me: "Who's he?" Dad: "The father of our laundry")—with the help of a few cues written on the blackboard I could figure out what my teachers wanted and give it to them. They didn't have much cause to complain. But outside of the classroom, hearing was one unending struggle of fast talkers and loud scenes.

After the frustrating experiences of childhood, I thought college might be a place to start afresh, past the limitations imposed by my ears. At seventeen, I applied to Yale. In my admissions interview, for the first time ever, I played the deaf card, and I played it, I have to say, like B. B. King plays Lucille.

INTERVIEWER: "What makes you different?"

ME: "Excuse me?"

INTERVIEWER: "What makes you different from all the other candidates?"

ME: (Takes out hearing aids, places them on desk. Nods, looks out window.)

But far from being a place where deafness was less important, at Yale it was much more of a problem than ever before. Classes were brutal; most of them were large lectures with instructors who spoke in thick accents or while facing the board. No matter how many times I asked them not to, they kept doing so. Great academics, in my experience, are usually shockingly lacking in elementary social skills. I spent many hours in one philosophy lecture course wondering how the German Kierkegaard expert onstage ate soup through his great beard. It was like a cotton candy machine was stuck to his face. He would talk for two hours straight through that beard, low guttural noises that sounded like he was trying to hack a pickle out of his throat, and then a student would stand up in the back of the room and ask a question in a squeaky voice.

"Rub-a-rub-a errgh rugga wub," said the instructor.

"Weee me we me, mee mee, wee?" asked the student.

"Ahh, glubba, glubba rugah erggh," answered the instructor, stroking his beard.

The afternoon sun slanted through the high windows and set floating dust on fire. A sea of students blinked in the sunlight, then bent over spiral notebooks and wrote their secrets. What great wisdom was being discussed? Who could tell me why the world was molded with such inequities? None and no one, I began to conclude. Everyone was ecstatic when the bell rang. Occasionally, if I was sitting next to a cute girl and wasn't feeling shy, I'd ask her to take notes for me. Otherwise I'd take my own notes, which were usually some variation of "Stop talking please." For papers I'd smoke a joint and write whatever came to mind, which usually tended to be the same sentence written seventy-eight different ways—always worth at least a B in philosophy.

I had hopes for a religious studies class. The professor was one of the few I could lipread clearly and was highly esteemed and spoke without an accent. However, he gave lectures of such complexity I could never tell if I was hearing them right. The readings for the class were no better—articles with footnotes as long as the articles themselves. The footnotes had footnotes, and the footnotes of the footnotes seemed to be written in a code from space.

If there was an easier way to take on the challenge of higher education as a deaf student, I had no idea. If there was help out there, I'd never learned to ask for it. About the only time I felt any kind of ease was when I was wasted to the point that I washed my feet by peeing on my shoes or when I had a lover in my arms— sex and drugs, two thirds of youth's holy trinity; the third, rock and roll, pretty much unavailable to me.

Senior year, as my classmates settled into their respective life paths placid as commuters making the last turns of a drive home— law school, biz school, med school, suit, briefcase, stethoscope, check!—I felt disconsolate. That's all we learn here? Yes, said the other students, with complete assurance, ready to pursue graduate degrees or don Batsuits. It was, I know, the height of arrogance to judge others for not having the answers for my own unhappiness, but still I questioned everyone on their motives: *How can you be so sure? What is true if everything changes? What's the point of ambition if we all die?* I was on the outside of all these students rushing noisily to their lives—I think that sound, bearing language from all directions, is the one sense that most grounds us in society—it all seemed bizarre to me.

Try Prozac, I was told.

Instead I went to Gallaudet University, the national university for the deaf.

AS I SAID, I DIDN'T KNOW A SINGLE DEAF PERSON AT THAT POINT besides my brother Sam and my younger cousin Ben, who seemed to drown his deafness in video games. I thought that by learning ASL, American Sign Language, at Gallaudet and meeting other deaf people, and entering a community where communication wasn't a constant, exhausting struggle that invariably came up short, life might open up in new ways. Also, maybe Marlee Matlin would be there.

At first at Gally, I could barely sign so I just sat quietly while others did, looking to snatch a word here and there and make up some remark off of that—pretty much the same strategy I followed in spoken conversations. At parties, I found myself a step or two behind, and relied on a dormmate to laboriously sign out the highlights. Often, not wanting to be a bother, I didn't ask for the details and nodded along like I understood—something I had plenty of practice doing.

I watched the students talk to each other in the cafeteria. Some threw signs like rappers, quick, harsh motions that had a bop and an edge. Others signed like orchestra conductors, their fingers hanging in space and then swooping down in long arcs, seagulls gliding in for a landing, the whole horn section quieting to one low plaintive note before exploding again. Others signed like shy mice, or out of breath grizzlies, or crouched over coal miners waiting for the walls to collapse, teenagers aping rock stars, eagles snatching dinner, rabbits scratching air, and rain falling in thick, luscious drops. It was beautiful, all of it, and I could barely understand a word. Still, I was sure what they said was poignant and profound. Only later did I begin to pick up that they were having exactly the same conversations as in the hearing world: who hooked up with whom, whose feelings were hurt and whose weren't, and do I look good in this shirt?

Still, Gallaudet was a unique place. Everyone, even the hearing people, used ASL—it was a law. Once a month there was a dance party in the school parking garage with six-foot-high speakers turned facedown on the ground. The speakers were turned so loud you could see sound waves rippling through the air and the students danced to the vibrations, which could be felt a quarter mile away.

This was an historic time at the school. The Americans with Disabilities Act had just been passed and the students had just successfully protested for a deaf school president. They held rally after rally to get deaf culture the respect it deserved. They were aware that they needed to maintain a constant vigilance against being marginalized. Where was the deaf person on the board of directors? On the conference call? On Capitol Hill? Deaf children would not grow up to be astronauts or soldiers, airplane pilots or newscasters, disc jockeys or rock stars. We would not strum guitars by campfires, hear movies in theaters, hear our children in the other room, hear our teammates calling to us on the fast break or the subway conductor announcing that the train would skip our stop and ride straight out to Brooklyn. Who was going to fight for us? Nobody. We'd hold the line ourselves.

If you could take a pill that could make you hearing, would you? was a question posed by the school newspaper, and a vast majority of the students said no, we are proud of who we are.

But who are we, I wanted to know? Who looks out from our eyes? Even here where working ears were irrelevant I felt out of place. To the deaf students I was hearing, just as to the hearing people I was deaf.

Let me say that Gallaudet's students deserved everything they asked for. For generations, the hearing world has unfairly treated the deaf community like a bastard child. It deserves equality. But if you get equality, then what? I had lived enough in the hearing world to know it was just as flawed as the deaf—if not, in its devotion to wealth and fame, even more so. Life had sixteen thousand different ways of being unsatisfying, independent of whether you heard it or not.

So for all these reasons, I couldn't relate to the protests sweeping the community. Some people told me that my ambivalence stemmed from trying to be hearing and not accepting who I was, that I should chuck my hearing aids and their attendant frustrations once and for all. But I wasn't ready to do that.

I ended up spending eight months at the university. I lived in a dorm on campus the first part of that, then I moved into a house across the street from the school with four other deaf men. At night we watched movies with fistfights and guns. The plots were easy enough to follow even if the closed captions were sloppy. One night, as we watched a Jean-Claude Van Damme flick, police lights started flashing through the windows. It took us a minute to realize where the lights were coming from because in the movie, Jean-Claude was riding his motorcycle in the bayou, outracing a dozen cops who unjustly fingered him for murder. Then the chase scene ended and he was emerging naked from a lake for an approving Rosanna Arquette and we noticed that police lights still shimmered around the room. When we opened the door to see what was happening, we walked into an armed standoff between D.C.'s finest and the crack dealers next door. This doesn't generally happen if you can hear. The mouths of the cops took violent shapes, and they lifted one hand away from their guns and waved us back inside.

Exciting, but the point is: this wasn't my home. It was another place where I struggled with the one constant in my life—being marginalized. In Mununga, however, I was right in the fray. Could I really be finding a home in the middle of Africa?

On the first of each month I had an experience that reinforced the notion that I was. I woke up early, brewed strong tea with Malama, gave him a handful of kwacha to watch my place, then went to the market and caught a pickup for the three-hour drive down the dirt road to Kashikishi. In Kashikishi, I caught a bus and rode all day down the freshly paved highway to Mansa and the bank where my pay was wired. It was a long relaxing ride. The view was of the same village repeated several thousand times. In its shades of green the land exactly reflected the rhythm of the seasons and in their unhurried routines the villagers harkened back to truths that would outlast all of us.

Sometime after dusk, the bus arrived in Mansa. I dodged child beggars and whores in the street, checked into a motel, and headed to the Mansa Club. A relic from the last days of colonialism, the Mansa Club was the only place in the entire province that served real scotch and real whiskey. It boasted high wood ceilings, a wall-length mirror over a varnished bar, a covered porch, and it had a dartboard, a Ping-Pong table, a snooker table, and, outside in the courtyard, even a tennis court. Most locals steered clear of the club because the drinks were overpriced and a one-eyed guard with a gun kept out whores. On the porch behind the bar, two skinny men barbecued chicken on a beat-up grill made from an old oil drum, and after a month of village fare of boiled fish and maize porridge, that chicken tasted like heaven.

It was refreshing to see Chris and everyone else, and to eat barbecue and drink cold beer. But I quickly grew to dread these monthly trips because in the noisy club I couldn't understand a word anyone said. Conversation was a jumble of personal revelations, breathless stories, random gossip, and news from the States, set to blaring rumba music from a cranked-up boom box—it was impossible to follow. I could hear laughter, but not the jokes.

By the time I'd been there an hour, I was ready to go back to Mununga. In Mununga, people really cared if I understood them. It was vital that I understood them; to the other volunteers it wasn't all that important. At the Mansa Club, it really struck me that never in my life had I felt so integrated into a place as I did in Mununga. Jere, the chief, sleepy Mulwanda, Malama, and Chiluba—I could hear them all.

As the months passed, I avoided other volunteers more and more, staying in Mununga as long as money held out, slipping into Mansa to pick up my pay only after the others had come and gone.

Alice

The days were full. There were Bemba lessons, community meetings, and at the clinic, I spent more and more time helping patients under Jere's and Mulwanda's guidance. Dysentery, malaria, malnutrition, tuberculosis, AIDS, grotesque tropical sores like exploded epidermal land mines—there was no end of work there. I was grateful to be of use although I'd had no experience with such things. Excitement hit up against suffering, and they had a difficult, guilt-filled relationship that I struggled constantly to clarify. Still, seven months in, the village felt like a home. So when I arrived at my hut buzzed from another night of banana wine and chess at Jere's insaka to find the beautiful Alice waiting on my porch, cleanly dressed and freshly bathed, it seemed, regardless of my earlier fears about STDs, regardless of Malama's warnings about the quality of her character, that the logical extension of all the warm feeling was to invite her inside. I didn't have to think about it long.

"You looking for someone?" I asked her in Bemba.

Alice pinched my arm. *"Eyy."* Yes.

I opened the door to my hut. Right inside the door my motorcycle rested against the wall and I whacked my shin on the footpad; the pain was like white explosions. I limped the motorcycle into a corner, shook Malama awake from his spot on the couch, pushed him out of the door before he was fully aware of what was happening. Then I extended an arm, presenting Alice with the two small front rooms, one with a table and motorcycle, the other with the couch.

"*Mwalilah*, Alice," I said. Welcome to my home.

In response, she took hold of her blouse and pulled it down to her waist. Her breasts rose like they were on springs. When I touched one, it pushed against my hand, challenging me. I accepted the challenge. I lit the kerosene lamp, and led her to the bedroom. With silkily composed movements, she stepped out of her white skirt and pink underwear and slid underneath the mosquito net. She didn't say a word. "Make yourself comfortable," I said, just to hear myself speak.

I looked for a condom. It took me a long minute to remember that the condoms were in the first aid kit, then five more minutes to find the kit. I had hid it from myself because whenever I saw it I started bandaging random body parts. Africa, big surprise, turns you into a hypochondriac. Alice waited under the mosquito net, smelling of musk, Rambo soap, and charcoal smoke. When I found what I was looking for, she reached up through the netting and pulled me on top of her.

"Oh!" she said.

But that was only because my elbow had landed in her ribs.

"Sorry," I moved to her side.

She lifted a hand up and slapped the condom out of mine.

"No, no white babies," I said.

As I put the rubber on, Alice leaned over the edge of the bed and blew out the kerosene lantern, but I wouldn't be able to read her lips without the light, so I felt on the floor for the matches and relit it. She blew it out again. I lit it again. This went on for a while, then she grunted and climbed on top of me and certain motions commenced—commenced, I have to say, by someone who seemed to possess some expertise. I'd had a couple of yearlong relationships in college and another one as a forest ranger, and it wasn't till this moment that I realized I was lonely. And not just for sex—I knew Alice and I didn't have much to talk about, but even so, I thought this could be the start of something more intimate than playing chess and joking around. After all, a drunken night of groping was how I'd begun most relationships.

Outside there was a vague pounding like a distant bass line. Alice slid off me and misinterpreting her, I rolled on top, pinning her against the mattress. The walls of the hut began to shake, and dust sprinkled from the anthills in the roof thatch onto my bed. Someone yelled, but I couldn't make out who or what.

"Jere!" I shouted, taking a guess. He was the only person I could imagine at my hut this late. "Door's locked! I'll see you in the morning."

But the pounding continued. More dust fell.

"Who is that?" I asked Alice.

"Ba ba ba," she said.

"Ba ba ba?" I mulled that over. "Is that a song?"

"*Batata, batata!*" she shouted. "My father, my father."

"Shit." I fell onto my back.

Alice leapt off the bed and out of the mosquito netting and grabbed her skirt, dressed without saying a word, and ran out of the bedroom. A few seconds later the pounding stopped. Just like that, I was lying alone in bed, not exactly sure what had just taken place. At least it didn't seem like a big deal: Alice had been in my hut for less than ten minutes, half of which we'd spent fighting over the lantern.

I took out my hearing aids and slept. When I look back at that night now, I think: what a rookie mistake.

THE NEXT MORNING, JERE WOKE ME BY KICKING THE FOOT OF my bed.

"Excuse me for coming in your bedroom," he said, after I put my hearing aids in, "I called your name again and again—Josh! Josh! Josh!—but you didn't answer."

"I can't hear," I said. "Remember?" I took a moment to orient myself, sat up, and noticed that Alice had forgotten her panties on the floor. Jere was bathed, shaved, and wore a long-sleeved shirt ironed till it creased. "Why are you dressed up?" I asked.

He shook out his sleeves. "Hurry up. It is time for your judging."

Without looking down, I kicked the panties under the bed. "My what?"

"Your judging."

"What judging?"

"Yours."

"Judging?"

"Yes, judging."

Sometimes, I don't hear, sometimes I don't understand. Sometimes both.

"What?" I said again.

Jere let out a long sigh. "Please get dressed," he said.

He led me down some side paths past mud huts and banana groves of all sizes, through an acre where all the plants had suddenly died and ghosts were now said to live, and into a part of the village I had never seen before. Malama and the mango tree boys followed a short distance behind us. As always, people froze and stared when I passed. I ignored them—one question filled my mind: *What the hell is judging?* I asked Jere to explain it as we walked, and he did, but he was in a hurry and wouldn't slow down and face me so I could read his lips and I missed what he said.

We stopped in front of a large hut with a tin roof and a walled courtyard. A crudely lettered wooden sign above the entrance read, in English: THE AFRICA FREEDOM CHURCH, MR. JACKSON BWALYA PRESIDING. A tall man with a shaved skull, salt-and-pepper stubble, and arms made from steel cables stood in the door; this, I learned, was Mr. Bwalya. He exchanged terse Bemba greetings with Jere and me, turned, and led us across the courtyard into a small dark room, empty save for three chairs and two short, muscular young men sitting on the floor. After offering us seats, Bwalya folded his arms, cleared his throat, and locked his eyes on mine.

"Mr. Peace Corps, White Man, Sir," he asked, in clear, deliberate English. "Did you take my daughter last night?"

"Excuse me?" I said. I turned my hearing aids to the loudest setting.

"I said, 'Mr. Peace Corps, did you take my daughter into your house last night?'"

I didn't answer right away. I wasn't sure what the right answer was.

Jere leaned over. "He's asking if you took his daughter into your house."

"Thanks," I said.

"Mr. Peace Corps," Bwalya continued slowly and forcefully. "Did you ruin my daughter? Did you ruin my eldest daughter in your house? Did you end her life?"

That worried me. "Are you talking about Alice? I saw her last night. Is she all right?"

"Yes! Yes!" Bwalya shouted. He clenched his fists, which made the cables in his arms writhe. "Mr. Peace Corps! You ruined her! And you will be judged!"

I looked at Jere; wide-eyed, he looked just as stunned as I imagined I did.

So began my judging. It felt unreal at first, almost a joke. Then, as the hours passed it grew increasingly unsettling. Bwalya glowered, paced, thundered, and occasionally stopped in place and swung his arms like he was preparing to throw a punch, and for what? Because his daughter had waited on my porch to collect on a six-month tease, had shed her clothes like they were infested with fleas, and gotten down to sex like she was being paid by the minute—for that, he was attacking me? It didn't seem right. I had a hangover too, which wasn't helping.

Phase one of the trial was the gathering of evidence and anecdotal proof. Speaking in loud, broken English, Bwalya did a fine impression of a district attorney, albeit one who smelled faintly of kerosene. *Did Mr. Peace Corps meet Alice on his porch? Yes, he did. Did Mr. Peace Corps take Alice into his house? Yes, he did. Did he take her into his bedroom? Yes? So then, she is ruined. Yes, I said, ruined, Mr. Peace Corps. For life.*

Bwalya smiled at this last statement, not the expression you'd expect.

"For the laws of our tribe," he said. "You now pay damages."

Jere was no help at first. "You had Alice in your bed last night?" he asked when Bwalya stepped to the other side of the room. "Last night? We were playing chess so late. You drank a lot of wine."

"You should talk," I said. He usually put away twice the wine I did.

"What did you do with her?"

"Nothing. I mean we started, but not much happened."

Jere blushed, chuckled, and coughed all at the same time. "Your maize didn't grow straight?"

"No, no, it grew straight. Straight like bamboo. It just didn't get a chance to, um . . . you know."

"*Ai,*" Jere nodded. "Ahh. *Ai.*"

"Why do you ask?" I hoped some legal strategy was behind his questions.

"Just curious," he said.

Around ten, we took a half-hour break. Outside the Africa Freedom Church men, women, and children had lined up five deep. When Jere and I came out, they scattered as if we were black mambas.

"Look at this," I said. "We should charge admission."

It was a weak joke and Jere ignored it.

"I don't think you understand the seriousness of the charges," he said.

"You're right," I agreed. "I don't. You know why? Because this is total bullshit. I didn't do anything wrong."

He frowned at that and insisted we go to the market bar for a beer. At the bar the generator and the music were shut off but a couple of drunks were in attendance, getting an early start. As I tried to tune out the bar smell of unwashed bodies and stale vomit, Jere explained to me the seriousness of the charges.

It went like this: in the bush, an unmarried virgin daughter is a very, very valuable thing. From sunup to sundown, she works like a slave, doing whatever her father and mother need without complaint. Such good service isn't cheap. It can take a young man in the village up to a year to raise the money to purchase the wife of his desires, and in respect for this diligence and patience, the virginity of his bride is guaranteed. On the wedding day, the man takes his wife to the bedroom, and immediately after that old women barge inside and search for blood. If they don't find any, the bride is sent back to her parents and the groom's payment is returned.

I hadn't been aware of that. Where I came from, virginity was something everyone ditched as fast as they could. Alice and I had been two adults doing adult things in privacy. I felt it wasn't anybody's business but ours. But Jere made it clear that if Alice were a virgin I would have to pay money for those things—a lot of money.

"Was there blood?" he asked.

"No, hell no," I said. "You saw my bed."

"Good."

After we finished a round of beers, Jere outlined what he thought was the trial's likeliest possible outcome. "Bwalya will charge you some cash. Twenty grand, maybe. I'm sure you can organize twenty grand." That was thirty dollars; my monthly living allowance was about seventy bucks. Though I now understood that I had made a mistake, that didn't seem fair.

"I'll pay," I said. "But I'm not happy about it."

But first, on our way back to the judging room, in one of those random, unexpected moments that over time I came to think of as quintessentially Africa—we came upon Alice squatting in the church courtyard next to a small charcoal stove, stirring maize meal into ubwali for the midday meal. Just us and her, she was all alone. "Give me a second," I said to Jere. I walked over. Jere stepped back to give me privacy and Alice squinted up at my face, her two-foot wooden ubwali spoon paused in its stirring. What we could have been, I thought. I double-checked to make sure no one was watching then tugged her panties out of my jeans pocket. With a beautiful, guileless smile, she stuffed them down her blouse.

BACK INSIDE THE CHURCH, MY JUDGING MOVED INTO THE NEXT phase: the negotiation of payment. Mr. Bwalya now sat on a chair, flanked by the same quiet young men, an enormous book the size and shape of a cinder block in his lap. When we were seated, he brought over the book, a Bible, Bemba/English, opened it to a page and pointed.

Deuteronomy 22, I read: *If there is a virgin and a man meets her in the city and lies with her, then you shall bring them out of the gate of that city, and stone them to death with stones.*

So they were going to kill me—wait, that was the payment? I'm not proud of what I did next. I coughed, once, twice, stretched it into a coughing fit, stood up and headed for the door. As I did, the two silent young men who had been seated on the floor popped up to standing positions. Mr. Bwalya also stood, the enormous Bible hanging from his hand like a weapon.

Jere followed close behind me. "Where are you going?"

"This is messed up," I whispered to him. "They want to stone me."

A doubtful look spread across his face; he turned and asked Bwalya a question in Bemba. Bwalya laughed explosively and then spoke to the two other men, who also laughed.

"It's the next line," said Jere, smiling. "You read the wrong line."

Still laughing, Bwalya handed me the book again. I sat back down. Deuteronomy 22:28: *If a man meets a virgin who is not betrothed, and seizes her and lies with her, and they are found, then the man who lay with her shall give to the father of the young woman fifty shekels of silver, and she shall be his wife, because he has violated her; he may not put her away all his days.*

So marriage, that's what Bwalya was after—marriage and shekels.

"Better?" asked Jere, reading the lines from the seat next to mine.

"Yeah, much."

"Mr. Peace Corps," Bwalya began and then he turned to Jere and, in passionate Bemba, counted off his demands. Jere translated: "For defiling a virgin and lowering her bridal price, for giving her a baby, for giving her Peace Corps diseases of venereals, the sum of ten million kwacha"—that's what Bwalya wanted.

I was stunned. That was fifteen thousand dollars.

"And your motorcycle," Jere added, dolefully clucking his tongue. He often borrowed it. He didn't like to walk far.

Ten million kwacha—it seemed like a monopoly sum. "Tell Bwalya I don't have ten million," I said to Jere. He did.

Bwalya loudly cleared his throat. "Nine," he said, holding out all his fingers but one.

"He says nine million," relayed Jere.

"I don't have nine."

"Eight, but that's as low as he'll go."

"I don't have eight."

"Seven," said Jere, "but you have to fuel the bike."

"I have to fuel the bike?"

"Yes."

I shook my head. "I'm not doing that."

Negotiations continued in this manner for a couple of hours: Jere relaying an amount, me saying that I didn't have it, and Bwalya lowering his demand while further describing my offenses. *Did you know, Mr. Peace Corps, that my daughter is ruined?* When Bwalya lowered his demand to one million kwacha and a motor- cycle, he dug in for a fight. He gave a vehement speech about the immense shame I had caused him, to the point where how, really, could he ever again show his face in the village? He was the laughingstock of Mununga, the man who had failed to protect his child.

"Hold on a minute." I had a sudden idea. "Jere, tell him I used a condom. A condom. You can't get diseases that way or babies. Maybe Bwalya doesn't know about condoms. Explain it to him."

Chuckling nervously and clearing his throat three or four times, Jere did.

Bwalya was unmoved. "One million, Mr. Peace Corps," he said.

"But she was not a virgin!" I exclaimed. "Sir, Alice came to my place last night without my asking and took advantage of me. I am just one man, one Mr. Peace Corps, alone, away from my family and my people, trying to help the people of Zambia, and she can't be pregnant, we never finished."

A pause. Bwalya looked expectantly at Jere.

"Are you sure you want me to translate that?" Jere asked.

"Yes, do it," I said.

Jere coughed and dabbed his forehead with his handkerchief. Then he translated. Bwalya listened intently, chewing his lips, the muscles in his jaw straining against his skin. When Jere finished, there was dead silence.

"I think that was not the best approach," Jere said, back at the bar. He ordered us another round of beers. The radio had been turned on since we were there last, it now blared Zairian dance music which through my hearing aids sounded like falling rocks, and through my headache felt like them. It wasn't much past noon. On an empty stomach, another Mosi to the two I had earlier was enough to get me buzzed, and the more I drank the more angry I felt and the more convinced I was that I had done nothing wrong.

Jere disagreed. He shouted to be heard above the music. "Telling a man that his daughter's having sex without a husband? Not a good idea. And it makes you look less strong, to blame a woman. That's dangerous for Alice also."

"But it's the truth," I said.

"That's not important. It's not our way to be so direct. Like our meeting with Headman Museka, remember? The snake-in-the-grass? It is better to be polite."

"I am polite."

Jere patted my hand. "We can still make a deal."

"How? My motorcycle? One million kwacha? Forget it. I don't make that much in a year and you know that the motorcycle doesn't belong to me. It belongs to the Peace Corps. They'll send me home if they hear about this."

"You could marry the girl," Jere said.

For a second, I pictured it. Would our kids be deaf like me? Would they be raised Jewish?

"I'm not marrying her," I decided.

"I didn't think so," Jere said. "That would be simplest, but that's okay. I have a plan." He took a long swallow of his beer. "But when we go back you have to be quiet, completely quiet."

I nodded. "Want to tell me the plan?"

"No."

I made a show of deliberating, picking at the label on the Mosi bottle with its photo of an MGM lion's head and then thoughtfully studying a soft-drink poster on the wall with happy white people sweating and drinking brown sugar water. Let Jere think I was only agreeing to humor him. But I was out of options. "Okay," I said. "Let's do it."

"Good," said Jere. "But don't say a single word. Really."

What did I do to deserve a friend like Jere? To meet and to know a man like him? Out in the deep bush in Africa, nothing is a given except that the strongest, most determined survive, and even that isn't always the case, so survival demands a fealty to your tribe—but Jere never put himself first. He wasn't even with his people. Eight years earlier, flush with idealism after graduating from clinic worker's school, he had chosen to serve Zambia before his tribe, and landed at this wild village far from home. He was college-educated, English-speaking, banana-wine–brewing, chess-playing, spy-novel–reading, and moreover, he knew whatever our skin colors, whatever our stories, we were the same—just people trying to get through the day. He saw that I'd made a mistake, and wanted to help.

All that afternoon, and continuing the next morning, I sat quietly on my chair in the middle of the tiny Africa Freedom Church crisscrossed by ribbons of sun while Jere presented my case to Bwalya. He never raised his voice. He made sure a smile and a kind word were never too far away from his lips. When Bwalya bellowed, Jere listened patiently, then told soothing fables about bush animals and national pride, made up stories about all the work I had done.

I'm guessing this is what he did. I couldn't understand a word. I tried, of course, but they were talking in Bemba and often talking so fast that if it were English, I probably wouldn't have understood either. I just watched Jere, watched his hands jab the air as he talked, and then I watched Bwalya and his hands going tense and slack as he clenched and unclenched them. They looked like they could crush diamonds. I made up my own dialogue to fit their movements:

"The white boy must be punished! My daughter is ruined! Yes, ruined! I will slice his nuts off and fry them with onions!"

"But how will he dig wells without them? We need wells. Your daughter needs a well. Let him keep his nuts."

This was deafness, chapter 148: helpless and clueless as my own fate was bartered right in front of me—I had no control, none. So I did the only thing I could do to get some power back: I turned my hearing aids off. In the silence, sunlight changed from gold to white as it crossed the earthen floor. Ant generals marched their conscripts across the mud brick walls and shepherded them into nests. Spiders scouted out corners for future development and killed their prey. I scratched lice out of my hair until Jere elbowed my arm to make me still.

IN THE END, IT WAS AGREED THAT I WOULD PAY MR. JACKSON BWALYA, director of the African Freedom Church, a hundred thousand kwacha for violating his virgin daughter and potentially causing an unwanted pregnancy. I had, back in my hut, beneath my mattress, eighty thousand kwacha saved up over three months for my first vacation, and I gave that much to Bwalya, promising to pay him the balance as soon as I could. For the next two weeks, all I could afford to eat was roasted corn and whatever food Jere could spare, but I didn't have to give up my motorcycle or my bachelorhood and I figured I'd borrow the vacation money from Chris, my friend from training, so I could live with the agreement.

When I returned to Mununga a month and a half later from a

Peace Corps conference and a trip to Victoria Falls, I was shocked to find Alice living with her husband—*husband!*—in that small hut across the path from mine. Jere had told me marriages took months to complete. By tribal law, once a man begins payment he is the legal owner of his bride, or else the parents could keep putting her up for bids. This meant that Alice had not been the property of her father on the night she had come to my hut. So Bwalya had no claim on the money I had paid him.

On top of that, Alice was pregnant, noticeably so. When she saw me, she patted her tummy and waved.

Motherfucker. I stood there and gaped like an idiot.

"Bad girl," said Malama, who was standing next to me. "You no listen."

"Shut up," I said.

I ran to the African Freedom Church to demand my money back, but, big surprise, Mr. Bwalya was gone to the Copperbelt, blowing my eighty grand on booze and whores.

When he returned to Mununga two weeks later with the dazed and satisfied look of someone who had scratched an itch with a blowtorch, I sued him in the chief's high council for my cash. A collection of seven elderly men who, by dint of their longevity, were accorded great powers of wisdom and witchcraft by the villagers, the high council convened one afternoon a week in an insaka in front of the chief's palace. They were Mununga. One member, Mr. Bule, a former school headmaster now in his mid-seventies, wore an immaculate pin-striped suit with a silk pink kerchief every single day, no matter the temperature. Through the years he had seven wives; the most recent, still a teenager, toted the youngest of his twenty-two children on her back.

On the appointed day, Bwalya and I each brought a live chicken, legs tied together so it couldn't run away, and lay it in front of the court. Mulwanda, the sleepy-eyed senior clinic worker, came to translate as Jere couldn't get away from work. I had sat up late the night before, planning what to say. But now I was after revenge more than money. Over the squawking of the terrified chickens, I told the councilmen that I was grateful for their time, that I loved Mununga, and that I had made a mistake with Alice and wanted to correct that mistake by their laws. The money wasn't really important to me, I told them (and it wasn't—a hundred and fifty bucks—nothing really) but I felt duty bound to retrieve it from Bwalya and pay it to Alice's husband, her rightful owner. Bwalya, when it was his turn, argued to the councilmen that they should not let a foreigner tell them what to do. We waited outside the palace while they deliberated.

They called us back after lunch. The ruling came out in my favor: I had been wronged, Bwalya had acted dishonorably, but they advised me to forget getting my money back, because he'd spent it all. To acknowledge the righteousness of my position, however, the seven wise men took Bwalya's chicken away and let me take home mine.

Within a few days, it became clear that Bwalya had not spent all of my money, as he took off to the Copperbelt cities again and reports drifted back of more drinking and whoring.

"I've been wronged. I hate him," I said to Jere.

"Forget about it," he said.

"When he comes back, I'm going to hit him in the head with that fucking Bible."

And then we heard that while living large on my dime, Bwalya was hit by a car and killed.

This Africa—who can tell the proper way to behave? You might be the greatest bush nurse ever, the kind of woman Mother Teresa looks up to, and still be raped by a platoon of children playing war. There are beauties like Alice and then at the clinic, the faces of angels are attached to bodies assembled from deflated balloons. Chickens and petty revenge and then moments when you can make diamond necklaces out of the stars. Why was I here? To learn everything I could, to find a place to gain perspective on my hearing loss, to live, and to help others to live. But when we heard of Bwalya's death, Jere and I looked at each other and laughed. It was too much to believe.

The Rains

After weeks of ominous thunderclouds, one October afternoon a cloud opened and rain poured, glittering in the sun like sequins on a dress. The dirt yards of the village, choked with dust for months, immediately flooded and rutted with fast-moving streams. Children stopped what they were doing and ran in ecstatic circles. Malama and Palije set my slipper down a flood stream roaring behind the latrine; it took off like a shot and we never saw it again. The forest grew six shades darker, maize seedlings shot up six inches a day, banana trees grew so fast they tipped over. Each evening, bullfrogs called out for their wives with desperate insistence. There was so much new life.

Then overnight children started dying in droves. Mosquitoes arriving on the heels of the first downpour brought meningitis and malaria and the youngest and weakest were hit hard. Villagers shuffled from funeral to funeral like shackled prisoners, dividing their grief into ever-smaller fractions. They huddled near each funeral fire, the men in one clump, the women in another. The women took turns to stand up and wail, but the men never stirred until it was time to head to the next ceremony. I was often asked to come and sit for a while and so I did, and we all sat with our thoughts of life and death.

Did they believe that death was the end or just a beginning? Did they believe souls recurred? I rued the arrogance of feeling at home in a place where people fought daily just to survive. The whole energy of the town became muted and I sunk into the background. At night, funeral fires dotted the night like traffic signals for ghosts.

Not knowing what else to do, I bided my time, waiting for the rain to stop, waiting for things to go back to how they were before. But like with everything else in the village, getting involved wasn't a simple matter of choice. One day as I sat on the porch with Malama eating boiled cassava and trying to teach him poker, the rain a slow drizzle, a thin man I'd never seen before ran up.

"Ba Joesh, you come? You come?" he said. He pointed toward a small hut nearby. A dozen men and women clustered around its door, squatting and holding themselves.

"What is it?" I asked. In response, the thin man took my hand and led me through the crowd. Inside the hut's one room, a half-dozen adults with tear-streaked cheekbones stood in a circle. They parted and in the center of the room a boy lay on the floor, groaning and thrashing. Half his body was absolutely still, paralyzed, and the other half struggled wildly as if trying to cleave away. The man who led me inside smiled weakly, announced something in Bemba to the others, and pushed me forward.

I knew what he wanted—for my powerful white magic powers to take the fever away. But I didn't have magic powers, or even basic medical training.

"I'm sorry," I said. "I can't do anything except get you a few aspirin."

The man bowed. "Please."

"Really, I can't help."

"Yes, please. Thank you."

He stepped back to join the others so I was alone with the boy in the center of the room. I took a deep breath and crouched down and looked at the dying child. His eyes radiated pure terror. He knew he was going. He knew he wouldn't be swimming in the river again. Half his body continued to try to escape. He was nine, maybe ten years old. I ran my hand up and down his forearm and it burned. It was meningitis; I knew the signs.

The thin man who led me to the hut reappeared at my shoulder. "What should we do?" he asked.

"I don't know," I said.

"You can't do anything? Don't you have medicines?"

"I'm not a doctor. Sorry."

"But you work at the clinic. You come all the way from America." Goddamn Peace Corps. "I do, yeah."

I squatted for ten, fifteen minutes more. There was a basin and a rag and I wet the boy's face. As the moisture evaporated off his forehead, I talked to him in my thoughts. I knew he wouldn't hear me if I spoke out loud—the fever had melted the hair cells in his ears. I tried to talk to him about that: silence, it's an interesting thing.

I turned back to the man. "We could pray," I said to him.

"Pray?" he said. "Pray?" He squatted down and pressed his fingers in the dirt. "Pray?"

"Yeah, I never . . . I don't really know what that means either."

A small child followed me back to my hut. He turned out to be the brother of the dying boy. Forgotten in the drawn-out illness, he ended up sleeping on my couch for a week, his face pressed up into Malama's armpit. What I remember most about him is that he had eyes so soft it looked like he was always dreaming. Whenever Chiluba looked at him, she shook her head violently and wiped away tears.

He was too shy to talk to me so I asked Malama to find out what he could about our new guest.

"He's from the bush," Malama reported back.

"Where are his parents?"

"They dead."

"Well, then, who's going to take care of him?"

"Someone coming from Copperbelt."

"Who?"

Malama shrugged. "He don't know. Someone."

The young boy stared at us unceasingly. To distract him, Malama gave him a pen and paper, but I'm not sure he'd ever held a pen before, and he put it down and resumed staring. At mealtimes, the boy wouldn't eat unless encouraged at least a half-dozen times, and even then he watched us between every bite. We had to pretend that we didn't notice he was there and only then would he bring the ubwali to his mouth.

Two days after my first visit to the hut across the way the thin man rushed over again. The boy with meningitis had slowed his thrashing, his eyes had closed, and his chest quivered, and so it passed that as we watched he arched his back for one last breath, his face finally relaxed, and for the first time in a while you couldn't tell the twisted part of him from the paralyzed side.

The funeral began immediately. Adults huddled in the dirt yard outside the hut, staring blankly at a fire. Sporadically, singly and in pairs, women rose from the crowd and wailed prodigiously as in the Old Testament where it is written, "They rent their garments and tore their hair and wailed." It seemed a little affected but they needed to hurry and empty their grief because the fields were wet and waiting for planting. There wouldn't be time to mourn the boy after his funeral fire had burned out so it had to be done now. Teenage girl-wailers stopped by my hut after yelling themselves hoarse and asked for candy and gum. Malama and I gave them everything we had.

It was just one death among dozens and after the funeral broke up, I never heard anyone speak of it again. I never again saw the thin man who had been so certain I could help him. Before dawn the next day, everyone shouldered their hoes and walked upriver to plant and weed their fields. They worked until they were too hungry to continue, then came home for the day's only meal. And one afternoon a week later, I returned to my hut from weighing babies at the clinic and the boy with those soft eyes who slept with his face in Malama's armpit was gone, just like that.

The rains continued. The villagers tended to their fields. Death, altogether at ease, strode through the village like it was his backyard, striking with impunity. I felt like I didn't know this place anymore.

I found Jere in his insaka. "This is some kind of malaria outbreak," I said to him. "Three more funerals today."

"What were you expecting when you came?" he returned. "A tribe that lived forever?"

"No, of course not."

He handed me a glass of wine, and sighed. "This is the rainy season."

We set out a game of chess. It was night, just blackness going on for thousands and thousands of miles. In the huts around us, children died.

TO GET AWAY, I WENT TO VISIT THE ONLY KENTUCKY RASTAFARIAN I knew.

I rode to his village on my motorcycle. Chabilikila, where Chris lived, was sixty miles south of Mununga, right on the paved Mansa-Kashikishi highway. Volunteers were forbidden to ride their motorcycles far from their villages but we all ignored that rule. Chabilikila was tiny and quiet, only a handful of huts surrounded by eight-foot-high bush grass and towering palm trees. Here the bush was a constant looming presence, always on the verge of swallowing up the settlement. When the rains fell, the villagers had to go out with their machetes and cut the forest back so their homes wouldn't be overrun. In Mununga, by contrast, the forest had been stripped of much of its energy—for miles around all the tall trees had been harvested for roof beams and the wild animals had been slaughtered for lunch.

Chabilikila's villagers were in no rush to dig wells either and

Chris had made his peace with that. He taught sanitation and hygiene classes and dug a couple of pit latrines, but mostly focused on integrating into village life. He hiked in the bush with his friends, canoed through the nearby swamps, hunted bush rat with a bow and arrow. He had been dating Helen, the village clinic officer's daughter, for four or five months. She was a beautiful and playful eighteen-year-old student who bit her lip when she smiled, and her three or four younger brothers overran Chris's small house.

"Guess what?" Chris said when I stepped off my motorcycle. "Helen's pregnant. I'm getting married."

"Wow," I said. "Congratulations." He seemed pretty matter-of-fact about the news. "You're taking this in stride," I said.

"I guess."

"You guess?"

"What should I be doing?"

"I don't know. Researching preschools? Getting a prenup?"

Chris grinned. He was matter-of-fact about everything, which I admired. He seemed to have figured out whatever in his life needed figuring out. You don't realize how rare such people are until you meet them.

"We got one," he said. "She gets the bed, I get the table. But come look, it's a good table."

I followed him inside his hut. It *was* a nice table: handmade, with legs of carved mahogany, covered with books, newspapers, and two or three magazines. There were quite a few books on Indians. One of them had black-and-white portraits of to-be-slain Indian chiefs staring accusingly at the camera, as if to say, you did this; another was Black Elk's book of wisdom. Chris was adopted and didn't know his birth parents and short and polite white people had raised him near Louisville, but he was tall and dark skinned and had long silky black hair—he could have been Indian, you could see it.

Also on the table was a small brown monkey. It startled when we came in and jumped onto a high bookshelf. While I gaped at it Chris explained that some boys had trapped it while hunting wild boar and brought it to him as a gift, and that his name was Herman. The monkey had been just a baby when Chris got him, a tiny thing that gummed his fingers, sipped milk from a saucer, and fit in his palm, but he quickly grew larger and now was about a foot tall and had a bright red butt.

"Hey, Herman, come here," I called, but the monkey ignored me.

"I'm still training him," Chris said.

We drank banana wine and talked about random things. There was no background noise, so it was easy to read Chris's lips, though he mumbled some. We flipped through the magazines and newspapers lying on the table, old issues of *International Newsweek* provided by the Peace Corps and papers from a trip to town. The O.J. story was getting big press; the magazines were calling it a new low. This was also around the time that in Washington, D.C., a man had his dick cut off and thrown into a field outside a 7-Eleven. That appeared to be a big deal in the States, but actually happened pretty often in Africa according to the Zambian *Times*.

"Penis dismemberment is popular in Cape Town," Chris said, pointing at an article.

That was my cue: I unloaded then, told Chris about the last few weeks in Mununga, all the funerals, the babies smaller than papayas, the boy with his head in Malama's armpit, how everything had changed, how useless I was. Chris nodded, but was mostly silent. A yellow parrot flew up to the windowsill, scanned our faces like he was looking for someone in particular, flew away through the trees. A few minutes later, Herman climbed onto the table from the bookshelf, coolly appraised each of us, grabbed a magazine, and then hopped out the window. After a while Chris said, "I want to show you something," and took me outside to the courtyard of the house next door where a litter of shorthaired puppies was playing. He picked up a tan puppy that snarled at his fingers. "This is yours," he said. "Her name is Scoopy."

"Snoopy? Scooby?"

"Scoopy." Chris put the dog in my arms. "She's got the best of both of them."

I held the dog to my chest, stroked her tummy; she wasn't much more than wrinkles and paws. She bit my thumb hard and I almost dropped her.

"Thank you," I said.

"I want to show you something else," said Chris. "Follow me."

We got on our motorcycles and rode up north back toward Lake Mweru. It was dusk, the road was empty, and our headlights cut through the gloom like scythes, occasionally startling a nighttime pedestrian who dove into the scrub as we passed. The pavement had given way to dirt and night had fallen when we stopped at a small village a little way up the lakeshore. We left our bikes under a tree and I followed Chris through the clearings between the huts to a cliff high over the lake. We walked right up to the edge.

"Behold," said Chris, "the eye of God."

The view was magnificent. Above us, stars flooded all four horizons. Below us, spread out on the lake, were thousands of twinkling yellow lights. The night fishermen had set up their lanterns, one on each end of their canoes, to draw chisense into their nets. The chisense, tiny bug-eyed fish, were like moths and kept heading toward the lights. Each boat had two lanterns, one at each end, so the paired lanterns, bobbing and twinkling on the invisible waves like runway lights for flying dinosaurs, stretched out for miles toward Zaire.

Christmas

Nine months had passed since my arrival in Mununga. In the mornings I worked at the clinic, weighing babies, bandaging infections and worm sores, rationing out vitamins for the most malnourished. After a lunch at home, I either went back to the clinic or held scantly attended meetings for well projects or went to teach bamayos how to prevent the spread of infectious disease. And, wonder of wonders, we actually started deepening the village well in Kaseke, lowering Jefferson the translator by rope with a pick and a shovel into the existing hole. He passed up buckets of dirt and also a human thighbone, which for some reason, possibly ndoshi related, had been thrown in there. It was slow going—the well floor was almost pure granite—but at least it was going.

If my Peace Corps volunteer experience was supposed to be about digging wells, then a borehole truck and a couple of million dollars could have taken care of the water problems of nearly the whole province. Think of it: five hundred thousand people spared from the worst of waterborne disease just like that. But that wasn't what being a volunteer was about, and I worked hard to make my peace with it or to at least not think about it too much. Sharing in the day-to-day in the village provided ample distractions, which, besides work, meant drinking with Jere, flirting with Chiluba and her sisters, and teaching Malama how to play poker.

Which wasn't easy. He had trouble with the concept of bluffing. He always said "uh-oh" if I matched his bet.

"It's not bluffing when you say 'uh-oh,'" I'd tell him.

"Sorry," he'd say.

"Don't be sorry—bluff!" But he couldn't get it down.

Some weekends I put Malama on the back of my motorcycle
and we took the east road up the river to a small waterfall and swam
beneath the spray. The water was full of nibbling fish and we
swam quickly in case crocodiles were lurking, but it was invigor-
ating all the same.

Around Thanksgiving, Chris and I took a trip to Harare
together. There, walking with a young Rasta who promised to
take us to a far-out club, we were jumped by fifteen men. We
fought our way to a passing taxi but the men surrounded the car
and Chris's window was open; someone reached in and raked his
eyes. I punched the three men closest to me, hard shots that hurt
my fists, and everyone ran away. We drove off, and I realized the
men had run not because of our fighting skills, but because they
had stolen my wallet. Dazed, Chris and I went to a hotel bar and
sat mesmerized for half an hour by a beautiful prostitute who read
our palms and explained our fates, each of us trembling too much
to talk. Her body was thick and ample and healthy-looking, but
we couldn't make a move. It was only when we went to our hotel
room that we realized Chris had two black eyes and I had a broken rib.

But we shrugged that off pretty quickly. "Africa," we said, and
toasted the continent with our South African beers.

Africa: this strange, wounded animal. Africa: where it was so
easy to reimagine yourself. Africa: where death—and laughter—is
never far. The Mununga villagers buried children like dogs bury
bones, but when you got past that you saw that they laughed more
and worried less than any group of people you'd ever hope to meet.
Sure, there were exceptions, most noticeably Boniface, but on the

whole villagers were friendly and I was grateful to call Mununga home.

Then on Christmas, everything changed.

CHRISTMAS EVE. I WROTE A LETTER TO MY FATHER GIVING HIM THE all-okay, then wandered over to an impromptu party for the clinic staff in Jere's insaka. There, I drank way too much banana wine. Jere had brewed the wine extra-strong in honor of the holiday, feeding sugar to the fermenting yeast for fourteen days instead of the normal three. After every sip, I could feel teeth wiggling loose. Apparently, it was village tradition to commemorate the birth of the son of God by getting stinking drunk. The brunt of the rains had passed and with it the worst disease outbreaks and we were all still alive: this was cause for celebration. We danced to South African reggae, holding each other up and ordering our feet to move. They disagreed and pitched us against the insaka's low mud-brick walls. Outside, drunken men wandered about the pitch-dark village like lost spacecraft.

An intense, if repetitive, discussion broke out about the sexual proclivities of Caucasian women.

"I hear they sleep with many men before they get married," Jere said.

"Some do," I said.

"You must find me one of those," said Patrick, the young junior officer at the clinic.

Jere leaned over and grabbed Patrick's arm. "Patrick, think," he said. "Where is Josh going to find you a white woman? Over at the market?"

Patrick set his jaw. He perpetually had the look of a man expecting bad news. "He will find one. He can do it."

Jere looked to me. "Well, Josh? Where will you be finding a white woman for Patrick?"

I tried to think of something witty to say. The Christmas wine and dancing had put me in an expansive mood, but the problem with banana wine is you start getting the hangover, the splitting headache like a trash compactor in your skull, only an hour after you get drunk. It had been more than an hour. I couldn't think.

"You see?" Jere said to Patrick.

Patrick shook his head. "You are wrong, Mr. Jere. I have faith in the umusungu. He can do it."

"I appreciate that, Patrick," I said. "For you, I will find two."

"Two?" Jere raised his eyebrows. "Two for Patrick, and none for me?"

"No, none for you."

Then a man appeared and whispered in Jere's ear. Jere's smile disappeared as he listened and he motioned for Patrick to turn off the music. Someone had just been killed at the market.

We shut up then. The dead man, Jere explained, had been arguing with a second man outside the bar and then this other man—Chitondo was his name—threw a lucky punch, or an unlucky one, that drove the first man's nose bone straight into his brain. He collapsed like a ripped sack of maize. First they thought he was pretending, then they thought he was knocked out cold, then they saw the blood pooling in the corners of his eyes. Chitondo ran and hid.

Men appeared at the insaka with more news every ten minutes or so and the situation got worse and worse. First, a vigilante mob was looking for Chitondo. Then, the mob couldn't find him; frustrated, they cornered two of his friends and killed them instead. They tried to kill a third friend but he took off and, the last anyone heard, was running barefoot through the bush in the general direction of Tanzania. He either started another life there or was eaten by a hyena on the way—no one ever saw him again.

Like that, three men were dead. It was wild and unimaginable, and drunk as we were, we tried to make sense of it.

"Do I know Chitondo?" I asked Jere.

"Yes," Jere said. "He helped move stuff at the clinic some. He's a big guy. Very big muscles like this"—he framed a body in the air. "Has a temper. Always asked for money. Remember now?"

"Yeah," I said, though I didn't remember. Jere had just described a dozen men. "How does a mob happen?"

"It helps to have a leader."

"Who's the leader?"

He took out his handkerchief and wiped his head. "There are rumors."

"Who is it?"

"They are saying it might be your friend, Mr. Boniface."

"Boniface? Holy shit."

Jere didn't say anything more. Patrick, more skittish than ever, got up and left to lock himself in his hut.

Around midnight, the updates on the vigilantes' progress finally petered out and I stumbled to my hut and fell into bed, holding on to the headboard until the room stopped spinning. I slept and dreamed tortured, bloody dreams, a side effect of the antimalaria pills I took. The pills burned like lit dynamite going down and then detonated inside my unconscious. Nights were full of screams, smoke, naked bodies dripping oil and blood.

Then someone was shaking me awake. Malama. He had never woken me up before.

He saw my eyes open and said something. But it was just his lips moving.

"Go away," I said.

Malama shook his head and flapped his lips some more.

"Hearing aids," I said, pointing at my ears.

He looked on the bed, on the floor, on the varnished tree stump that served as my night table, and then found them near my flip-flops in the living room. His oval face was excited, burning, brilliant white teeth shining. I had never seen him so animated before.

I moistened an earmold with my lips and slipped it in my ear without lifting my head from the bed.

"Okay. Speak." I waved to him. "No. Wait"—I still tasted banana wine in my throat: sickly sweet, grainy and vinegary, like Kool-Aid cut with kerosene and sand—"Get me some water."

Malama ran to the kitchen and returned with a glass and I sat up.

"What, Malama?"

"Ba Joesh, you must come!" he said. "You have to see! We have caught the killer and are drag him to death! In Solange. The killer! They bringing him now."

"Killer?"

"Yes, killer."

"You mean Chitondo?"

He grabbed my arm and tugged. "Yes, let's go."

And so we hurried over to the market at seven-thirty in the morning on Christmas day. When we arrived, the market was empty. Nobody was there. Not a single cig boy or bamayo, no customers, no travelers, toutboys, nobody. No vendors had set up, no fish sellers, no cooking oil salesmen. It felt like the morning after the world had ended, like Ebola had finally made its way over from the Zairian rain forests and killed everyone as they slept. A breeze blew off the river and the mango trees and cassava fields were verdant green—the rains had been good. The huge sky seemed, as always, quite impressed with itself.

"Where is everybody?" I asked Malama. He was looking up the hill.

I felt it before I saw it, before I heard it obviously. A terrible, heart-stopping feeling like when a nightmare suddenly jolts you awake. Malama pointed and I turned to see an enormous train of people, cresting the hill and rolling down the road toward the market, dancing and screaming; and at the head of the train, right where the conductor would be, two men were dragging a naked body. It bounced on the rocky road like a Super Ball.

This was Chitondo.

One thing about deafness is you come to develop an intuition based on physical observation. Body language—posture, motion, expression—reveals so much. The loneliness in the way a woman waves good-bye; the anger in how a man opens and closes his fist—people are open books. They give their secrets away every moment: in how they study their reflection, how they check the time. Thing was, that moment when the parade of villagers came over the hill, their energy, the energy I sensed before I saw or heard them—that energy was clean. It felt like happiness.

The mob had searched for Chitondo at first light. They trashed his home village a few miles to the north, threatened his mother with exile to Zaire, kicked his wife until she cried and until she stopped crying. At dawn they finally located Chitondo cowering in the roof beams of a girlfriend's hut. They threw rocks at him and knocked him to the ground. He begged for his life, offered them a thousand dollars if they would spare him. A thousand dollars! More money than any of them would ever see.

"Where would Chitondo get a grand?" I asked Jere after it was over. "Was he a thief?"

"He didn't have it. He was trying anything. He knew he was in trouble."

"Why didn't they take it?"

"Nothing would have stopped them," Jere said. "He was not a good man, but this was a little much."

After the mob dragged Chitondo out of his girlfriend's hut, they stripped him naked and tied ropes to his wrists. The bravest in the crowd darted forward and belted him across the jaw. Then men coiled the ropes around their forearms and took turns dragging him back to Mununga, three miles away. It took them an hour. Dawn broke as they ran, that sudden equatorial dawn, the sun hustling to get started like a man running from a snake. When the mob passed the market where Malama and I stood, Chitondo was already dead. But the men towing his body still ran hard, panting and sweating, handing off the ropes every hundred yards. The crowd behind them danced and sang and spat on the bucking corpse and dogs followed behind as close as they dared, gobbling the bits of flesh that tore loose.

I could hardly breathe. I looked at Malama. He was grinning from ear to ear.

"What are they singing?" I asked him.

He looked at me hesitantly. "'We killed the killer. The killer is dead.'"

"We killed the killer?"

"Yes."

"That's a song?"

"Yes."

"That's great, Malama."

"Yes," he said again, still smiling. Sarcasm and bluffing both eluded him.

The parade followed a wide arc across the road and then cut behind a row of stores to a dirt field where three other dead men lay beneath mango trees—the man Chitondo had punched and Chitondo's two unfortunate friends. Malama and I walked over. Hundreds of people milled about, moving excitedly from body to body like schoolchildren viewing stuffed animals at the museum. Groups of women tittered and pointed, covering their mouths when they smiled. Fathers lifted young boys on their shoulders for a better look. *That's an elephant, son. That's a monkey that lives deep in the rain forest. This is a man with sixteen different fractures in his face.* The atmosphere was good-humored, satiated. Here now, for once, justice had been served. The government down in Mansa didn't do a thing for Mununga, the stoned soldiers at the checkpoint could only be roused to collect tolls and bribes, and dysentery and malaria had pounded the town all rainy season— but here the villagers had won. The killer was dead.

Chitondo's body lay naked on the ground, arms spread-eagled, huge road-scraped penis resting on his left thigh like a half-peeled mango. The shadow of a jackfruit tree shimmered across his legs. For a face, he had only the idea of a face left, a first draft. Malama and his friends squirted through the crowd to look at each body, pointing and whispering. I saw Boniface standing with arms crossed, chin high in the air, the villagers giving him a wide berth. He nodded to me. I stared at him, but if this was his doing, he didn't give a sign.

A man stepped out of the crowd and stood over Chitondo's body with a machete. He wore a white T-shirt praising Zambian democracy: I LOVE MULTIPARTY, it read. The man bent forward slightly, then raised the rusty two-foot blade over his head. At this point I turned to leave, pushing through the crowd. I turned off my hearing aids. And so I missed, thankfully, the blade cutting through the body, the thunk of it, the second blow with its spray of blood, Chitondo's intestines flooding the dirt like so much dirty water and the yelping dogs kicked forward to take their fill.

Back in my hut, I collapsed on the couch. For a long time I just sat. I knew that brutal things happened here and that children died suddenly and randomly, but I had believed without question that men I knew did not murder other men, nor feed their livers to dogs. I was wrong. The mob had left a blood trail down the center of the main road, and people were strolling about with an almost postcoital joy. Malama came in the open door and took a seat on the floor against the door frame. I looked at him but he avoided my gaze, chewing his knee. He was shirtless this morning, rib-popping skinny and shiny with sweat. For eight months he had slept on the couch, sharing my meals, reading my magazines, practicing his English by writing letters to my brothers. But

I didn't know him. And if I didn't know him, how could I know anything about the village?

"What do you want?" I demanded.

He stuttered a bit. "D-do you want today to eat *isabi* or *inkoko*?"

Fish or chicken? I pointed an accusing finger at him. "Malama, you don't do that. You don't do that to people. That was not a good thing. You know better than that. There is never ever a reason to do that. Ever! You should not be happy."

"But he was a killer."

"So what? You don't just go killing people."

"Why?"

"Because"—I couldn't think of how to put it. I'd recognized so many faces in the mob. Faces I depended on: Mubanga, who helped build my latrine; Lucky, who rented me this hut for one year in exchange for five bags of cement; the Museka headman who kissed me for beers. "Because what does that make you, Malama? If you kill a killer, what does that make you?"

"It's different," he said.

"No, it's not—think about it!" I was yelling now. "What does that make you? If you kill someone, what the fuck does that make you!"

He cowered against the door. "Okay."

I wiped my eyes with the back of my arm. "Now you're just agreeing with me, Malama. But you better think about what I'm saying." We sat in silence for a minute. I wanted him to leave.

"Fish," I said. "Tell Chiluba we'll have isabi today. Now go away."

After dinner that night I went to see Jere in his insaka. We sat staring at a chessboard for an hour without moving a piece. He held a sleeping Beauty in his lap the whole time and tenderly stroked her arm. I'd never seen such open parental affection in all my months in the village.

"Did you see the bodies?" I asked him.

"I did not want to," he answered.

"But did you see them?"

"It is not relevant."

"But did you see them?" I asked again, louder. I needed to hear him say it. He was my truth-teller. His words would confirm what was burned into my mind's eye. He looked across the field toward the clinic where the tin roof glinted in the moonlight, his round face compressed and tight. I'd seen that look before, at baby weighing now and again, and it had always lifted quickly, but there was something different, something I couldn't place. It took me a while to figure out what it was. Fear. He was afraid.

"I saw," he said. "This town is crazy."

New Year's

The next week was a long one. The first two days I went to the clinic, weighed babies, then left early and went home to bed. Jere kept his head down at work, avoiding conversation, and at night he ate inside his house with his wife and didn't seek out my company for chess. I'd never seen him that antisocial before. I'd never seen him afraid either, and I didn't know if we were allowed to talk about that.

By the afternoon of the third day I couldn't keep to myself anymore so I went to Jere's office to make him talk. He was seeing patients; I walked in and crouched by his desk so he couldn't avoid me.

"We have to do something," I said.

"No we don't," he replied.

"Jere, we have to tell the police about Boniface. We have to file a report. We have to tell someone."

He shook his head firmly. "I'm not doing anything."

"And everyone just kills everyone whenever they feel like it? I thought we were trying to help people."

"These are not my people." Jere spoke without looking at me. "It's not my tribe. It's not my responsibility. You figure it out."

But I couldn't figure it out, hard as I had tried. And I tried. It was all I could think of. But what did I know of mobs, of the alchemy that turns peaceful people into killers? My brain was fried: every question I sent it came back with the same error message: DOES NOT COMPUTE. The next morning, the fourth day after Christmas, I took two steps out of my hut toward the clinic, thought, "The hell with this," chased away Malama and Chiluba, and lay on the couch all day eating through a stack of pygmy bananas and reading a book I had borrowed from the rather threadbare Peace Corps library. It was on the secrets to a harmonious marriage. "Forgive, and your problems will be healed," it said, and that seemed like a beautiful concept, but I didn't know how to apply it to the current realities.

What would set them off next? What if they needed to eliminate witnesses and came for Jere and me? What if, this very night, Malama would lie awake on the couch in the living room, listening for my breathing to slow and deepen, so he could unlock the door and let in the men with ropes? What would happen to Scoopy then? What would it feel like to have the skin peeled from my back?

I was driving myself nuts, obviously. Okay, then, what to do?

Make fish soup, I decided. I lit a fire in the cooking stove, threw five small Mweru bass in a pot, added double heapings of onions and garlic, two fresh and succulent tomatoes. I carefully tended the concoction, keeping the liquid at a low rolling boil, covering and uncovering the pot. But I missed a strand of guts while cleaning the fish and when I finally tasted the soup, it was like moldy dead leaves. I backed up and kicked the pot and stove clean across the courtyard and cursed everything in sight. Then I got on my motorcycle and went to see Chris.

"Good timing as always," he said when I rode up. "Keep your helmet on. We're going on a trip."

"I saw hell," I said.

Chris raised his eyebrows and I thought I detected an eye roll. "There's gas in the storage room," he motioned. "Fill up."

"Where are we going?"

"It's a surprise."

Together we rode our motorcycles to a bush hospital in the town of Mbereshi twenty-five miles farther south; there, we met up with a Peace Corps volunteer named Joe, who in two years of service never unpacked his duffel or took off his fanny pack, and a burly, hard-drinking German doctor whose name I didn't catch. The doctor had a bloated red face and blond hair over every inch of his body. He had numerous opinions about Zambia, most of which ridiculed the superstitions of the natives and the procedures of the Peace Corps. I couldn't understand much of what he said, his thick accent reminding me of the burbling of my old cotton-candy–faced philosophy professor, only louder and with more spittle.

Yet Herr Doctor hadn't, far as I knew, murdered people, and he supplied our small party with cold beer (Joe only drank Fanta) so I endured his company, nodding and smiling at what I guessed were the right moments. I wanted to pull Chris aside and pour out the story of watching my village drag a man to death but it never seemed to be the right time (is there ever a right time for such a thing?). After a couple of hours listening to Herr Doctor, the four of us piled into his Land Cruiser and drove east. It was ten hours before midnight and Herr Doc wanted to ring in the New Year by visiting a fabled waterfall deep in the bush.

The road was paved for the first hour, dirt for the next hour, then a two-lane track for another thirty minutes. The landscape was typical plateau savannah: mpanga forests and swamps and occasional villages, beautiful but familiar. Gone was the romance. In every passing face, I saw a killer. We ran out of road when we reached where, according to the map, the waterfall was supposed to be. It wasn't, nothing was: no people or huts, just a jeep track dead-ended in the bush. It felt like we had time-traveled straight into the earlier Jurassic.

Stepping from the Land Cruiser, I was greeted by an indecipherable white noise. Herr Doctor opened the rear gate and handed each of us a machete and we hacked our way into the forest, following the sound, which was the waterfall, not that I could tell. As we walked, Herr Doctor, leading the way, suddenly turned back and hacked violently at my shoulder. I dove to the side, visions of mutilated bodies thrust across my brain—this is how it ends? I knew it: never trust the Germans!—and a beheaded black mamba fell at my feet.

"Poisonous," said Herr Doctor. He picked up the still-twitching head with the end of his machete. "Very dangerous." He flicked it into the bush.

Chris helped me stand up. "Man, you jumped fifteen feet," he said.

Then the forest cleared and we were standing on a grassy knoll before a huge hill of thundering water, a long white curtain, a hundred yards long and a hundred high—it looked like God was dipping a paintbrush in the river. From fifty yards away, I had to take off my hearing aids so the spray wouldn't soak them; without the aids, the thundering water seemed just as loud. Chris walked toward the falls, climbing over several boulders, emerging on a hillock not thirty feet from the waterfall face. There, buffeted by the winds, he could barely keep his feet.

Far away from the reach of men, nature had tossed this off without even trying. So us poor souls kill each other, drag each other to death, and feed each other to the dogs—that's fine, I told myself, that's just arms and legs, that's the ten-thousand-year-old story. But look at this. This is true.

IT WAS A SMALL BIT OF SOLACE AND I TRIED TO HANG ON TO IT, but right after I returned to Mununga, Jere came to my hut and announced he was leaving the village for good. Once again, I was at a loss.

"I am finished," he said.

"Uh, happy New Year," I responded.

"No. I am tired of this place. It's dangerous and it's not healthy. I belong with my tribe. I've talked it over with my wife. She, as well, is missing our home. I am putting in my notice for a transfer at the district tomorrow. I wanted to tell you first."

I was stunned. "Jere, where will you go?"

"Lusaka or Eastern Province. Back to Nyanja tribe."

"No, wait," I said. "You can't leave." The thought of being in Mununga without him was terrifying. "Let's talk calmly about this," I pleaded.

Jere acquiesced, sat down, and laid out his plan for going. As he spoke, I saw that the plan was really a fantasy. Transfers were frowned upon in the Ministry of Health, which oversaw all the country's health clinics, and leaving one province for another would mean starting all over at a new clinic, God knows where, as a junior clinic officer, with a junior's pay and status. All Jere's accrued seniority and experience would be wasted—it would be like switching from a corner office to a cubicle. He wasn't going anywhere. His plan devolved into a string of bitter complaints and gloomy predictions and I commiserated, inwardly breathing a sigh of relief.

He was too worked up to sit and paced the hut. "Who are they going to kill next? You? Me? Probably me—they wouldn't touch a white man."

"They're not going to kill you, Jere. Everyone likes you."

"You don't know that. They'll kill anyone here. Mununga is famous all through Zambia for killing. When I travel to see my father in Lusaka and I tell people where I live, they all say, 'You live there? That place is full up with ndoshi!' In Lusaka everyone is afraid of this place—how can you say that they won't kill me?"

I held up my hands. "Hey, I'm not arguing. I'm just trying to help."

"Did you see the dogs? They fed the dogs!"

It was his turn to unload and be anxious, I gathered, so I sat quietly and he feverishly recounted the whole Christmas episode, filling in many details I had missed. That Chitondo had only been in town a half-dozen years or so, like Jere, and that his limbs had been cut off and thrown in the road for the dogs to fight over. Then Jere described other frightening incidents from his eight years in Mununga. It was quite a list. Once, in Matwishi fishing camp, a duck thief had been beaten senseless, stuffed in a fifty-gallon drum, doused with gasoline, and set on fire.

"How many ducks did he steal, fifty?" I asked.

"Three."

"Three? Three ducks?"

"Yes. Three ducks."

"Did he live?"

Jere snorted. "Of course not. And now we're next."

I punched him lightly on the shoulder. "Okay, now you're being ridiculous," I said.

Malama, banished for about a week now, was slinking around the porch, hoping I'd let him inside, so I called for him, gave him kwacha, and sent him to buy banana wine. He returned from the market with two plastic liter bottles of cheap booze, and Jere and I drank these quickly. The gooey buzz kicked in with all the subtlety of a high fever. We sent Malama to get the chess set from Jere's insaka and set up the game when he returned, though neither of us was really in the mood.

I put my hand over the board. "Jere, one thing, before we play. One last question. Was it really Boniface in charge of the mob? Does he really run this town?"

"I'm not sure."

"Come on."

He was about to say more when the front door of the hut flew open with a bang. We jumped up, knocking over the chess set, hearts in our throats, fists clenched, ready for anything, ready to fight to the death. Scoopy snarled from under the couch and Malama cowered on top of it.

It was Patrick. He had run from the clinic and was out of breath.

"Sorry, I tripped," he panted. "There's a boy, he had his leg cut off."

"What? What? A boy what?" I yelped.

"Had his leg cut off," said Patrick. He made a cutting motion across his knee. "Mulwanda's passed out. We need you, Jere."

Jere shook his head. "Ai, Patrick, you really should have knocked."

The Night the Boy Had His Leg Cut Off

We ran through the dark village to the clinic. It was a moonless night, the stars without limit, the footpaths empty, and every hut dark. From a treatment room a weak light shone and we ran to it; on a table inside a shirtless boy of about fifteen lay, and an older man, his father by the looks of it, stood at the head of the table with his arms crossed. The father excitedly turned to us when we entered. Jere went right to him, shook his hand, and spoke to him in a low, urgent Bemba I couldn't follow. I stopped at the door and took in the scene. The shirtless boy was muscular but unfinished, like a half-grown cornstalk, and lay calmly on his back without moving or speaking. The room's single kerosene lamp flickered, casting him into darkness like there was something shameful about him.

"Where's he cut?" I asked Patrick, who stood beside me, panting hard from the run.

"Left knee." Patrick pointed. "Someone swung an ax through the back of his leg. It went through the skin and the muscles, then stopped right against the kneecap."

I saw it then—a yawning black crease where the back of the knee should have been. Two inches up, a tourniquet fashioned from a ripped shirt circled his thigh.

I stepped back. "Holy shit. Why'd they do that?"

"He stole a fish."

"He stole fish?"

"Not fish," Patrick corrected. "*A* fish. He stole *a* fish. Stole it out of someone else's net in the river."

"He stole a fish so he got his leg cut off?"

"Yes. That's what happened."

I didn't know how to respond to that. Patrick had nothing further to say. Across the room, Jere and the boy's father had stopped talking as well. For five, ten minutes the four of us just watched the boy in silence. I tried to digest the idea of trading a leg for a fish, for a single, more or less tasteless, river bass, but like the Chitondo business, I couldn't get my mind around it. Yet here it was. The boy's large eyes searched the ceiling with such intensity that we all followed his gaze, but there was nothing to see there save rafters, cobwebs, metal sheeting, and, in the back corner, a hanging shape that may or may not have been a bat.

Jere asked Patrick some questions, fell silent again. Amputating a leg was far beyond their capabilities.

"So what's the plan?" I asked Jere.

"The district ambulance passed through on the way up to Puta this afternoon," he answered. "If it comes back through the village tonight they can pick up this patient and take him to the hospital in Kashikishi. We must hope they show before the gangrene." He shook his head. "I don't think he will play for the Eagles regardless"—that was the national soccer team.

I turned to the father. "Batata, I am so sorry," I said in Bemba.

"It's an honor to meet you," he returned, crossing the room to me and clasping my hand in both of his. I understood him because I heard this greeting a dozen times a day.

"Thank you," I said. "The honor is mine."

The father continued to hold my hand and speak to me in Bemba; I caught one other phrase I had definitely heard before: *umusungu umuti*—white medicine.

"I don't have that," I said. "No white medicine. I'm sorry."

He pleaded, his voice a low murmur. *White man, can you heal my boy?* I kept saying I was sorry, hoping he'd ask me to bandage a scab or shoot a layup, something, anything, I could do. No such luck.

The father finally ran out of words and we all looked at his son again. The boy's eyes remained trained on the ceiling. Patrick took a rag out of a cupboard and dipped it into a basin full of water and started washing the boy's legs and feet, first the attached one, and then, with some hesitancy and with great delicacy, the one that hung by a flap of skin. The boy looked down with an expression of curious bewilderment as Patrick ran the rag over his left toes. It took me a minute to realize he was wondering why he couldn't feel a thing.

Jesus. Enough already. I mumbled an excuse and left the room.

I stumbled down the long outdoor hallway of the clinic, almost stepping on the mothers and drunks resting there. I felt a surge of admiration for them: they were trying to bring life into the world or trying to make life go away—everyone else was just failing each other. I found myself at the door of the pharmacy, the bathtub-size room that held all the medication for fifty thousand people. A few weeks earlier, hunting for multivitamins, I had discovered the village's Valium supply, a single bottle; now I used my key to open the lock and groped for the bottle in the dark. I tapped out three pills and swallowed them dry.

Then the screaming started. I didn't know they were screams at first, of course. There was a low and steady repeating noise muffled by the pharmacy door, it might as well have been a passing zebra horde. I had no idea, really, what it was. The door swung open and there stood Patrick, holding a flashlight. He looked very surprised to see me.

"What's going on?" I asked. Five times louder with the door open, the screaming began to take shape. "Hey, is someone yelling?"

"Shock is wearing off," Patrick said. "He has big pain. I am getting Valium for the pain."

"Here." I handed him the bottle. "I thought he might need some."

And when Patrick—this kind and nervous young man—extended his hand to take the bottle, the beam from the flashlight he held illuminated a mottled forearm.

I grabbed his wrist in alarm, pulled his shirtsleeve up. The purplish sores continued evenly past his elbow. "Patrick, what is this?" I demanded.

"Oh, it's nothing," he stammered. "Really." He turned and ran back toward the screams.

Then things got hazy. I was standing in the courtyard of the clinic beneath the mango tree that grew there, resting the back of my head against the trunk, listening to the screaming; turning my aids off and listening to nothing. Turning them back on, back off. *He's screaming; look, he's stopped. Oh no, he's still screaming. Wait, he stopped.*

Then I was in another dark clinic room standing next to a young woman wearing a green citenge sprinkled with goldfish. I wasn't quite clear about how I had gotten there. The only light came from a single candle on the floor.

"Ba Joshua, Ba Joshua," the woman covered in goldfish was sobbing.

On a mattress at our feet lay a wide-eyed man. Next to him, two small children were sleeping the lights-out sleep of the young. The man was so thin he seemed, save for his head, to have melted into the floor; all that remained was the shortest, barest nouns. Ribs. Skull. Knees. Hands. His body was like the bare framework of a house.

"Ba Joshua, Ba Joshua."

"I'm sorry, I'm sorry," I was repeating over and over for the second time that night. Those words should have been tattooed to my forehead.

"Please," the woman cried in Bemba. "Please, Ba Joshua. Umuti umusungu. Ba Joshua, please."

The dying man didn't look much older than I was. His eyes had grown enormously large and white as the skin dehydrated around them, and as I watched, they appeared to detach from their sockets and hover sadly in the air above his face.

I felt thick, insane. "What can I do?" I asked the wife in Bemba.

She poured water from a pitcher into a cup and handed the cup to me, then reached down and lifted the man to a sitting position, his clean white shirt falling off his bamboo stick limbs. Water leaked into my palm from a crack on the side of the glass.

"Water. Great idea," I said to the wife. "Good evening, sir," I said to the man. "You want a drink?"

He nodded with his eyes. Resting the back of his head in my palm—weightless really, an origami sculpture of a head—I tilted him backward, then brought the glass to his lips and began to pour the water into his mouth. Slowly, carefully, I poured three quarters of the glass into his mouth, then lifted it away.

I turned to the wife. "He drank it!" I said. Maybe there was something to umuti umusungu after all.

Then we watched as three quarters of a glass of water slid right back out of the man's mouth, down his chin, over his clean white shirt.

An apologetic expression crept across his face. "No, don't, it's not your fault," I said. I lay him on his back. He turned his head in my hand and rubbed his lips, wet with spilled water, against my wrist. "Ba Joshua," cried his wife. The boy with his leg cut off screamed from down the hall.

Outside again.

I turned my hearing aids off.

Everything had gone crazy—when would it stop? The more I knew of the village the less I saw I could help, and the less I could help the more hope villagers seemed to place in me. "Our first three sons died," one friend from Museka village had said to me when I joined him and his wife for a meal, "but we know you will keep our last alive." What could I say to him and his wife—"I will do no such thing"? To them, I was proof that a better world existed.

Come on, I wanted to say, to them, to the father of the butchered boy, to the men and women huddling in a circle as the child died in the hut across from mine, I'm untrained and my motives are selfish. Indulging in my few burdens, thinking of deafness as a terribly unfair blow, escaping to a new life as far away from the old one as possible. . . . Don't you see? I don't keep children alive. I joke. I adjust the volume in my hearing, I struggle to parse the garbled sentences of oddly shaped mouths, I drink banana wine when all else fails. These are my resources. My skills. Accept this apology and let me go.

But I couldn't say that. I tried to meet their hope. And so, next, I found myself standing in the middle of the road yelling furiously at two men in front of me.

They were the ambulance drivers. They didn't drive an ambulance really, but a dusty Land Cruiser that the government of the Netherlands had donated to the Ministry of Health, with no sirens on top or medical equipment inside. Jere had tracked down the drivers at the market bar and implored them to take the boy to the hospital in Kashikishi but they had refused—the ambulance was loaded with sacks of dried fish to sell in the cities, and they would have to take many sacks out to fit the boy inside.

Jere was upset at the men, but not as upset as I was. My gauzy trance had given way to full-bore, cathartic rage.

"What is wrong with you? This is a fucking ambulance!" I yelled at the two men. "Take the boy to the fucking hospital!"

"We are full," the taller of them said.

I went over to the vehicle, ripped open the back gate, and started throwing sacks of fish in the road.

Jere followed nervously. "Easy, Josh," he said.

"Hey, hey, hey," the taller driver said.

"No, hey," I shouted, still throwing out fish. "No, hey! Take the fucking boy to the fucking hospital!"

The driver relented. "Okay, we'll take him. It's no problem. Please, no problem." He warily stepped forward to close the ambulance door. "No need to take out anymore. See, there is enough room now."

"Great," said Jere, clapping his hands. He pointed at the sacks in the road. "We will sell these here for you in the morning."

"No, not great," I corrected. "There's someone else."

Jere paused, stared at me doubtfully. I brushed his look aside, pointed toward the clinic. "There's a man in the last room," I said to the driver. "You're taking him, too."

"Him?" said Jere. "They don't need to take him."

"Wrong, Jere!" I yelled. "They need to fucking take him! They are going to fucking take him! It is their job to fucking take him!"

"Ba Josh," said the tall driver. "We already took out some fish. We get a much better price for fish in the city. The fish we sell here, we don't hardly make any money."

I walked over and stood very close to the driver. We were the same height, but I had grown up eating cold cuts and fish sticks, three squares a day, and outweighed him by at least thirty pounds. "Hit me," I said to him, clenching my fists. "Please."

"You shouldn't have done that," said Jere, after the ambulance had driven away down the hill and over the bridge, the crippled boy and the dying man lying in back, strapped onto planks lain above the few remaining sacks of fish, their noses almost touching the ceiling. Just the two of them and the drivers inside—there was no room for the boy's father and the man's wife, who would have to try and find a ride to the hospital in Kashikishi in the morning.

"Why not?" I retorted, still pumped from the confrontation.

"That man needed treatment. An IV or something. Fluids. Antibiotics. He needs a doctor. There's a doctor from Norway in Kashikishi."

"Treatment?" Jere frowned. "The poor man's dead. They'll stick an IV in him and he'll live another twenty-four hours. We've just added twenty-four hours to his life. Twenty-four hours alone in a dirty hospital, away from his family, with a doctor who probably hopes he dies sooner rather than later so someone with a chance can use the bed."

I thought about that. I knew he was right.

"Well, so what? Maybe he wants those twenty-four hours."

"Would you want them?"

I didn't answer; the question lingered.

"Goddamn it, Jere," I said, defeated. "Why didn't you tell me before they left?"

"I tried to," he responded. "It's been a long day. Let's get some sleep."

He picked up two sacks of fish and walked back toward the clinic. I picked up a couple more and followed behind him. After a few steps, I stopped and called out, "Hey, what's that rash on Patrick's arms?"

Jere dropped his head, turned around. I could hardly see him; the only light was from the stars, shining like tiny, leering eyes.

"Kaposi's," he said.

"What?" I didn't quite hear, but I had guessed.

"Kaposi's," he repeated.

So on top of everything else, our friend Patrick was a dead man walking.

There was nothing more to say. We stood there for a bit, feeling the wind, the sleeping village, the hard-fought silence, thinking of Patrick, or of the boy, or of Chitondo, or of the dying man, of ourselves, rivers, malaria, Rambo, dugout canoes—who the hell knows? What the hell sense did anything make out here? We locked the fish in Jere's office and walked home together without speaking. It was so late, even the mosquitoes were asleep. We stunk of fish and starving dogs gathered behind as we walked, snarling at one another as they determined who would have first crack at us. Jere went into his house and I picked up a few rocks to chuck at any dogs that got too close and walked on.

part
two

Kolwe tapusuka mipya ibili.

The monkey will not escape the burning grass two times.

Starting Over

While all this drama played out in Mununga, I was pursuing a relationship with Maria, the Peace Corps nurse. It was slow going. We didn't get to see each other much so it took a long time for us to get to know each other; we had that weekend together in Mansa during the first volunteer conference (the one where we were encouraged to focus on cultural exchange), but then we only saw each other once in the next nine months. That was for two quick nights in Kashikishi while she was traveling around the country giving vaccine booster shots. Our relationship was mostly letters, phone calls of course being out of the question.

In February, one year and one month after I arrived in Zambia, there was a volunteer conference in Lusaka. This mostly involved sitting around a U-shaped table in the conference room of a hotel, trying to read the lips of fast-talking development experts and volunteers who had grown scraggly mustaches—which meant going back to being deaf again. Did Joe say his project was going well or he was doing no wells? How long till lunch? A waste of time, but at night, after the day's meetings ended and Administration drove home to his beautiful girlfriend and enormous TV and the other volunteers gathered in the bar to drink and catch up, I walked out the motel gate to where Maria waited by the side of the road in a little red car. I ducked inside and she drove us through the darkened capital, past the shantytowns, the padlocked office buildings on Cairo Road, the street kids sleeping on the sidewalks underneath billboard advertisements for a fantastic national future, and down Saddam Hussein Boulevard into the district where the diplomats and ex-pats lived, with its armed guards, golf courses, and cinder-block fences topped with broken glass and razor wire. I held her hand as she drove.

Technically, our relationship was against Peace Corps regulations—volunteers and staff were not allowed to have personal relationships and could be fired for it. So we could only meet this way. But these were beautiful, strangely hopeful drives. Stretched out and almost completely empty of all human gatherings or movements, the unlit capital felt like it could be anything it wanted come morning. And by extension, so could we.

Once we got to her apartment, Maria and I tried to talk about what we'd seen while we'd been apart. But that was largely a mistake. You could go crazy thinking and talking about Africa, trying to process it, trying to make sense of a continent of boys with their legs cut off, punished for their hunger, waiting for the ride that may or may not come in time. Next to them, other boys missing hands, arms, and heads, girls torn to shreds for a passing trucker's pleasure. Much as we may have thought we wanted to, Maria and I quickly realized we couldn't really talk about these things.

So instead, she asked me about hearing loss and I, for the first time in my life, really did want to share my experience of it with someone else. In the States deafness was a touchstone for every experience but it wasn't that in Mununga, so I had some distance and was much more at ease with it. We did an experiment: Maria produced a pair of earplugs and put them in her ears and I took out my hearing aids, and we cut the lights and went to bed and made love in darkness. Each of us was blind and deaf, down to three senses from five, the three expanding like gases in a vacuum, everything concentrated in a fingertip—lovely, but when it was over I felt like I had betrayed something.

I put my hearing aids back on and Maria turned on the lamp.

"That was strange," I said to her, and it was. I didn't know why.

She took off her earplugs. "I just wanted to see what it was like," she said.

"What was it like?"

She threw the plugs in the direction of the trash and they bounced soundlessly on the carpet. "I liked it," she said. "But it's weird being in my head with all that quiet. I felt like I kept bumping into myself."

We tried another approach: I turned one hearing aid to its lowest setting and moistened the ear mold with a dab of lotion. Maria put it in her ear, and then I read her a poem I'd written about a village baby who had been born with a green butt. (A true story: the women blamed it on the mother eating too much cassava while she was pregnant.)

"What do you think?" I asked her when I had finished.

"It's loud," she said. "And your voice sounds mechanical, like off a record or a microphone. And I really hear every background noise"—she pointed at the ceiling—"like, I really hear that fan now."

"Aids are like that," I said. "They can't differentiate. But what did you think of the poem?"

Maria smiled. "It needs more work. It needs more work. It needs more work." She repeated herself a few more times. "Wow, I can really hear my own voice."

She got up from the bed wearing just a T-shirt and repeated words and phrases over and over, now cupping her hands like a trumpet, now holding them flat over her mouth. I stretched out and watched her. She was petite and dark-skinned and her face was lit up like a child's with a secret.

"Needs more work," she said again. "Neeeeds moooooore wooooork. NEEDS more WORK." She breathed loud and quick. "That sounds like a storm." She growled. "Whoa, that's loud."

She whistled, jumped up and down, groaned like she was having an orgasm.

I watched her and drank South African wine from the bottle. Finally taking off the hearing aid, she turned it over and over in her hand—a tiny little thing, smaller than a lighter, lighter than four quarters—it looked so fragile, she said, like a snail missing its shell. I took it from her and put it in.

"When I was at Gallaudet," I said, "living with other deaf and hearing-impaired people, the school newspaper had a survey: if you could take a pill that would make you hearing, would you take it?"

"And?"

"The vast majority of the students said no. They were happy with their lives."

"And you?"

It was a hard question to answer, now more than ever, which was why I brought it up. "I don't know. If I say, 'Yes, make me hearing,' isn't that some kind of failure of will? Does it mean I couldn't find happiness with all the gifts I've been given? I have money, family, education, hearing aids, and I didn't grow up in a shack in the bush. Shouldn't that be enough?"

"There's nothing wrong with wanting more," Maria said.

"Yeah, but here's the thing," I said. "I've already taken that pill. I'm no longer deaf."

She frowned like I'd told a joke that didn't make sense. "You're not deaf? You didn't hear a thing I said before when you had both aids out."

"I'm not deaf," I repeated. I told her then of the miracle of discovering in Mununga a place past deafness and hearing. How in the open village spaces, in the quiet insakas, and by the hushed river, unencumbered by radios, subways, passing cars, ringing phones, or beeping appliances, I heard better than I ever had before—five, ten times better; how the villagers looked at me when they spoke so I could look right back at their lips; and how they talked slowly and repeated themselves freely and kept conversations simple, rarely going off on complicated tangents that were difficult to follow. I could hear them all. And above and beyond all that, the fact that I was a white man was so astonishing to the villagers that my being deaf didn't register. It made no difference whatsoever in my daily interactions—I'd taken the pill.

"I'm telling you, it's like living someone else's life," I told Maria, "someone who hears."

"That's pretty cool," she said.

I shook my head, drank more wine. "No," I said. "It's actually been worthless."

And I told her then about the rainy season and its diseases, about the boy with one leg cut off and other such things. What did it mean that I had found a place—for all I knew the only place on the planet—that could fulfill just about every hearing fantasy I had ever entertained, and the staring eyes of a half-dead infant canceled it out immediately? Even with this new and long-sought and amazing sense, I still got angry with people and hurt by them and jumped to conclusions and said inappropriate things. I could hear, but nothing had changed.

"Deaf or hearing, it doesn't seem to make a difference," I summed up.

Maria nodded, thinking, tapping her nose with her finger. "If it's true that it doesn't matter," she finally said, "then that means blindness doesn't matter, paralysis doesn't matter, health doesn't matter, or wealth or fame." She exhaled deeply. "Shit, or even living and dying."

I hadn't considered that. What was important then?

"It means this world is without meaning," she said. "Pretty heavy." She pulled off her T-shirt. "Let's make love. Now. You can keep the stupid hearing aids on."

Later, we cooked a steak and ate fresh vegetables—a cucumber, lettuce, a green pepper—the only produce I had during my two years in Africa. Then we filled the bathtub with hot water from the stove and sat in the water until it grew cold. We went to sleep, but I was having nightmares all the time those days and Maria woke me and we lay talking until the roosters cawed and I walked down the road and woke a taxi driver asleep in his vehicle for a ride back to the hotel. Maria told me stories about being an emergency room nurse back in Montana, the teenage heroin addicts and the car accidents and the teenage heroin addicts in car accidents. I told her about the shock of seeing how a violent mob is more driven by joy than rage. Such is pillow talk in the developing world. I was grateful for these nights. Unused to the fresh vegetables, I passed gas so foul it knocked us off the bed. We held each other and made plans to go away together when her contract with Peace Corps ended.

SOMETIMES, EVEN WHEN YOU DON'T EXPECT IT, YOU JUST SHAKE stuff off and move on. After the madness around the holidays, life continued in Mununga and there were no more mobs or impromptu amputations, so I got back to work.

It helped having Jere's great example. His work ethic was astounding—and surprising. He'd changed the night the boy had his leg cut off. After bursting into my hut, swearing that the Chitondo violence was the last straw and he would leave Mununga for good, not an hour later, he was finding the ride that would save the boy's life. After that night, he became more driven. It seemed like an idealism had been reawakened in him, one that years spent in Mununga had plastered over. And with the idealism came great energy—no matter how late we stayed out at night, Jere was always first at the clinic every morning, unlocking all the offices, triaging the patients for when Mulwanda and I arrived. He expected me at the clinic earlier and earlier and grumbled when I left town to spend a weekend with Chris. Every morning, Malama woke me with a shake and word that Jere was waiting.

"Five more minutes," I'd say.

"Ba Jere say hurry," Malama would reply.

One day, Jere and I were crossing the bridge, returning to the clinic from a meeting of some sort, probably about wells (though I'd pretty much given up on those after Christmas) or to teach a group of bamayos to practice better hygiene during meal prep, and I asked him why he was working so hard. He stopped in the middle of the bridge and looked downstream, to where the river slunk past a few last rocks into a fecund, mosquito-breeding marsh. A half mile further on the marsh merged with Lake Mweru.

After a few minutes, he turned to look at me so I could read his lips. "I know this town is Gomorrah," he said. "I know it. There's nothing for anyone to look forward to here so people go crazy. There's no development, no development coming, no government help, no government help coming." He took out a handkerchief and dried his face. There was no shade on the bridge so he was dripping sweat. "But this is still my country," he continued, "and I still want it to work. Nyanja, Bemba, Tonga, Lozi, Shona, Zulu— Kaunda once said, 'What do tribes matter? Tribes do not matter, we are all brothers.' Now I know Kaunda had his failings. But he is right. We are all brothers."

It was a beautiful speech. Jere wiped off his face again and started walking, and I fell in next to him, inspired.

"Let me know how I can help," I said.

Not long after, as another day at the clinic wound down, Jere sent for me to come to his office. It was late afternoon, the morning line of patients had all been lectured, medicated, consoled, or ignored. From the office's one window, you could see the market vendors boxing up unsold bubble gum and cooking oil and bamayos gathering leftover tomatoes, balancing bundles on their heads, and, trailing children like swimming ducks, heading home. I could tell that Jere had something on his mind, but he had trouble getting to the point. He wiped and rewiped his face.

"What's up?" I prompted.

"I have been thinking about our conversation on the bridge," Jere began. "And I have had an idea. An idea for a project that will transform Mununga. This project will bring together Peace Corps and Zambia and will help clean the market and will help our patients and will even slow infant mortality during the rains."

Quite a buildup. "What is it?" I asked.

He didn't say right away. A born storyteller, he did love a dramatic moment. He took my hand and led me outside and down the clinic steps, and pointed across the courtyard at the enormous, decrepit AIDS ward. The walls of the ward were crumbling earthen brick and flaked plaster and women wrapped in their citenges sat on a pile of rubble that passed for stairs, staring at nothing. It looked like a single well-placed sledgehammer blow could have knocked the whole building over.

"You want to fix that?" I asked. "That's your big idea?"

"No. It was built wrong," Jere said. "Too much mud, not enough cement. What we'll do is build a new one. A completely new AIDS ward and"—he turned to face the side of the clinic—"and here we'll put in new stairs and a new hallway and build an alcove where all the pregnant women can sleep."

"That's a great idea," I said. And it was, I could picture it— more than just providing space for the patients, a new ward would close the clinic in on itself, give it privacy from the bustle of the market. "Who will build it?"

"I've worked that part out," Jere said. "We'll build it very quickly by paying people."

My heart sank. "You know I can't get that money, Jere. I'm not allowed to pay people. Peace Corps won't let me."

Jere looked at the crumbling ward, turned back to me disappointed. "So don't tell Peace Corps," he said. "Why do they have to know?"

"It's their money."

"Can't you tell them it's for something else?"

"No."

I wasn't enjoying being a killjoy and I understood why he wanted to pay workers—for almost a year I'd been trying to convince villagers to dig wells without pay and I'd gotten nowhere, but paying people would mean going against everything I had been taught in training—community development, self-reliance, sustainability, all those things. It would just foster further dependency.

Jere looked down, kicked the ground with his foot. When he looked up again, it was at a spot over my right shoulder, which was unusual—he had always looked me in the eye before. "I didn't want to say this," he said, "but people in the village are saying you are a spy. They say there is no way a strong man like you could have been sent all this way from America without supplies."

I stared at him. "I'm a spy?"

"Yes, CIA."

"Come on, you know I'm not a spy."

"Yes, I know. Others are not so sure." He took in my disbelief and laid a fatherly hand on my shoulder. "But a new clinic would convince them."

I left, telling Jere I needed to think his idea over. Without waiting for my decision, he went ahead and drew up plans for the new ward. He showed me the plans every evening when we met for a chess game or drinking session. On large squares of taped-together writing paper, new buildings were sketched out with an architect's eye. The attention to detail was impressive: Jere must have spent hours shadowing in the ripples in the roofing tin. In one diagram, he even drew a pregnant woman sitting on a bench with a hand over her stomach. "You see that," he said. "She is waiting to go into your office."

He was rolling.

"You think if we did this project they would bring electricity up from Kashikishi and send us a doctor?" he asked.

"I don't know," I answered.

"What color do you want your new office?"

"Light blue."

"If I win this game of chess, will you ask Peace Corps for the money?"

"No. But I'll buy you a beer."

He finally put down the drawing. He was still a much better player than I was and beat me in less than fifteen moves.

April marked one year into service: one down, one to go. It was harvesttime and villagers were happy: the rains had been good. Some afternoons while floating on my back in the river, enjoying the sweet exhaustion of a long day's work, the sun dappling through the leaves, the thought came to me: I could do this, I could just keep doing this and I think that's why I was leery of Jere's project—things were going okay and I didn't want to mess with that, didn't want to mess up something else. Mununga wasn't really a bad place, witchcraft or mobs or not, just a place that had bad moments. And this year I would just go away for Christmas.

Game Park

What brought me on board with the clinic project, randomly enough, was a lost ambulance. The ambulance, carrying the nurse from the Mununga clinic (Malama's hard-drinking childless aunt, actually) and a cooler full of vaccinations, along with a driver, was last seen headed down a seldom-driven road into the deep bush. They were due back at sundown and when they hadn't returned by the next morning, Jere grew concerned.

"Maybe crocodiles got them," he worried, "or bandits."

We set off on my motorcycle to search for them.

The road the ambulance had taken went past the chief's palace, became a jeep track, and bore through miles of swampy grasslands interrupted by mopane groves and clusters of huts. The mopanes with their wild, electrified profusions of branches looked like they suffered from painful inner fires; the droopy huts looked like sickness. After forty-five minutes, the trees cleared and the track dipped down into a wide marsh, bowled in on all sides by forested hills, a speck of white in the middle. From closer that speck turned out to be the ambulance sunk right up to its rear bumper in the mud—it looked like a shih tzu dog-paddling in a lake. A dozen men and one woman squatting around the vehicle turned to watch as Jere and I pulled up. I cut the engine. The ambulance driver sitting behind the wheel rolled down his window and waved.

"Good morning, Ba Joshua!" he said, in English. He was from the Copperbelt, where men often knew some English.

"Morning," I replied as Jere and I got off the motorcycle. The mud immediately pooled up to our ankles.

"It is a nice morning, isn't it?" the driver said.

"It is," I agreed.

"And you are feeling healthy, Ba Joshua?"

"Yes, I am, thank you"—and we continued the now familiar salutary exchange as he sat in a car sunk four feet in the mud. The others sat on their haunches and watched us. No one seemed to have any other ideas.

Except Jere, who tapped my shoulder, interrupting the greeting. "Take the nurse back to town on your motorcycle and get the roads crew," he said.

"Yes, sir," I said.

After dropping the nurse at the clinic, I rode to the army checkpoint at the south entrance of town. Next to the checkpoint was the roads camp; the half-dozen men living there maintained the hundred miles of dirt roads ringing the Zambian side of Lake Mweru. However, like the soldiers next door, they rarely got paid and therefore rarely worked. The roads reflected it. During the rainy season, giant potholes appeared on the road surface, and these holes, large enough to hide a fridge, slid stealthily back and forth across the surface with each rain, like lions stalking prey. Once or twice a month old pickups got separated from their axles and the roads crew was roused to clear the wreckage—they had a tractor. The rest of the time, they got high, napped, farmed maize, and waited for their pay.

A day after I told them of the situation, the roads crew arrived at the swamp, surveyed the stuck ambulance with the cocky assurance of crime scene detectives, turned their tractor around and backed it up to the vehicle, hooked up a strong chain and pulled; the tractor promptly sank four feet into the mud.

"I don't understand this technique," Jere said to me.

"Me, neither," I said. "Is this quicksand?" I'd always wanted to see quicksand.

"That's further in the bush," Jere replied. "I think you should go back to Mununga and get shovels." He was in a bossy mood.

We dug for three days: Jere, myself, the driver, roads crew, and a dozen grimy barefoot men who materialized out of the swamp each morning. Most of these men lived nearby; some were just traveling through, hiking to Mununga from villages so far in the bush they might have been on other planets—regardless of where they came from, they put down their packages, stayed for a day or two, and helped us out. There was no food or water to offer them, viscous mud oozed into every hole we started, and the sun beat down like an angry heat lamp, but they picked up the shovels and dug.

Jere had taken charge of the situation. He strategized, gave directions, and complained about the heat, all while wearing, God knows where he got it, a blue one-piece mechanic's jumpsuit with the name Mike stitched over his chest. He looked like he had just walked off a Sunoco station. I kept asking him for an oil change but he didn't know what that was.

We freed the tractor on day three. The roads crew thanked us, immediately piled on, and left for their camp, leaving us right where we had started, with an ambulance sunk up to its bumpers. For a long time Jere and I stared in disbelief as the tractor slowly made its getaway across the swamp, but the locals kept right on working. They took turns on the shovels or got on their knees and dug with their bare hands. They walked off to the distant hills, returning an hour later with armfuls of branches and stones to place under the wheels. Their generosity was a beautiful thing. Natural, like breathing. It seemed to never occur to them that they needn't help us and if they sometimes asked me for a few kwacha, it was done so sheepishly that I always gave more than they asked. Why can't we find guys like you in Mununga, I wondered.

One afternoon, as we took a rest, the ambulance driver (whose name I never heard correctly, but it might have been Robert) made Jere and me an offer. After his car was freed, he would be delivering vaccinations up to Kaputa, a remote and fabled city to the north and east, halfway to Wapita, and he invited us to come along with him. Kaputa rested beyond more than seventy miles of unexplored forest, on the eastern edge of Lake Mweru-Wantipa, a vast, shallow lake that disappeared during dry years. Because of its isolation and lack of depth, Robert explained, Wantipa's waters were filled with the most delicious fish in the country.

"So please you will come," he summed up. "We will buy fish and sell it back here or in the Copperbelt. Wantipa chisense are the best in the world. Wantipa bream taste like goat steak. Everyone knows this."

I thought it sounded like an interesting diversion and a nice ending to a week of shoveling our asses off in a swamp. Jere thought so, too, even though he'd recently confessed to me that he was sick of eating fish.

The next day, once we finally had all four of the ambulance wheels clear of the mud, Robert tried to gun his way out of the marsh, the rest of us pushing, but the wheels spun and spun on the branches we'd put down. Robert reached his limit right then—he had been sleeping in the ambulance all week to protect it from thieves while Jere and I returned home each night for a hot meal and a bath—he threw open the door and staggered, groaning, out into the marsh. I was just as desperate at the thought of resuming the dig so I climbed into the driver's seat. Back in the States, I had freed my share of cars from snowdrifts and I applied the same technique here. I pumped the gas to start the car rocking, working up a rhythm as well as a cloud of smoking tire rubber. Suddenly the ambulance shot forward and skidded out of the marsh.

"I didn't know you could drive ambulances," Jere said when I climbed down from the driver's seat.

"It's part of my CIA training," I replied.

He stared at me, surprised. We left for Kaputa the following morning.

THE DIRT ROAD TO KAPUTA WAS WELL MADE. NO ONE DARED TO PUT up a hut in the forest and no one wanted to get stuck driving through. Unlike the rain forest in Zaire, which was too lush for big game (and big people—it was the land of the pygmy), the Kaputa forest was just right for lions, leopards, and hyenas—all the big predators that lurked in village legends. And unlike Luangwa National Park, Zambia's largest and most famous wildlife park, no safari tourists or game hunters ever came out and surveyed or shot up the Kaputa game park—it was simply too remote. We didn't pass another vehicle the whole ride out.

My first inkling that the trip would not be a smooth one came about a half hour after we left Mununga. Cruising through the game park at fifty miles an hour under Robert's practiced touch, we blew the right rear tire, the same one that I'd smoked in the swamp. While Jere and I kept a cautious eye on the woods, Robert put on the spare. That soon blew as well, but he fixed up a patch on the first tire and pumped it up with a bicycle pump—that held.

Midday, we arrived at a fair-sized bush city with neat streets and a clean market laid out in an organized grid. A steady lake wind kept all of it cool. Kaputa was bigger than Mununga but felt gentle in comparison. Peaceful, clean, electrified—it was in fact everything I'd imagined in my Peace Corps dreams of a better Africa. It even smelled good, like fifty miles of freshwater, instead of the usual bush city smell that one finds in Kashikishi and Mansa and other places: the smell of fermenting trash and hidden turds.

While Robert went to have the tires repatched, Jere and I bought a hundred pounds of chisense, made plans to pick them up when we left, and then strolled through the town. A dozen or so children flocked to watch the white man walk but they respectfully kept their distance and held their tongues.

I couldn't hold in my admiration. Kaputa was a revelation. "This town is like a dream," I said to Jere. "It's perfect."

"Remind you of America?" he asked.

"No, it's better. This is Africa being Africa. It's not trying to be something else. Africa can't be anyplace else, but foreigners are always trying to change it, trying to make it match some place they came from."

Jere clucked his tongue. "I wouldn't mind if it was like America."

We came upon a large crowd outside a school; a man in a three-piece suit was giving a speech and Jere stopped walking and listened attentively. "Wha-ee-ohh, wha-ee-ohh" is how the man sounded to me through his bullhorn—I couldn't even tell what language he was speaking, but whatever he was saying, it made Jere upset.

"It's not right," he said. "He says he will bring more development here. Well, why not to Mununga? Mununga doesn't even have electricity."

So it was a political rally—that or some kind of sermon. "Is that a chief?" I asked.

"It's the governor. Have you ever seen him in Mununga?"

"No." I'd actually pretty much forgotten there was a governor—or a government.

Jere shook his head. "You're right, no. He's afraid of Mununga like everyone else. He won't campaign there, won't even show his face. And we need help more than anybody."

I shaded my eyes and looked up at the man on the porch. He wore a gray suit the color of rusty cooking pots and a gold watch chain hung from his vest. As he spoke through the bullhorn, he gestured forcefully with his free hand as if he was pounding maize meal.

"Maybe he doesn't know what's happening in Mununga," I said to Jere. "Tell him about your clinic idea."

"No," Jere said firmly, lips pursed, nostrils flared.

"You want me to say something?" I offered.

"No," he said again, without offering any explanation. "Let's get lunch."

We met Robert at a lakeside restaurant for a meal of Wantipa bream—not quite the goat meat he boasted of, just another bony white fish, but not bad—then Robert went to visit a lady friend and Jere and I wandered around town a little more. We came upon the governor speaking at another rally and again his speech made Jere furious, but again it just sounded like gibberish to me, like the din of six fish sellers calling out at once. I ignored Jere, aggravated as he was, because there was something about standing there, feeling the breeze off the lake, that felt like a fresh start—I was enjoying my day away from Mununga and I was enjoying this town. I turned off my hearing aids and took in the rally. The governor with his expensive suit seemed from another century than the audience of several hundred bedraggled, barefoot men. A shirtless old man held a looping umbrella of banana leaves over his head. Children darted through the crowd like mice in a maze.

Jere poked my arm, started flapping his lips. I halfheartedly turned my aids back on.

"Promises and lies," he seethed. "He never does anything for us. Did the governor visit after the Chitondo situation? Did he call for an investigation? Did he do anything at all?"

"Not that I remember," I replied.

"Eight years I've lived in Mununga," Jere said. "And the governor's never visited there one time."

He had a point: why was Kaputa, with electricity and clean streets already, being promised more government support? Even during the deadly rainy season malaria epidemic, not a single extra nurse had been sent to the Mununga clinic, nor a single extra dose of quinine.

"You really should say something to him," I said. "Raise your hand, ask him a question. It's a public gathering."

Jere waved me away. "Forget it. He will just ignore me."

I should have left it there, but I couldn't. I wanted something to happen for Jere who was working so hard, caring so much, against Sisyphean odds. Also, to be honest, as much as I was enjoying the peacefulness of the town, I wasn't enjoying standing around for speeches I couldn't understand—it reminded me too much of college lectures and temple and childhood. The instinct to make a commotion when things fell too far out of my grasp kicked in.

"He won't ignore you," I said to Jere. "Watch this."

I picked up a little boy in my arms. Pale but friendly, he had followed Jere and me in a crowd of other boys since lunch. Now I spun three-sixty and dipped him ballroom style. The children surrounding us cheered. More of them flocked over. I feinted at grabbing them, shook my hips, and their laughter was a tinkly, rising roar.

Jere's lips were pressed tight. "What are you doing?" he said.

"Rumba." I did another move. "Malama's been teaching me."

Almost instantly, the entire rally, about 150 people, turned away from the governor to watch me. The governor stopped talking and lowered his bullhorn.

With a flourish, I stopped dancing to more cheers. "There," I said to Jere. "You said the governor wouldn't pay attention. He's paying attention now."

"Yes," he agreed.

"We have the floor. You want to ask him questions or should I?"

"You ask," Jere said without hesitation.

I took a deep breath. "Hello!" I yelled up to the governor. He was about fifty feet away. *"Mulishani mukwai. Mwalilah?"*

The crowd, surprised to hear a white man speaking Bemba, broke into applause. The governor smiled a pained smile. While I waited for quiet, I considered what to ask him.

"Uh, *mukwai, twafuma Mununga ee tufwaya* electricity," I managed to get out—we're from Mununga and we need electricity—but then I was stumped for what to say next. Talking in Bemba in front of all these people was making me nervous.

"Let's go," Jere said, pulling roughly on my arm.

Then I thought, hey, the governor knows English; I could just ask my questions in English. "No, wait, Jere," I protested. I hadn't really said anything yet. But just then I saw the soldiers. There were four of them. They wore dusty fatigues and wraparound shades and were walking toward us. Smooth and unhurried, gliding like crocodiles, they nudged people out of the way with the tips of their rifles. They were real soldiers, with real African soldier glower, not the stoned and scared Mununga kind.

"Holy shit," I said.

The crowd, catching on, went totally silent, and for a long second no one moved at all, and then everyone started to run in all directions. Jere and I were frozen to the spot. The soldiers stopped about twenty feet away from us, their eyes inscrutable beneath their shades. I was stunned. A moment ago I had been dancing goofily; now these men were pointing their guns at us.

Just then Robert drove up behind us in the ambulance.

"Bop-ba! Tires all better," he said.

Jere and I nodded politely to the soldiers. Then we hurdled inside. "Go, go, go!" we yelled.

A minute later we were speeding out of town, whooping and hollering. From my spot in the backseat, I leaned forward and clapped Robert on the shoulder. "You're the best ambulance driver ever," I shouted. He beamed.

"That was foolish," Jere said, but he was excited, laughing.

"We got his attention for sure. Thinking he can just ignore Mununga forever. Thinking Mununga doesn't matter. Still, I can't believe you—those soldiers looked ready to kill you."

"Fuck them," I said, surfing on the adrenaline. "I danced for one minute, I asked one question, and they wanted to shoot me? The whole thing was too fast. He probably doesn't even know who we are."

"Oh, the governor knows who *you* are."

"We should go back."

"We're not going back," Jere scoffed.

"But we forgot our fish. The Wantipa chisense, best in the world."

Jere laughed until he couldn't breathe. "I'm sick of fish."

I settled back in my seat for the long drive through the forest.

Robert drove fast, sliding at the edge of control. He and Jere shouted back and forth about what had happened at the rally and about other things, but I couldn't hear them with the noise of the road or read their lips with all the car's bouncing, so I slumped in my seat and looked out the window. Outside, miombo trees, looking like the mutant offspring of ferns and palms, crowded up against the road. I turned back to the front and saw Jere still gesturing and laughing. I had a small ache at not being able to join in the conversation and shut my eyes as it grew. We had just pissed off a governor and his soldiers back in Kaputa—or, more accurately, I had pissed them off—but what I thought right then was that I kind of wished we were back there, because in the middle of that situation, in the middle of all high-octane situations, I could at least follow what was going on. People in mobs or missing legs or carrying rifles make their meanings clear in their actions. It was the full contact way out of loneliness. So okay, I probably shouldn't have danced, but no one got hurt.

The right rear tire blew again, breaking my reverie. Robert replaced it with the spare the toutboys in Kaputa had patched up, but that blew too—they had done a half-assed job. By now we knew the drill: we got down from the ambulance, jacked and removed the flat, pried out the inner tube, and spread spit on it to find the puncture. After finding it, with rough-surfaced rocks we scraped up a scruff that a new patch would stick to when glued. The scraping took a while—it was tough rubber.

We fixed the two tires, put one on, it blew; the other, same thing. We climbed down to do it all again. Vultures gathered to watch us in a towering nearby jackfruit tree, its trunk as wide around as a small hut. Not a single vehicle or person had passed since we left Kaputa several hours before.

Jere jerked his head toward the forest. It was noisy with sounds I couldn't quite make out.

"What was that?" I asked him. "What did you hear?" I was feeling jittery all of a sudden.

He frowned. Robert kept scraping a tube. I peered into the shadows and thought I saw something move.

"Who's out there?" I called. No one answered.

Suddenly the bright disc of sun high-dived behind a ridge and it was night and we were sitting on the road in inky darkness without any food or water and with two flat tires. Stars appeared with the suddenness of a magic trick, blotted out here and there by circling vultures.

"We're not going to make it home in time for dinner," Jere said.

Hell, we might become dinner, I thought. "We almost done, Robert?" I asked.

He looked up from his work and shook his head. "Almost. I want to do it perfect this time. Just this one tire, and I'm going to get it perfect."

Something roared at us from close by. I jumped.

"Hey, was that a lion?" I asked Jere.

"No, that was an owl," he said. He sighed dramatically and kicked a rock in the road. "I wish I never came. I don't even like fish."

Robert lifted the tire upright. "I think we're ready."

We set the tire in place, wrenched on the lug nuts, and got inside the ambulance. "Drive carefully," Jere pleaded, and Robert did, creeping softly down the dark road, but then a rabbit scampered across the high beams and Robert slammed on the brakes, threw the car in reverse, and tried to run it over. The tire blew with a loud bang. Jere dropped his head in his hands. Robert got out and peered under the car.

"Missed," he said.

An hour passed. It quickly grew colder. I had forgotten how cold it got on the Central African plateau. On the chilliest nights, if I exhaled slowly I could see my breath, which always made me think of New York. This was one of those nights and I wondered what my folks were doing. My brothers. I wrote letters to them in my head: *Dear Ma, I can hear so well. Dear Zev, I finally got to see a game park!* We rolled up the ambulance windows and I curled in my seat to sleep.

Jere turned to face me. "Can you hear my stomach?" he asked.

"No," I replied.

"It's empty."

"Sorry."

"If we were home it would be full."

"Okay. Got it," I said. "What do you want me to do?"

I drifted off. In my dreams, forest shadows gathered into leering, howling hyenas, vultures grew to the size of rhinos and carried a man in each talon, then brilliant white dots of light grew brighter and brighter until I was completely blinded. Shielding my eyes, I sat up. A white Land Cruiser rolled up, followed by another car. They were coming from Kaputa, a midnight convoy. The odds were tiny that we'd encounter cars at midnight—people avoided driving at night for the exact reason of not wanting to end up like we had. The cars drove fifty feet past us and halted.

Gleefully we jumped out of the ambulance—they could loan us a tire, share some water!

Four soldiers climbed out of the first car, followed by the governor.

Jere, Robert, and I froze.

The governor walked toward us, his stride purposeful and heavy. The soldiers followed him, cradling their rifles. My legs started to shake.

"Trouble?" the governor called. He had a broad smile.

I didn't say anything. Jere and Robert didn't say anything.

The governor walked around the ambulance, bending down to look at the flat tire when he came to it. He was a tall man, bald with a fringe of white hair, and a bowling ball stomach jutted proudly in front of him. He was in no hurry and rubbed his belly like he had just polished off a huge meal.

"What a disaster!" he finally said, drawing out the words. "A flat tire right in the middle of the game park. Such a dangerous place. So dangerous! So unfortunate!" He took his pocket watch out of his vest and peered at it in the light from the headlights. "And so late. Anything could happen to you men out here. Like me, us," he motioned to the soldiers, "we could have been bandits. Bandits with guns out for your money! And your lives!" He laughed.

I had a vision: the governor tapping the side of his nose, his soldiers nodding at the signal, marching us into the forest, and putting their guns to our heads. The percussive gunshot, the startled birds taking flight. Vultures would pick our bones clean before anyone knew where we were. The rules of society were worthless out here in the forest at night—the man with the gun made the rules. We knew that and the governor knew we knew that. Five feet behind him the nearest soldier unstrapped his rifle and pointed it in our direction.

I peeked at Jere for a cue, but he had his head down.

"White man," the governor barked. "Excuse me."

The governor had my undivided attention. I had been looking at him all along so I could read his lips.

"Sir?" I said.

He grinned fiercely. "The famous Mununga white man . . . I don't know how you do in America. But in our country we do not dance when others speak."

I mumbled some kind of apology. He snorted. The soldier behind him kept his rifle trained on us. I looked down, saw ruts in the road. Rocks buried in the ruts revealed just their tips like icebergs. What else was there to say about standing in the middle of the forest, in the middle of the night with a gun pointed at me?

It was quiet for a minute, then the governor broke the silence with a deep laugh. "I'd give you a ride to Mununga," he said. "But I have no room. No matter, strong men like you can fix a tire." He nodded and turned back to his Land Cruiser, followed closely by the soldiers.

"Good night," he called as he walked away, or maybe it was "Good luck" or maybe even "Nice life."

The governor and his men piled back in their car. One of the soldiers paused, turned, raised his rifle, and fired off a round over our heads. Jere, Robert, and I dove to the ground; the crack of the gunshot knuckled against the car windows and went screaming down the road. This soldier then pulled something long and dark from the car and threw it in our direction. It tomahawked through the air. Still crouching low to the ground, we scrambled behind the ambulance, scraping our knees and elbows on the road. But it was only a stick of sugarcane. The convoy started up and drove away.

I fell back against the ambulance bumper. Each limb in my body shook independently and I badly had to piss. I felt like I couldn't breathe.

Jere picked himself up, brushed himself off, and let loose at the taillights disappearing down the road.

"You are a disgrace!" he yelled at the cars. "Abandoning your people in the bush. We will tell the newspapers how terrible you are! It will be a huge scandal. Huge! The biggest ever."

His anger surprised me, scared me a little. But mostly I was relieved it wasn't pointed in my direction. I had danced at the rally after all.

"Jere, sugarcane," I pointed, hoping it would calm him down. "If you're still hungry."

He ignored me, picked up a rock, and threw it after the cars, then climbed into the passenger seat and slammed the door. Robert shrugged, picked up the sugarcane, and got into the ambulance as well.

I was alone outside. I took a couple of ragged breaths, trying to catch a good one, but wasn't able to. I decided I needed to get away from the ambulance, the menace and contempt swirling around there, so I walked down the road. I went a hundred feet or so and stopped, turned off my aids, and peed like a bull elephant. How nice to take a piss without anything explosive pointed at my chest! My breathing slowed. The silence turned the dark shadows of the forest into soft blankets. Walking back to the ambulance I saw its headlights flicking on and off. I ran over, switching on my aids.

"What? What is it?" I said.

Jere was leaning halfway out the window. "Where did you go?" he shouted. "There are lions out there! There are hyenas!"

"Oh." My heart dropped four feet. "I forgot."

"How could you forget? Didn't you hear us calling?"

"Sorry, I didn't hear anything."

"I was calling and calling," he said.

I opened the back door and climbed inside the ambulance.

"Sorry," I said again, feeling even dumber than before.

We passed the night shivering in the ambulance. Then at first light Jere and I started hiking along the road toward Mununga, probably a two-day walk away, without a plan really, just a hope that we might pass somebody. Robert caught up with us around noon, having stayed with the vehicle while we went for help, and having, remarkably, finally worked up a good patch. By that point none of us had eaten or drank anything in twenty-four hours save for a few bites of sugarcane, and none of us had anything to say. We climbed into the Land Cruiser and drove for home, our prayers to the God of tires for once were upheld.

As we rode home, I reflected on the night that had passed and, having reflected, was emboldened to make the decision that set in motion the events that would lead to our final confrontation, the one with the drunken mob that wanted Jere and me dead. Part of my motivation was simply Jere: how he soldiered on and on in his efforts to improve his country, despite outbreaks and breakdowns, drunken chiefs and crooked governors, despite getting no recognition and scant pay. Part of it was my old urge just to stir things up and see what happened. But mostly, I wanted to do it because I was ashamed. Deafness was no excuse for always arriving at the point where risk and stupidity met. Jere was rightfully upset and I craved his forgiveness.

"I've been thinking. We should do the clinic project," I called out to him as we bumped along in the ambulance.

He turned back to me so I could read his lips. "Yes?"

"Yes. Definitely."

"Good," he said. "It will be great."

"I'm not CIA," I added.

He nodded. "I know."

Waiting

So after that long night in the forest the clinic project became
my focus, just as it was Jere's. And while this shift sometimes
didn't feel so much a decision as a capitulation, and I still felt
uneasy about going against Peace Corps guidelines, I knew that
the additional clinic space would have a huge impact on the quality of life in Mununga. It would go far beyond any notion of
cultural exchange. I devoted as much time as I could to helping
Jere. We drew up more scale model drawings of the clinic, as
well as detailed cost estimates, lists of potential workers, and a
construction schedule; we measured out the field where the new
structures would go; we debated the placement of windows and
doors and the benefits of oil versus latex paint and tin versus
asbestos roofing; then I wrote everything up into an application,
rode my motorcycle down to the post office in Kashikishi (the
one in Mununga only received mail twice a month, if that),
and mailed our papers to the United States Agency for International Development (USAID), the branch of the State Depart-
ment that funded all Peace Corps projects. As I handed the packet
to the sleepy post office clerk, I had the thought, "This is a big
mistake," but I handed it over nevertheless.

Then we had nothing to do but wait.

It would be at least two months before we found out if the project was approved. In an air-conditioned, wood-paneled office in Kenya, a USAID officer would open our packet, shake out the dust, read over the reams of information, and decide the project's fate, posting—or not—a check to my bank account. Until then, waiting.

An hour floating in the river counting leaves. Two hours rubbing grease off my motorcycle with a rag dipped in kerosene. Three hours bent over a chessboard, trying to save a trapped queen. A whole day spent on the couch poring over a single book I'd found about the American Civil War—God knows where it had come from—sinking into another continent and another time, the pictures of men with fantastic mustaches.

In many ways, waiting is the true experience of village life. Yes, the planting days are frantic and then there are the dramas of violent mobs and seductive virgins, disease outbreaks, a rabid dog clearing out the market every month or so, but most days in the village passed in a lulling rhythm with lots of downtime. Work, eat, bathe, drink, and wait. Wake up at dawn, lie down at dusk, do it again the next day.

I took up jogging to pass the time. For a week, I woke up early every morning and ran a few miles down the road. But just about every boy I passed dropped whatever sticks, tools, or animals he held and ran with me, and with his stick legs and bare feet lapped me like I was running in sand. That got embarrassing. So I took long evening walks in the fields with Scoopy instead. She'd grown big and muscular and had turned out to be a sadist, leaving her evening meals of leftovers untouched in the front yard so she could torture the starving village mongrels. After hours of agony they would make desperate lunges for Scoopy's food and she would tear them to shreds with her teeth and claws.

At dusk, Malama and I went to swim in the river, walking down a path through a cassava field and a banana grove, past the mothers calling their children to the evening meal, the dogs correcting one another, and the young women tending the cooking stoves.

Jere and I worked at the clinic. After work, in his insaka, we played chess and drank. Friends—Jefferson the translator, Mubanga the African doctor, Patrick, fighting a cold—came to visit and gossip for a round or two. Everyone spoke loudly and clearly and I was enjoying being hearing. Even if, as Maria and I had discussed, it didn't matter in the larger scheme of things, hearing well made day-to-day life a hell of a lot easier.

And then those random exhilarating moments: a man at the market wearing a T-shirt from my high school (a Salvation Army donation), a blue lizard falling from the roof thatch right into my water glass; a sickly baby at the clinic suddenly sending a healthy stream of piss out over everyone within range.

I had fallen back into a leisurely routine and whenever business related to the clinic project arose, I felt a twinge of unease. Would Peace Corps applaud the bold risk we were taking or were we going too far? Who would make that call? I pushed these thoughts aside when Jere decided that, for the next step, we had to get the chief's support. If the project was approved and got under way without the chief's knowledge, it would be an affront to his authority, one we couldn't expect him to let slide. Furthermore, if we could get the chief excited about the project, it would be so much easier to do—just one of the chief's kapasos loitering around the worksite each day would make for huge gains in productivity. Workers would arrive on time and work until told to stop. And if the chief were really into the project he could conscript a few men from each village in his rulership and we wouldn't even have to pay anyone. I was aware that it wasn't really in the spirit of community development to have the chief order people to work, but that seemed a minor point compared to the other liberties we were taking. Jere and I requested a meeting at the palace.

We arrived there after lunch on the scheduled day. Unfortunately, the chief was hammered—when he offered us his greetings, he poked himself painfully in the eye. He was also full of nostalgia about his boxing days. He loped around his insaka in a pugilist's crouch, eyes peering out from beneath his crown and told us to call him "The Copperbelt Boy."

"Ba Joshua, one time I punched my brother in the face so hard his nose split in two," the chief said. He threw out a straight right. "Woosh. One side of his nose went to each cheek."

"Wow, Chief, you must be very strong," I said. "Did he go to the clinic? If he needed stitches it would be good to have a good, clean clinic nearby. A clinic with mosquito screens. Otherwise he could get an infection."

The chief glared at me. "He did not respect my wife."

"That's a shame, Chief," Jere piped in.

The chief looked me over. When he was sober, he was always anxious, discomfited by the fawning respect people gave him, and his irises jittered in their sockets, and he often stuttered. Sober, he seemed perpetually embarrassed. When he was drinking, however, his voice was loud and his eyes were rock still. He was usually drinking.

"You are not an ugly man," he finally said. "My court took care of your situation last year with that young girl. Why don't you now have a wife?" He took a few steps to the entrance of the insaka and called out in Bemba and a young woman fifty feet away lifted a water jug off her head and jogged over. "This is my third born," said the chief when she arrived. He said her name but I missed it. "She is very beautiful."

I nodded in agreement. Standing before us was a lean-limbed young woman, seventeen or so, with cheekbones so sharp they pulled her lips into a permanent kiss, and with the full, taut ass that all Mununga women had.

She stared at a spot far in the distance. The chief pushed his crown up his forehead. "She will make a good bride," he said.

I had been offered daughters before—it happened pretty regularly actually. Malama and I would be sitting on my porch, talking, playing cards, or reading, when a man dressed in his Sunday finest would appear trailing a girl with her head down. The man would introduce himself and we would exchange greetings in Bemba, an endless and increasingly ornate string of them as he built up his nerve.

"And your mother, too, is well?" he would ask.

"She is well, thank you," I'd answer. "And yours?"

"Yes, thank you. And your father?"

"He is well, thank you. And yours?"

"He is with the ancestors, thank you. Such is life, thank you."

And on and on. Then there would come a point where he peered around to make sure no one besides Malama was listening.

"Sir, your servant is here?" he asked.

"No sir, Chiluba's at the river."

"Thank you. And you are not happy with her?"

"No sir, I am happy with her."

"Sir, you have not married her?"

"No sir, I have not married her."

Another pause. Now he would smile a that-is-unfortunate-but-I-have-just-the-thing smile, and turn back and put a hand on the young woman behind him, pushing her forward. Malama would always get very nervous at this point, as if advancing to this stage in the conversation—the presentation of the shy virgin—meant that the marriage was a done deal and the bride would be moving in immediately and kicking him off his favorite place on the couch. If that happened, he would have to move back in with his aunt, the nurse, and he would be lowered in the eyes of his friends, and the teachers at his school across the river would make him tend their fields with the rest of the students after lessons instead of buying his excuse that he needed to go and help the white man. He stressed a lot, Malama did; you could see where the worry lines were going to form when he was older.

But after allowing myself a good look at the young women presented to me—all of them beautiful and bathed so clean they shone—I would cut the father off. I do not want a bride now, sir, thanks for offering. Or, if that wasn't sufficient: Sir, that other volunteer, the white woman who visited last month, she is my girlfriend, maybe even my wife. The man would nod, smile, drink a glass or two of water, and work his way through the elaborate farewells, and then he and his daughter would walk back to whatever distant village they had traveled from. Afterward Malama would be extra attentive for a day or two, sprinting to the market if I needed anything, before relaxing again over the swimsuit issue and peppering me with questions like: How could Rambo kill so many people without going to jail?

So now Jere and I had come to the chief to present our great project and instead of trying for the chief's approval, I was trying to politely decline his daughter.

I explained to him that I wasn't looking for a bride. The chief turned to face Jere. "Ba Jere," he said, his eyes two angry points. "Your friend thinks he's better than us. He thinks white is better than black. He thinks a black woman isn't good enough except for a quick quick sex. Like a South African man!"

"Yes, Chief," Jere agreed.

"That's not true," I protested.

"No, it's okay, Josh," Jere said, giving me the faintest shake of his head.

The chief had been turned down and was not happy about it. In the awkward silence he walked back to his throne and sat down. Jere took out his handkerchief and wiped his face, cleared his throat, and took this opportunity to tell the chief about the clinic project. He gave a long speech about all the good it could bring. Did the chief not know that one third of all Mununga babies passed away before they were five years old? Was the chief aware that expectant mothers had to sleep on the same clinic porch as drunken men? Wasn't the chief himself upset with how the government offered Mununga no support?

Jere spoke in Bemba, having switched over to the chief's native tongue. I knew the points he made because I had come up with many of them the night before. And I think the chief knew all these things and was concerned about them, he just hadn't yet learned how to lead. He slumped on his throne, holding his head in his hands, said, *"Ee, ee, ee"*—yes, yes, yes—to Jere, but it was obvious that he just wanted us to hurry up and finish so he could sleep.

Afterward Jere said, "He doesn't know what he's doing. We'll just do it without him."

"Good idea," I responded.

"It's a shame."

"Yeah."

"His daughter was pretty, wasn't she? He must be eager to find a good match for her."

"Jere—" I started.

"I know, I know," he said.

Bro

Right during this period of waiting my brother Zev arrived in Mununga for a visit. He appeared at my hut one evening covered in road dust, carrying a rucksack, an Israeli army flashlight, and new muscles that looked like bricks. The last time I'd seen him, twenty months before, he'd been little more than skin, bones, and attitude. He'd been living on a kibbutz near Tel Aviv, dredging fishponds and drinking protein shakes and his body reflected it. But he'd gotten fed up with kibbutz life.

"There are some psychos here," Zev had written me a few months earlier. "Living a life they don't want and resenting you for it, always lecturing you about your country's flaws and your personal materialism. Ragging you for enjoying life more than they do. And my girlfriend's got a manly voice. What do you do with that?"

"Come see this place," I had written back. "Everyone loves America here. And the women all sound fine to me."

"Of course they sound fine to you," Zev replied. But he said he would come.

Now he was here. We hugged each other tightly.

"You smell," he said.

He shrugged off his pack, introduced himself to Malama and Chiluba, then went to bed and slept for fourteen hours straight.

When he woke up, Chiluba brewed him a pot of bush coffee, acrid, paint-peeling stuff, then Malama and I took him to our favorite place for a swim, a secluded spot where a row of water-loving musondo trees grew right in the middle of the river and met other trees overhead to form an intimate canopy. The seclusion of the place made it, theoretically, perfect for a croc ambush, which was probably why there were never many bathers there. But you couldn't worry about that. There were so many ways to die in Mununga it was pointless to fixate on just one. While you scanned the water for crocs, a black mamba could come up behind you and bite you on the ass. If you didn't pull it off within five seconds, it would pump enough venom to down a hippo. Or maybe a mosquito carrying cerebral malaria was probing your neck at this very moment and schistosomiasis larvae were slipping up your veins toward your intestines and the tunnels they would eat there; or maybe some flesh-eating bug was in the goat meat you'd eaten the night before, Ebola even—come to think of it, the meat that had been sitting in the sun all day at the market before Chiluba bought it tasted kind of funny. Point is, if the water was cool, it was best to enjoy it.

Malama and his friends, showing off for us, gleefully cannonballed off the rocks. Zev and I stood in the river, water up to our waists. I watched him taking it in—the kids, the river, the sun paused directly overhead for its midday nap—it was definitely a long way from New York, from Tel Aviv and its tourist-strewn beaches. Over coffee earlier he had told me about his last weeks on the kibbutz: disillusionment, heavy drinking, and then breaking up with his girlfriend for reasons he couldn't quite articulate. It may have been that she liked Zev too much for him to trust her judgment.

"Some people call that love," I had told him.

"Ehhh," he said, and changed the subject, talking about his trip to the latrine that morning. He liked the economy of reading the newspaper and then wiping his behind with it.

"It's brilliant," he said.

"I like it, too," I agreed.

I decided then not to tell him about the disturbing events of the last few months. I didn't know how. What did it mean that people cut off legs for fish and the next day pawned their wives with a smile? To be honest, I just wanted Zev and me to get along for his three-week stay. If we made it half that long without any major blowups, it would shatter all records.

Suddenly he jumped a foot in the air.

"There are fish biting my legs!" he yelped. "These aren't man-eating fish, right? Piranhas?"

My hearing aids were in my shoes up on the riverbank so they wouldn't get wet and ruined, but Zev knew how to enunciate so I could read his lips effortlessly.

"I'm afraid they are," I told him.

He lowered his head down so his face was underwater and peered closely at the fish.

"Liar," he said when he came up for air. "These aren't piranhas. They tickle."

"Piranhas are in South America."

"African pirahnas. Whatever, jackass."

I had missed him.

The next morning we went to the clinic to help Jere with baby weighing. Zev and Jere ("the only chubby guy in Eastern Africa" is how my brother described him) hit it off. Jere was impressed with my brother's muscles. Zev told him about dredging fishponds on his kibbutz.

"Fishponds?" Jere said, turning over this information. "Maybe you can teach people here how to raise fish? At the rate things are going they will fish out Lake Mweru in five years."

"I would do it," said Zev, "but I have no idea how. They never really explained it to me."

"They didn't tell you anything?" Jere asked.

"They did a little. They said, 'Go over there and jump in the water.' And then they said, 'Pull on that, push that, shovel this.' But they didn't really explain why."

"Why not?"

"I wasn't important enough. They have guys like me coming through all the time. They just threw me out there."

"Kind of like Peace Corps did with me," I pointed out to Jere, trying to be helpful.

A look of doubt crossed Jere's face. I guessed he was trying to reconcile this level of organization with Western civilization's ability to produce cars and trains and planes. It bothered me, too, but Zev didn't seem to mind his similar situation. Though he had gotten sick of the people at the kibbutz, he had liked the physical labor—he always had; during high school his summer job was hauling garbage.

Jere led Zev out to the empty field next to the crumbling AIDS ward and described the plans for the new building. He marched off the new ward's dimensions, explained how it would be turned just so to catch the evening sunlight, showed Zev where the porch for pregnant mothers would be built, and produced from his desk a swatch of the gold paint that he had chosen for painting the outside of the entire clinic, old buildings and new.

"It will glow in the sunset like a chest of treasure," Jere said. Talking about the project always made him excited.

"Cool," Zev replied.

But that night, after dinner, while my brother sat on my couch reading an old *International Newsweek* and I played poker with Malama, I had another wave of anxiety about the project. Jere's pride and eagerness had left the role of worrying to me and there was a lot to worry about. I asked Zev to hear me out and give me some advice about what to do, though we'd never had that type of relationship before.

I told him my main concern: Peace Corps projects were

supposed to build groundswells of support in communities, and get their labor there, but instead of doing that, for this project I'd made up figures to filch money to pay people who weren't supposed to be paid.

Zev flipped the pages of his magazine. "I don't see how that's a big deal," he said. "If people need money, give it to them. It can't be that much."

"You're right. It's not the money," I said. "It just feels like we're cutting so many corners that the project is going to fall apart for sure."

"So don't do it," Zev said.

"I can't not do it."

Zev sighed. He lay out on the couch, his feet propped comfortably on an armrest. "I know what your problem is," he said. "You want to know what your problem is?"

"What is it?"

"Your problem is you can't let yourself succeed at anything."

I was taken aback. "What does that mean?"

"Don't worry, it's not your fault. You were raised wrong." He buried his head back in the *Newsweek*.

I was struck dumb—then I was angry. I hadn't asked for much. It's obvious now that my anger that night and over the next two weeks actually had nothing to do with Zev, but I didn't know that then. He was family, meaning he was a familiar and accessible target, and in the end I knew he wouldn't set a mob after me.

"God, you can really suck," I said. "Could you be any less helpful?"

"Yes," he replied.

I went to bed more or less in that state. The next morning at the clinic, Zev and I ran the baby weighing, scores of infants crying hysterically at the sight of not one but two white faces peering down on them and lifting them into the produce scale. Their crying was like sirens so I turned my aids off, but that was no defense against the babies wrinkled and shriveled like old mango pits. They watched you lift and jab them into the scale like it was happening to someone else. You prayed for them to start crying, just to show some energy. Chastened, Zev and I put aside our disagreements. Afterward, we met Jere and Patrick in Jere's office, ate a snack of boiled cassava, and talked more about the clinic project.

But first Patrick had some questions about America.

"Is it true you have a pill for every disease there?" he asked.

"A lot of them," I answered.

"A lot of pills or a lot of diseases?"

"What?"

"It's true," Zev cut in. By reflex, he spoke up when he knew I couldn't understand something. "They have pills for everything, for diseases, for sleep, for waking up. They even have a new pill just to make you happy. You take it and it smoothes out your thoughts so you don't get too high or low. It's very popular except it's impossible to get a woodrow with it."

"To get a what?" said Jere.

"Like bamboo," I explained. Jere blushed and coughed into his fist.

Patrick was in awe. His eyes widened as he contemplated this utopia: happy, healthy people swallowing pills, never growing old or sick or sad. He took a cloth out of his pocket and blew his nose: it was warm, but he wore a sweater and a handkerchief tied around his neck. He was out of the office more often than not those days, but no one talked about it and Jere had him over for dinner every day to make sure that he ate.

"So everyone in America is happy," Patrick said. "How wonderful. I would like to see it. I think in October, right, Ba Josh? That's when the autumn is, your favorite?"

"Yeah," I said.

Zev held up his hands in a calm-down motion. "No, wait, that's crazy. People aren't happier in America. I think people are happier here actually. Malama's friends at the river definitely are.

The reason so many people in America take Prozac is because so many people—"

I kicked his foot under the desk and gave him a shushing motion. "What?" he mouthed.

I ignored him and changed the subject to the project. Tomorrow, I told the others, Zev and I would be leaving for Mansa, the provincial capital. I was going to pick up my paycheck, then we would scout out the best places to buy project supplies and to hire transport. Jere suggested a store to visit, asked again when I thought the money would arrive. Zev rubbed his shin where I had kicked it and glowered at me.

"A new AIDS ward is a very nice idea," Patrick said. "Will it have warm blankets?"

Jere caught my eyes, looked at the ceiling.

That left one last key piece of business: the project committee. Peace Corps development guidelines insisted that all projects have committees drawn from the people of the village. Jere and I had thrown the guidelines out the window but we had recently decided we should still have a committee. It would cover our rears—nominally (but not really) having authority over the project, a committee of respected village men would be a strong buffer if something went wrong.

"We'll hold elections when the supplies come," Jere said. "Everyone will see the truck and they'll be curious. We'll do it then."

"Okay," I said. "But the right people have to get elected, Jere. Not people like Boniface. They'll just mess it up."

"Yes, of course."

"I think we should pick the candidates beforehand."

"Yes."

Zev coughed and coughed until a piece of cassava fell out of his mouth. Then he laughed until his face turned red. We all turned to stare.

"First you steal money and now you're going to rig elections?" he gasped. "I'm proud of you, bro. You do America proud."

ZEV AND I ARRIVED IN MANSA AFTER DUSK THE NEXT DAY AND crashed at a cheap motel full of drunken, skeletal prostitutes. For two bucks or less these poor women would do anything you asked. If you made the merest eye contact they would trail you for hours until you slammed a door in their faces. Our room was a filthy, airless pillbox and giant turds overflowed the communal toilet next door. Across the street, a darkly lit bar blared Zairian dance music until dawn—which was Zev's problem, not mine. We woke up hot, with angry red zippers of bedbug bites criss-crossing our stomachs, and dragged ourselves through the city under a broiling sun. The heat was ridiculous, the air as thick and pungent as water left in a ditch. I sank into a thin-skinned stupor, as did Zev.

After a full day of arranging for supplies, we needed relief. At the Mansa Club we ran into a group of volunteers having beers. I knew Zev would be happy to hang with other Americans, to hear their stories and talk about the latest in the O.J. trial and the baseball strike, but I also knew that with the bar's boisterous crowd and blasting stereo, I would barely be able to hear a word of their conversation. Also, most of the assembled volunteers were part of the second group to the country; they were a whole new group I had to explain my deafness to and I wasn't up to doing that, wasn't up for studying how ten new people spoke. Most of them spoke fast, as Americans generally did. I was reminded of why, no matter how bad things got in Mununga, I avoided the Mansa scene.

While Zev and the others talked, I waited on a bar stool and counted whiskey bottles, ceiling fan revolutions, scars on my fore-arms from scratched mosquito bites, things like that. The sounds of conversation and music and drunk men playing snooker came through my hearing aids as a single wall of noise.

"So what did you talk about?" I asked Zev afterward, as we walked down a pitch-dark road to our motel.

"A lot of stuff," he said. "The guy Rob, from Indiana, taught me how to give the Hungarian evil eye."

"The Hungarian evil eye?"

"Yeah."

"What is the Hungarian evil eye?"

Zev stopped in the middle of the road, turned his flashlight on his face, lowered his head, and stared at me from under his brows.

"You look constipated," I said.

"Well, it wards off curses," he responded. Then he told me that he had described the clinic project to the new volunteers. They were fresh to the field and eager for information and hoovered up everything he said.

I grabbed his shoulder and pulled him to a hard stop. "Are you an idiot?" I said. "You told them? Every part of the project is against the rules."

"Take it easy, man," he said, knocking my hand away. "They were teaching me the evil eye."

"You're an international fucking idiot," I snapped.

He scoffed. "Must be like looking in a mirror."

Back in Mununga twenty-four hours and 200 miles later, the tension between us ratcheted to a fever pitch. We tore into every character flaw we could think of or make up, every mistake, every excuse. I called him a lazy washout; he called me a frustrated martyr. It was absurd to be ripping on each other in the middle of all of Mununga's poverty and we knew it, but it was also sane. It kept us from obsessing about what we saw, while letting us express how much it hurt. We just couldn't turn it off, was the problem. Malama and Chiluba were terrified watching us go at it.

"You come for water sanitation, but I've never seen you even wash your hands," Zev jeered one afternoon in my hut. "You know why? You don't actually want to get anything done, you just want to feel excited and victimized."

"Shut up," I said.

"Suffering is your entertainment. Why ruin your entertainment?"

"When did you start talking like this?"

He stood up from the couch and gave the room a round of applause. "Josh says: Two thumbs up for Mununga! Better than *Cats*!"

He hit a sore point there. Mununga was my life but I could have walked out of my hut any single day since I'd arrived there, walked to the bus stand, caught a ride to Lusaka, arrived at Peace Corps Headquarters, and said, "I'm done." Within a week I would have been on a plane to New York, eating salted peanuts out of a foil packet while reading an in-flight magazine article about the nightlife in Miami Beach. The village would be gone forever. But did that mean my being here was just some kind of voyeurism?

No, that wasn't it. Mununga was my home. But Zev reminded me that I hadn't delivered on the Peace Corps promise. Other than my work at the clinic and a few other small projects, I might as well have just been a tourist. So when Zev sat down after his round of applause, I kicked him in the shins; in response, he picked up a glass of water and threw it in my face.

I wiped myself off. "At least let me take off my hearing aids before you do that. The water will ruin them. You know that."

"Waah, waah, waah," he said.

Then we were outside in the dirt yard, shirtless, throwing each other to the ground. I wanted to kill him, and I wanted it to hurt. It was hot; the sand on the ground scraped my limbs like cut glass. We were alone in the yard save for a startled Malama and Chiluba. Zev, using his new muscles from the fishponds and old moves from four years of varsity wrestling in high school, snapped me in a headlock and twisted my arm back until it felt like it would tear out of its socket. And when I lifted my head in one last-ditch attempt to wrench free, all I could see, in every direction, covering every free space, was people. They stared at us, rows and rows of them, up the path and across the hill, every single one slack-jawed in shock. Zev saw the crowd at the same moment I did and released his hold on me. I knew instantly the story of the battling and bloody umusungus would spread around the village like wild-fire, up the valley and down to the lake, and within the hour the chief would be told. I collapsed onto the ground.

"Holy shit," Zev mouthed to me, so I could read his lips. I had pulled off my hearing aids on the way outside so they wouldn't get crushed. "There must be five hundred people here."

"I know," I responded. I didn't need to look again. How would anyone work for the crazy umusungu now?

"This is like being a rock star," Zev mouthed.

I dragged myself over to the porch, chest heaving, pools of red forming around the sand in my elbows. "You're strong," I said.

Zev nodded. "Yeah, I kicked your ass."

Malama brought my hearing aids from inside and I put them on. Chiluba brought a pitcher of water and I poured it on my elbows, trying to wipe the sand out, and they stung when I touched them. I kept my head down, hoping that if I ignored the crowds, they would disappear as quickly as they had formed.

A few nights later, on Zev's last night in the village, we stayed up late beneath the kerosene lamp and reflected on his three-week stay. Our anger was long gone by then, spent in the dirt outside the hut. We were already joking about the fight—it was no big deal, we agreed, nothing like that time when I was seventeen and had a broken ankle and we destroyed two windows and a screen door while fighting with my crutches—nothing at all like that.

Zev and I sipped banana wine and reminisced. My elbows were raw and full of pus from wrestling in the dirt, and I had them slathered in Bactine so I didn't get one of those bush infections that turns your limbs into balloon animals. The Bactine was rubbing off all over the couch. Malama watched us, not wanting to miss anything, though he didn't understand much of what was said and after a while he fell over, fast asleep, his head coming to a rest on Zev's knee.

We tried to keep the conversation light. Zev brought up how, even though he was shorter than I was, and had twenty pounds more muscle, longer hair, and grew a pretty much full beard each afternoon, when he walked through the village all the children called my Bemba name out to him—Joe-shoe-ah.

"Strange," I said. "They never do that to me."

"Of course they do."

"I've never heard it."

He rolled his eyes. "Such a genius."

We reminisced some more—about playing chess with Jere and poker with Malama, about finding Palije under the bed in the morning; about how, on his first try on my motorcycle, Zev, with Malama sitting behind him, had ridden it straight into a banana tree—but I could see, in Zev's expressions, in his pauses between words, that something weighed on his mind. Something was on mine, too. With the film of our constant arguing now removed, we all of a sudden had no defense for the realities of the village. Things like the infant old-men—you could try to avert your eyes but if you turned away, who would bear witness to those brief lives? You had to do it; you were there.

"You need to write about this," said Zev. "Tell people what's going on here. Tell them about baby weighing, about Malama and his friends. Tell them about the clinic workers. They're the real heroes. Jere—that's a man. Doesn't ask for anything from anybody. Going to build a clinic by himself. And the skinny one—what was the skinny one's name?"

"Patrick?"

"Patrick. He showed me how to take blood pressure, really nice guy—write about him. How he thinks everyone in America is happy. Hey"—he paused, suddenly remembering—"why did you kick me when I was talking to him? That hurt."

"Because America is his heaven. You were going to take that away."

Zev looked at me, dubious. "America is his heaven? Come on, it's as insane as anyplace else. He should know the truth."

"He has AIDS."

My brother smacked himself in the forehead, pursed his lips, and looked up at the thatch ceiling for a long couple of minutes.

"God, that sucks," Zev said. "I wish I could do more. I feel like I don't know what I'm doing with my life."

"I'm sorry," I said.

"I mean, at least you're doing something. You're helping people."

"It doesn't feel that way."

"Fuck. I leave tomorrow and what's the point? Go to grad school? Buy a new car? Get an American Express card? What's the point?"

Zev would drift for a few years after returning to the States, trying out several careers and growing disenchanted with each, before ending up a teacher in a Compton, California, elementary school. There, too, he was one of the first white men many children had ever met. Sometimes over the years we didn't talk for months, sometimes we talked every day, but this night we didn't so much talk as just sit together, just us, no phone calls to take, no television shows to watch, only a kerosene lantern, a few mosquitoes, and a teenage boy drooling in his sleep for company, and a world that made no pretense at fairness stretching in all directions. We sat up late into the night.

Committee

A few weeks after Zev left (his parting words: "I love you and wash your hands more, fucknut"), a letter arrived from USAID—the clinic project was approved. A wild night of celebratory inebriation followed and, after a quick trip to Mansa, a huge flatbed truck arrived with supplies. The truck was easily the largest vehicle to pass through Mununga in my time there. It was a spectacular sight: nearly as long as the bridge, it made the ground vibrate a quarter mile away. Scores of curious men came to watch its arrival and some of them helped us unload. Jere was right—the truck grabbed their attention in a way that all of our cajoling never could. Capitalizing on the moment, he called for an immediate meeting for committee elections.

We stood on the clinic porch while the men gathered in the courtyard below us.

"What is happening? What are you building?" they asked.

"The future," Jere told them (and later translated to me). "The future is being built. This is your time. Do you want to paint it golden? Do you want to have a beautiful clinic, a beautiful market, a beautiful village? This man from America has given us the opportunity to make things better for ourselves and now we need a new generation of leaders to step forward and lead the way."

The crowd murmured excitedly and nominated four candidates to chair the committee, young men with serious faces who strode up to the clinic porch and gave bold speeches about Mununga's future. They had been to the Copperbelt, these men said (the vast majority of villagers had not), and had seen there how important good clinics were. They spoke well and were well received, their eloquence probably due to the fact that Jere had personally convinced several of them to run and had pretty much told them what to say.

But was it any surprise that Boniface, my original nemesis, was a near-unanimous selection to lead the committee? I hadn't seen him in months, had nearly forgotten about him, but he was just biding his time. As soon as he climbed the stairs to announce his candidacy, the other candidates raced to withdraw theirs. The vote was a pure formality. Victorious, Boniface shook hands with Jere and me, bowed to the crowd, and spoke for an hour. He talked and talked. I couldn't understand what he said and Jere, staring glumly at the ground, refused to translate. There was no one to persuade, he had won the election, the sun appeared to stall overhead frying the crowd, but still Boniface talked. No one dared to leave. Why? Why him? I thought, watching his enormous warship chin bob up and down.

"I will make sure my project is well run," he said to Jere and me afterward. "All of Mununga will know of my project."

"Your project"—I started to protest—"your project?"

Jere cut me off. "Good, good," he said to Boniface.

And so, just like that, after all of our planning and waiting and dreaming, fate, African fate, with its dramatic and macabre and rather unfair sense of humor, had intervened and the clinic project was now completely at Boniface's mercy. I couldn't believe it; didn't want to believe it. But maybe, I hoped, it wouldn't be all that bad. I did a little research, asking Malama and Chiluba and Jefferson the translator and other village friends to tell me everything they knew about Boniface—and it seemed that rumors were all they had, vague ones that no one could verify. No one could prove he had anything to do with the Christmas killings or that he kept a teenager's heart in his store.

But it was bad; it was worse than we feared. Boniface immediately took absolute control of every aspect of the project. The financial records, the blueprints, the keys to the storerooms: he removed all of these from Jere's office to his home. The workers Jere had arranged were sent home and Boniface hired his own men, who barely worked.

The first part of construction was to bake earthen bricks for the new building: a big hole would be dug in the field next to the clinic and filled with bricks and charcoal fires, and then it would be covered over with dirt and left to cook for a few days. The process should have taken a week, two at most, depending on the number of bricks, but after a month the Boniface-led workforce had only managed to dig the hole. It sat there like a bomb crater, filling slowly with trash.

Then came news that a dozen bags of cement were missing, as well as a few sheets of roofing tin.

I found Jere in his office. "You know whose fault this is," I said.

"What do you want me to do?" he said. "I can't do anything."

"Stop him somehow. This is your dream. This is the future of Zambia."

"You're right, you're right," he agreed. But he didn't do anything.

It was weird seeing Jere so unassertive. I'd seen him angry; I'd seen him afraid; I'd seen him dead drunk one moment and delivering a baby the next, but I'd never seen this: an unresponsive daze. He sat in his office for whole afternoons staring vacantly like something inside of him had been ripped out. Forget the project, for so long, Jere had been the undisputed king of the clinic, the man with the answers, the man everyone went to in a crisis, health-related or otherwise, but the clinic was quickly turning into Boniface's little fiefdom—it, too, was slipping away. I didn't know what to do.

Then the clinic sewing machine disappeared.

In the back of one of the treatment rooms, there was an ancient pedal-powered Singer sewing machine—God knows where it had come from—on which the wife of Mulwanda, the inpatient clinic officer, and the nurse, Malama's aunt, repaired bedsheets, curtains, and other clinic linen. When they had time, they mended clothes to augment their lousy pay. Soon after taking charge of the clinic project, Boniface insisted that for safekeeping the sewing machine be moved from its regular spot to the room that stored the roofing sheets and paint. The only room he had a key for. Two days after the machine was moved, it was gone.

"We can't let this stand," I said to Jere.

He nodded vaguely. "Yes, you could be right."

With no help from him, I came up with a plan. In a few days there would be a meeting of the project committee. The committee consisted of Boniface, Jere, Patrick, myself, an officer from the roads crew, a representative of all the village headmen, and old Ba Bule of the pin-striped suits and twenty-two children, who represented the chief's high council. I decided that at this meeting, we would challenge Boniface to admit his crimes.

The project committee met in the insaka of a large church half a mile north of town. The church was on the top of a hill, a good distance from both the river and the lake, so there were few people around. Jere, Patrick, the roads worker, and I met there an hour before the meeting; with much prodding on my part, we pooled together everything we had heard about the thefts and worked out a strategy for presenting it. That I would do the talking was pretty much the strategy.

I was fine with that. I wanted the confrontation.

"Just don't be too direct," Jere warned.

"Whatever," I replied. Jere had slipped so far into the background that I resented his advice.

Boniface arrived and called the meeting to order. In English, he recapped the project's progress, recited long lists of schedules and figures and promises. He spoke for an hour. Of course, there was no mention of the missing supplies or the missing sewing machine. I have to admit his verbiage was actually kind of impressive, in a Don King–language-bulldozer kind of way, and with his bellowing voice he kind of sounded like a ring announcer, but it also gave me a pounding headache.

"I am vital. I am the only one who knows all this information," Boniface summed up. He sat back and thrust out his chin.

For a long minute, there was total silence in the insaka. My turn to speak and I didn't know how to begin so I just did. Forgoing any pretense at snake-in-the-grass indirectness, I launched straight into a point-by-point rebuttal of everything Boniface had just said. All his numbers, all his promises, and then I detailed the overwhelming evidence of his criminal activity—that he had the only key for the storeroom; that he had asked the clinic watchmen their schedules; and, most damningly, that people had actually seen him carrying the sewing machine down the street the night it disappeared.

"It needed repairs," he said.

"No, it didn't," I scoffed.

"I brought it back."

"You're lying."

It felt righteous to call him out. It felt so good I couldn't stop, and I repeated my points over and over. Boniface sat and took it all in with no change in expression save for a slight narrowing of his eyes. I ran out of things to say, assuming from our earlier strategy meeting that Jere and the others would chime in at this point with suggestions for a new division of responsibilities or maybe for a co-chairman to help Boniface out—but no one spoke. No one even moved. My speech trailed off and Boniface thanked me for my input, thanked the others for their attendance, closed the meeting, and left. He was still the project chairman and the mystery of the missing sewing machine remained officially unsolved.

Unbelievable.

"Why didn't you speak?" I railed at Jere and the others as we stood around afterward. "You know he's guilty!"

Jere coughed into his hand. The other men pawed the ground. "We were going to," Jere said, "but we were afraid of his juju. He has a very powerful juju."

"Juju?"

"Yes, juju. You know, black magic."

My head was still pounding. Out of sheer frustration, I thought. Rubbing my temples was no help.

"Oh, man, I'm tired of that," I said to Jere. "Did he actually say he had a juju or did you just make that up?"

"He didn't actually say it," Jere admitted.

"Exactly! Juju? You should know better than that! This was our project, Jere. What about all our work? What about all that talk of the future? I've broken a lot of rules for this and if Peace Corps sees nothing done and all the supplies gone, I'm in a lot of trouble."

"Are you all right?" Jere asked. "You look sick."

"I'm fine!"

"Are you sure you understand?"

"Understand what?"

He took a deep breath. Patrick and the other men shifted nervously. "Juju. You might be cursed."

Cursed with friends who don't keep their word, I thought. My headache got worse. I couldn't believe I was having this conversation with Jere of all people. He was by far the most educated man in the village and while he had told me many tales of witchcraft starting on the very first day, I never really thought he believed them. They're just a language for explaining deaths and failures, he had once said.

"We should go home and talk about this," Jere said.

But I had only one thing I wanted to say to him.

"You're a fool," I told him. "And you're not my friend."

I said it to hurt him and it worked. In two years, it was our only real falling out. Patrick and the other men looked away. I took off on my motorcycle, and the next morning I packed a bag for my long-awaited going-away vacation with Maria, boarded a bus, and left the village.

Buses

Unless you were rich and could afford your own car or you worked for an agency funded by guilt-ridden ex-colonizers with more cash than ideas, traveling in Zambia meant taking a bus. Bus was a fluid term. Anything running that could hold more than fifteen people was a bus. A pickup was often a bus. A flatbed truck was a bus. A bus was what was there.

Tatas were the most prevalent buses, ancient Russian vehicles that looked like scrap-iron mastodons, and they fought against their sweating, straining drivers—bus whisperers—like wild horses. They did what they wanted. The first trip we volunteers took back in training, for our initial visit to our villages, bore this out—first, the Tata that never even bothered to arrive, then one that could barely be persuaded to move before it broke down in the middle of nowhere.

Stuffed to the gills with men and women, children and small animals, the lumbering Tatas were like moving nations with their own governments and economies. The driver was king, of course. Two to four conductors made up the coterie. The head conductor handled money and guarded his seat next to the king; secondary conductors manned the door, called out destinations to potential passengers standing in the road, and loaded packages onto the roof; and at the lowest rung, conductors who were really just toutboys worked for passage around the country by doing whatever was asked. Needless to say, the conductors were always male.

A bus ride was full of unknowns, the major one being that you never knew how long the trip would take. You could tell a little from the looks of the vehicle, but not really. One volunteer caught a sixty-mile ride on a South African bus that looked fresh off the assembly line, green paint gleaming, but every five minutes the bus slowed to a crawl and a conductor ran down to a swamp next to the road, filled two gallon bottles of water, and ran back. For the duration of the trip he sat on the hood, pouring water into the radiator. The sixty miles took all day.

The morning after my confrontation with Boniface, I caught a pickup to Kashikishi; from there I rode a Tata to Mansa, where I met Chris; by chance he was also going to the capital, to visit Helen, now eight months pregnant. Chris and I overslept the next morning and were the last passengers to board the Lusaka bus. Passengers and their wares occupied every inch of seat, so we had to stand in the aisle for thirteen hours straight and then, around ten at night, still hours from the capital, the driver dozed off and ran the bus head-on into the side of a bridge. We weren't going fast so no one was hurt, but the radiator was driven straight into the engine. Which made for another kind of bus, the dead bus. You saw those sometimes, too, steel skeletons by the side of the road, picked clean for scrap.

We piled down the stairs and watched fluorescent green radiator fluid drip from under the grill and run beneath our shoes. Nothing to do then but wait. We were far from any city, river, or village, surrounded by scrub brush and heat-stunted trees. Passengers spread out and lay down along the edge of the pavement, not too close to the woods and its snakes, and not too far into the road that they would be run over on the off chance a South African freighter barreled through. Chris and I sat against a tire and talked. The sonogram had showed a healthy baby boy, but there were complications and the doctor ordered Helen confined to bed. She and Chris had gotten married not long before in a traditional ceremony on the road that ran through their village, during which men and women danced at each other like taunting and neither bride nor groom was allowed to smile.

"What's up in Mununga?" Chris asked me. "How's Jere?"

I told him a little, but not much. I was still upset about what had become of the project and didn't want to think about it unless I had to.

Around midnight, a bus passed by, and Chris and I paid whatever the conductor asked, leaving behind the other passengers who couldn't afford the extra fare. This bus was like nothing I'd ever ridden before or since in Africa: a ghost from another continent, nearly empty, clean as a church, running smoothly—a bullet train would not have been any more out of place. We lay out on long bench seats and slept the remaining hours to Lusaka, where I met up with Maria and parted ways with Chris.

I felt awful when we arrived, but thought it was just fatigue from the long journey combined with the headache I'd been carrying for a couple of days; it seemed to pass. In the morning, Maria and I flew to Dar es Salaam and took a hydrofoil across the choppy Indian Ocean to Zanzibar. In the boat's indoor seating area, a giant TV played movies of martial artists amputating each other's heads and limbs with their bare hands. Blood spurted from the wounds in bursts, like water from a pump well. No one on the boat could take their eyes off the screen. I lay on the floor and held my head. A little seasickness, I thought.

A small island that was the trading post for three continents, Zanzibar was packed with more variety per square mile than seemed possible. Every conceivable fruit and flower, spice and sea animal was for sale at the market, sold by vendors of every skin color. Arabs, Asians, Europeans, North and South Africans, street urchins, albinos, tourists, lost and drunk ex-pats, sailors from Sri

Lanka, indigo sellers from India—all of them and more jammed the narrow streets of Old Town. They had diamond necklaces; they had skin sun-wrinkled into rhinoceros hide. The streets were one wheelbarrow wide so everyone was pressed together and pickpockets did great business. Outside of town: white beaches shining like fluorescence, palm trees with coconuts the size of soccer balls. It was fantastic—but I felt like death.

"This is something else," said Maria, watching a man cutting the tentacles off live octopi and serving them raw.

I tried to push the sickness away. "It is."

"I'm so glad we got to see this together."

"Me, too." I took her hand. "Let's go lie down."

It dawned on us then that I had malaria. I had already caught it once, three months after moving to Mununga. Rave, my old basketball friend from training, was visiting the village when the fever came on, and he watched over me as I slipped in and out of delirium for a day and a night. The next morning when the fever broke, he asked me what a *dreydull* was.

"A *dreydull*?" I said.

"Yes," he replied. "You made one out of clay. You sang about it all night."

I didn't remember any of that. My mind felt like it had been melted down and regrown missing key parts. Jere had given me a massive dose of quinine, and by afternoon I was well enough to hobble over to the clinic and shoot the breeze with him, Patrick, and Rave, though it looked like they had painted their faces gray and it felt like someone had kicked me hard in the liver.

The problem was, antimalarial pills sucked. They tasted like burning sticks and pumped my dreams full of Technicolor violence—gunshots, car crashes with dripping red blood, piercing screams. We were supposed to take the pills once a week and the day I took them my stomach felt potholed with ulcers. So I only took them during the rainy season, an imperfect system.

"Take this, you'll feel better," Maria said, handing me some pills back in our Old Town hotel room, but I vomited out whatever this was.

"Nothing wrong with your esophageal muscles," she joked.

I wiped my mouth. "I'm sorry. Your last week in Africa. I wanted us to have fun."

Maria wiped my forehead with a wet towel. "It's not your fault. Sometimes it slips past the antimalarial pills."

The illness made for honesty. "Well, I kind of didn't take them," I admitted.

She frowned. "Why didn't you take them?"

"The dreams."

She nodded; she knew what I meant.

When the fever broke for a bit, leaving behind a mouthful of fever blisters, I begged Maria to make the most of her last week and to explore Zanzibar without me. Then I took the hydrofoil back to Dar es Salaam and went to the hospital. As soon as I had absorbed two liters of IV solution, the world came back into focus. I slept for two days, then took a swim in the warm green ocean, savoring the often underappreciated state of just being healthy, and made plans to go back to Zanzibar and surprise Maria; I even made plans to apologize to Jere and find a way to make the project happen yet. But while I was in the water two young thieves stole my bag from the beach. From fifty feet out, I watched them—I might have been a mile away. I gave chase, but they had way too much of a head start. Their haul: my money, my passport, my sunglasses and shoes, a notebook with everything I'd written in a year and a half, and last, and most important, my hearing aids.

I ran barefoot through the streets, praying that the thieves had discarded the aids somewhere, tossed them in a gutter as they ran—but nothing.

"Boniface!" I called out at the intersections. "You can do what you want with the project. I renounce all claims. Tell your juju I take it back. I don't think you stole anything!" But I don't think he heard me.

By chance I passed a police station. I went inside. Underneath a low roof and a slow fan, six men sat and sweated in short-sleeved blue uniforms. I told them what had happened, but I hadn't gotten a good look at the thieves or the direction they'd run and when I described the hearing aids, the police looked perplexed. *A little machine that makes you hear? What will the white man think of next?* They asked me questions I couldn't understand, so I asked them to write down what they were saying, but they refused. Maybe my voice was too loud because I couldn't hear it, maybe they were embarrassed by their writing skills or maybe they thought I would use their handwriting to steal a part of their souls—regardless, the policemen wanted me out of that station. Smiling broadly but gripping their blackjacks with tense fingers, they pushed me out of the door.

Back in the street, boys emerged from behind palm trees to stare at the bare-chested, barefoot white man. I sat down under a tree, my mind churning. So hearing or deaf didn't matter? Liar! Think about it: strip away the technology and speech therapy, in the end, always deaf. *Always* deaf. Yes, the sound my hearing aids gave me was a poor facsimile of the real thing. But maybe the flaws and limitations made it that much more precious. Because sound was so thin and so elusive, I had never taken it for granted. Because words were so hard to understand, I hung on every word of even the most mundane conversation. Now they were gone.

My skin started to burn. I was talking to myself out loud, which made the boys around me back nervously away. Enough of this, I decided, I'm still healthy, I'm still here. Let's get back to Mununga.

Somehow, I can't remember how, I found the Tanzanian Peace Corps office and in forty-eight hours I had a new passport, travel money, and a pair of running shoes. A day or two after that, I met Maria at the airport and we flew back to Zambia. It was different between us. Her lips trembled and I had trouble reading them without the cues from hearing aids, so she had to write notes— *I took a boat to a reef and scuba-dived. I ate a durian and rented a moped*—and this made us feel embarrassed. Our previous intimacy felt like something that belonged to strangers. We didn't hold hands. We didn't kiss like lovers kiss. The deafness was a wall between us.

Chris was still in Lusaka when we landed. We ran into each other at a small party at Administration's house, standing over the strangeness that was a cheese tray. Neither of us had seen cheese in at least a year. Helen hadn't given birth yet, but Administration had gotten tired of Chris hanging around the capital waiting for her, not even given the pretense of working, and had ordered him back to his village. I got him a piece of paper and a pen.

"*They won't let me stay. Let's ride up together,*" Chris wrote.

"Screw them. Stay with one of the drivers or Maria until Helen gives birth," I said back.

"*They say I have no more vacation days.*"

"Take mine. I'm done with traveling."

"*Can't. 'There are rules.'*" He paused, then wrote: "*Do you have to do this writing thing with everyone?*"

"Just you," I said. "I'm not talking to anyone else."

Watching Maria, Chris, Administration, and the others flap their lips at the party, back in my long-standing role of the deaf child at the dinner table, I wondered what part of ourselves is formed from our communication with others and what part is untouched by it. And where could one find the untouched part? Because it seemed like the untouched part might be able to make sense of the way things played out, while the touched part was completely at their mercy. Or maybe I just mean that, as much as we want to connect with people, could we ever truly do so? And if we couldn't, and we were all ultimately alone, why do we so desperately keep trying?

Every answer I came up with led to another, deeper question. My mind gets like that sometimes. But as it always did, Africa would shortly make questioning irrelevant. I stuffed my face with the crayon-colored cheese.

ANOTHER BUS TRIP: MARIA DROPPED US OFF AT THE LUSAKA STATION early the next morning. Her brown eyes shone with what was probably regret, but I mistook it for pity and was eager to take my leave. She faced me and spoke slowly, but I still only caught a few phrases, good luck, I'll write to you, have a safe trip; her mouth kept moving in silence and I pretended to understand.

"Have a good life," she mouthed. I caught that.

"Hey, you too," I said.

Of course there were many things I wanted to say to her about what we'd shared but it may have just been that the Lusaka station paralyzed me. It was an extraordinary exhibition of humanity at its most wretched: drunken men and wasting women, piles of shit, feral dogs eating piles of shit, starving street children dressed in sheets of dust, holding each other's hands, begging for kwacha. I couldn't think of what to say to Maria besides good-bye. We kissed each other on the cheek. I never saw her again.

Chris and I caught a bus that took the shortcut through Zaire and arrived at Mansa that evening. The next morning we boarded another bus for our villages. We were early, the first passengers (having learned from our experience of standing in the aisle), and, taking seats near the back, we watched the other passengers board, not realizing how much depended on where they planned to sit. Some of the passengers carried their whole lives with them, down to their pots, charcoal stoves, and strung-up live chickens tied to their bags. They were headed upcountry to start over in the fishing camps and they wore their best clothes for the journey. One middle-aged man looked quite dashing in his brown three-piece suit. He smiled and introduced himself to me, his white teeth flashing. I had long ago memorized the Bemba greetings and ran through them without hearing a word he said.

"Good morning . . . from America . . . good health . . . good health to your family . . . good luck on your day."

A terrible feeling brushed against me. I ignored it—we were getting an early start on a Chinese bus, the most dependable kind, much better than a Tata, and it was going all the way to where the pavement ended. Then, a couple of hours on a pickup and I'd be home to my friends and my dog, my spare set of hearing aids, and I'd finally be done with this unlucky trip of malaria and theft and crushed romance.

Chris sat next to the aisle and I sat next to the window. My seat was over the right rear wheel well, so I had no legroom; my knees were up in my chest. We started off; after a couple of hours my legs started to ache so I stood up and went to the front of the bus. Next to the debonair brown-suited man I had exchanged greetings with, now fast asleep, a boy of about twelve sat looking at his hands.

"Switch seats with me," I said to him.

He looked up, nodded. Can I describe his face? Young, smooth, trusting—I will never forget it, though I can't quite remember it. The boy wore his school uniform, a light blue checked shirt and a dark blue tie, too short black pants that ended high on his ankles. I remember watching him as he walked to the back: he hugged his bag to his chest like it was a child of his own. He was the perfect size, the lack of legroom in the other seat wouldn't bother him. And besides, children in Zambia had to do what adults told them, just as women in Zambia had to do what men told them. And everyone did what the white man said, just because.

But that doesn't explain it.

The driver gunned up to seventy miles an hour, an amazing speed on that bush highway, where you never knew when a goat or dog or child might jump into the road. Brown thatch huts and tall green trees flashed in the windows like flip-book photographs of themselves. Barefoot pedestrians with bundles on their heads dived into the scrub as we hurtled past. Chris stood up to let the boy sit in the cramped seat next to the window.

Later, he recounted their conversation to me.

"Where you going?" Chris asked him.

"School," the boy said, in halting English. "My first time away."

"Nice," said Chris. His Bemba was poor but he was friendly, easy to talk to. "Where is school?"

"Mbereshi."

"You like your classes?"

"I like studying English. It is my favorite."

"Mine, too," said Chris.

"I think the driver's been drinking," the boy said. "He should not be doing that."

"It's okay," Chris reassured him. "We're almost there."

But the boy was right: the bus driver had been drinking. And he wasn't a real driver—he was a young conductor watching the bus for a day while the real driver took the day off to get drunk in Mansa. Thinking he could make some money by taking the bus quickly up to Kashikishi and back, he had borrowed it. So far so good—the young conductor and his friends had made a lot of kwacha, more than any of them had ever made before. Tomorrow, who knew what would happen—maybe he would get back and no one would be the wiser or maybe the real driver would beat him for taking the bus unasked. So he was celebrating his success now, as he drove, with a fresh Mosi at every stop. Soon after the boy and I switched seats, the conductor lost control.

It happened fast. The bus lurched into the bushes on the left side of the road, bounced through the undergrowth there, then quickly swerved back onto the pavement. But it had swerved too hard, toward a big drop-off on the other side of the road, and swerved again. Two big swerves and we tipped at seventy miles an hour and the pavement came soaring.

I came to covered in blood and flesh and clothing and shards of glass like broken teeth. I ran out the front windshield, through jets of spurting oil, swept up in a mass of panicked passengers. Men and women sprinted wildly up the road, fearful the bus would explode. Others, clearly injured, pulled themselves a couple of yards clear of the wreckage and then fell shuddering to the pavement. A woman sitting in the very back row had her head caught in the rear window and sliced in two, right across her cheekbones. She was dead, the two halves of her head flopping loosely against each other. A man tied a rag under her jaw to keep them in place. The friendly man in the brown suit had a deep puncture in his skull through which gray brain tissue oozed out like soap bubbles. He winced and gave me a thumbs-up.

Chris grabbed my shoulders.

"Are you okay?" he said. I read his lips. I didn't know the answer. I looked down. My T-shirt was crisscrossed with jets of blood and body tissue, but other than a gash on my arm, I was untouched.

I looked back at Chris. "Your mouth is full of dirt," I pointed.

"No, it's not," Chris said.

"Yes, it is."

"No, it's not." The dirt fell out of his mouth and onto his shirt as he spoke. I held his arms tightly.

Chris let go of my shoulders and turned back to the bus. I watched him go, then climbed up a small hill next to the road. I walked through a grass meadow and entered a cool maize field, the maize plants taller than my head. There appeared an old man, thin and barefoot, with a crown of white hair. Without a word, he took my hand and led me out of his field. Down on the road, the bus lay like a dead animal dropped from a great height, twisted grotesquely, leaking fluid in all directions. Now men were lined up against the roof of the bus, pushing against it. Could they possibly be trying to push it upright? Pointless. Then one man reached underneath the bus and pulled out the boy with whom I had switched seats. I ran down the hill.

The boy was still alive, badly broken, but alive. His chest moved in separate pieces as he struggled for air. Blood ran like tears from his eyes. We all stood, staring at him, watching him leak. Everything in total silence without the hearing aids. After a while, everyone—Chris, myself, and others—began to reach inside the bus for our bags. What else could we have done? There was nothing else to do.

A pickup truck passed by, and another, and we climbed up on them to ride to the nearest town, which was Mbereshi, where the hairy red-faced German doctor ran a hospital. And so, not twenty minutes after the crash, Chris and I were crouched in the back of a pickup doing sixty miles an hour, our hearts leaping into our throats at every turn, while in the center of the truck bed, the crushed boy left his life. He didn't jerk or death rattle or anything. You could just tell he was dead.

"No!" I shouted then. No one looked at me. "No!" I shouted again, just to see if I could get a reaction—I couldn't hear myself and who was that old man in the fields?—I thought I might be a ghost.

Here's one thing I can say for sure about that crash: the driver's life ended then. He didn't die—he survived the crash and ran with his friends into the bush before anyone knew he was gone, but for the rest of his days, if he ever tried to make contact with his old life, the bus owner would have killed him, or else the relatives of the dead would have, or the police. I like to think that he found a village deep in the bush, away from the roads, and quit drinking, showed his worth to the village men with hard work in their fields, gained the headman's trust, married, had children, asked whatever supreme being he believed in for forgiveness, lived right. But I doubt it. I'm sure they found him.

And the boy, what of him? The driver of the pickup didn't want to take him to the hospital, which was a mile or two out of his way, but Chris gave the driver money and he went. Two weeks later the boy's body was still in the hospital morgue and his family came to pick him up, but Herr Doc refused to give it to them because he had been away on vacation and had not yet completed the autopsy. Autopsy! What do you need an autopsy for? The bus fucking fell on him! Do your mad scientist thing on someone else! Chris was in Mbereshi that day and argued with Herr Doc until he changed his mind. The old woman who had her head cut in two, however, was never picked up and was buried in an unmarked grave behind the hospital.

Chris and I stayed that night with Joe, the volunteer who never unpacked. For hours, Chris talked with Joe and Joe's friends about what had happened, about the blood, the terror. Or maybe the accident pushed them to the other extreme and they talked about love and God, and the fullness inherent in any given moment, even the moment you hit the ground. These are things I would have wanted to talk about. But it was dark in Joe's hut and without my hearing aids I couldn't read lips well enough to follow a thing they said, so I lay down in the bedroom and curled up against the wall.

In the morning, I boarded another bus.

Superfish

I arrived back in Mununga late in the afternoon. I went straight home, hurrying past the men who stopped in the paths and bowed to greet me, ignoring their perplexed expressions when I didn't respond. With Chiluba, Malama, and Palije's help, I tore apart my hut looking for the spare hearing aids. Malama found them in the first aid kit and I put them on. An old set, weak and moody, they gave voices a tinny echo so that everyone sounded like powering-down robots. It was wonderful to hear nevertheless.

"Talk to me, my friends," I said to them. I spoke English, needing to hear it then.

"Do you want isabi or inkoko for dinner?" Chiluba asked. Fish or chicken.

"Isabi," I said.

"Okay, isabi."

"Invite your sisters to eat with us," I added. "I want to see them."

"Okay," Chiluba agreed. "Five hundred kwacha for isabi. And hundred kwacha for tomatoes." I gave her the money and she left for the market.

Malama nervously bit his lip. "Scoopy miss you," he said. "She sleep next to bed at night."

"Did she? Where is she?"

"I find."

"Yeah, go, go," I said. He turned to leave. "Wait, Malama—"

He stopped in the doorway, half framed in sunlight, wearing an old red T-shirt of mine that reached to his knees. I had something to say, but how to put it? I wanted to thank him for sharing his life with me; I wanted to know him and I couldn't really—but we were alive.

"I love you," I said.

This confused him. It wasn't something anyone had ever said to him before.

"Palije," he said, avoiding this unpredictable version of me, and the small boy emerged from behind the couch, walked over to Malama, and took his hand. "We find Scoopy," Malama said and left.

I took off my shirt and sat down. Jere came running through the door, dripping sweat and wiping his face with a handkerchief.

"My friend! You were in an accident," he panted. "They said a bus exploded. Many people died! They said you were hit so hard, your ears fell off."

"Not exactly," I said.

"Yes, they exaggerate. Are you hurt? I heard you were hurt."

"I'm not hurt."

"So you are okay? I was worried."

"I don't know. I don't feel okay."

Jere wiped his face again, confused. "But nothing's wrong with you."

Other than my housekeeper, my right-hand man Malama, and my best friend, no one in the village talked of the crash. It had happened seventy miles away; that meant it might as well have been across the Sahara. All the villagers knew was that I was back and looked pretty much the same. Across the path from my hut a funeral was taking place for a young man, a brother of my old paramour Alice, who had died mysteriously a few nights before. After dinner with Malama and Chiluba and her sisters, I went and sat by the funeral fire, listening to the wailers get up and force out their woe for all of us so we could get on with our lives.

But it wasn't enough.

Over the next few days, even though the spare aids worked well enough to hear, I avoided people. I woke up late and stayed in my bedroom until after lunch, then took Scoopy on long walks into the bush, staying clear of the village until dusk, when we could slip back largely unobserved. In the forest, I passed a man harvesting a small field of marijuana plants. With my hearing aids off we negotiated with our fingers: for what it cost to buy ten sticks of Bazooka Joe he gave me a half pound of pot. It was bush weed and made you dumb more than high, and there was so much of it, it felt like it had to be something else, but I rolled giant joints using sheets of the *Zambian Times* and smoked them until I couldn't move. That wasn't enough either.

Jere came over after dinner the first or second night back. He wanted to talk about the clinic project. More roofing sheets and bags of cement and tins of paint had gone missing while I was away. The storage rooms were now half empty and all the money set aside to pay workers was gone. Jere said that he was sorry for not helping me during the committee meeting when I had confronted Boniface, that he was sorry that I had been in an accident, and that while I was gone he had thought some more about the project and come to the conclusion that we had to find a way to do it. It really was the last best chance to save the village from itself. The new Zambia depended on us, he said. It sounded like he had been preparing this speech for some time.

"How can we get more supplies?" he asked when he was done.

"It's not my problem," I replied.

"Look, we can't let Boniface stop us. The project can still happen if we just get some cement."

The whirring of my spare hearing aid blended with crickets, a steady white noise canceling thought. In the canceled space, a bus was falling.

"It's not my problem," I said again.

I got on my motorcycle and rode to see Chris.

"Hey," he said when I drove up to his porch. He was frying okra. "I thought you would come today."

We went inside his house and sat down at the table, the one that would be his if he divorced. Helen was still in Lusaka waiting to give birth and the room was a mess: T-shirts were strewn about, magazines were on the floor, a layer of dust covered everything. Something else felt off, but I couldn't tell what. Chris told me about a dream he had had, a dream of four moons. They were lined up in the sky over the lake like a string of enormous pearls and in the dream he pointed the moons out to me, but I couldn't understand him and blew him off. Four moons and it had been four days since the crash. Chris thought this had to augur something but he didn't know what.

"Maybe I couldn't understand you because I didn't hear you," I said.

"Maybe."

"You mumble a lot. You could talk louder in your dreams."

"Four moons! Four days!" Chris yelled.

I threw a *Newsweek* at him. Then I realized what felt so different about the house. Herman the monkey, the chattering, red-butted book thief, was nowhere in sight. Now that I thought about it, it was obvious that he was gone, because there was no way Chris could have left so many magazines and shirts lying around if Herman was there. They'd all be in the trees. But Chris was evasive when I asked him about it.

"You said he's a house monkey," I pressed. "You said there's no way he'd run away—he'd die in a day in the bush."

"I know what I said."

"You dumped him in the bush."

Chris shook his head. "He's not in the bush."

What Chris had done was have his neighbors kill the monkey because he had become bigger and more aggressive. Soon Chris would have a baby in the house and he worried that in an unguarded moment, Herman might grab his son and carry him out the window and off into the trees. After killing Herman with an ax blow over a tree trunk, his neighbors had cooked him for lunch—meat was meat.

"They burned off his fur after they cut off his head," Chris recalled. "Held him over a fire and seared it off. It smelled terrible. He looked just like a person without the fur. All the muscles in the same place. Little shoulders, little hamstrings. Little penis."

I could tell he was hiding something. "Did you eat him?" I asked.

Chris shrugged. "Just a taste."

"Oh God, you ate your monkey? What'd he taste like?"

"Like chicken. Who knows? I couldn't be rude."

Of all the volunteers I'd come to Zambia with, Chris had become the most native; this was just another example. It wasn't about language: others spoke Bemba better—I spoke it better. Nor was it about completing projects: Ros from Pennsylvania finished more projects than the rest of us volunteers combined. It wasn't even that Chris had fallen in love with a girl from the village, married her, and any day now would be the father of her child. It was about the way Chris was. They cooked the monkey so he ate it.

He turned suddenly in his chair toward the door, stood, and went outside. I followed him out. In the dirt next to Chris's insaka a huge white pickup I had never seen before pulled to a stop and a tall white man I didn't recognize stepped out and walked toward us. This was unusual. Curious children emerged from the tall grass.

"Are you Chris Hayden?" the white man asked me.

"I'm Chris," Chris said.

"I'm Lars Voor-Something from the Netherlands Volunteers in Kashikishi. I bring you an important message from Lusaka."

He handed Chris a folded piece of paper. Chris opened it and in big block letters was written, "A BOY. HEALTHY. COME TO LUSAKA."

"A boy?" Chris said.

"Yes," nodded Lars, whatever he had said his name was. He smiled deeply, his teeth crooked and green. Chris stood there stunned. Seeing his expression, the children around us became concerned.

"Hey, you knew it was a boy." I grabbed Chris's arm and raised it over his head. *"Batata!"* I yelled. There was a huge cheer.

The news spread rapidly. Men and women rushed from all corners of the small village to congratulate Chris. Helen's parents appeared, weeping forcefully, and embraced him. The tall stranger from the Netherlands shook Chris's hand, waded through the crowd to his truck, and drove away. A man passed Chris a glass of maize spirits, and other men urged him to drink. "Batata! Batata!" they sang.

Chris wasn't really in the mood to celebrate and I wasn't either, but we tried to anyway. "A baby boy!" the men cheered. "Son of America and son of Chabilikila! Together forever!" A group of them dragged us to the village saloon, where we drank bottles of teeth-loosening home brew and sang made-up drunken gibberish. The saloon was really just the front room of someone's hut, with a single table and two full-time drunks, and after each round Chris and I felt worse and worse. We grew quiet, felt each bite from the mosquitoes, wondered whose idea it was to go there. We bought a half gallon of wine and took it back to Chris's house. It was night by then and sitting in the dark next to a kerosene lamp felt much more appropriate.

This is how it was: a village in ecstasy, a death avoided, and a newborn child, yet we couldn't feel a thing. Yes, Chris had a son now, but what was this world? What was the meaning?

"What did it sound like?" I asked him.

"The loudest thing I've ever heard," Chris said. "But I didn't really hear it. It all happened so fast."

"Yeah? It seemed slow to me. Like it took a really long time. Like we were just hanging and hanging."

"Yeah, it did," Chris agreed. "Slow but fast." He sighed deeply and told me the story of his conversation with the boy. "That poor kid. If I'd just reached out . . ." He trailed off.

Yes, that poor kid. A wave of guilt flooded over me, so strong I could barely breathe. Why hadn't I died?

"Chris, I made him switch," I said.

"No," he said. "Never, ever say that."

Here's how I knew Chris would be okay: it came back to the way he was, the guy who would eat his monkey. About a year before, when we were fresh and much more innocent volunteers, Chris and I had met for a weekend of R & R at the village where Ros, the volunteer who actually finished projects, was living. Late at night, we were sitting around a lantern, talking of nothing, maybe playing cards, when there was a knock at the door. It was a man bringing us the gift of a fish. A shy man, he could barely bring himself to enter the room. He placed the gift, wrapped in writing paper, on the floor in the corner, thanked us for coming to his village, and backed out of the room.

Thing was, the fish was still alive. For an hour, it flopped in the corner without pause. Finally we decided to kill it. We took it outside and lit a charcoal fire and Chris sliced the fish open and gutted it and threw the guts to the dogs—but still it was alive. It flopped its way off the porch and appeared to be trying to slide down the hill toward the lake, where its brother fish were. It didn't know it was supposed to be dead. We carried it back to the charcoal stove but it flopped off again and again and struggled down the grass. We were filled with awe. It was unkillable. When the fish finally grew weaker, Chris picked it up and held it over his head so that it could pass its last minutes smelling the breeze off the lake. It died in his hands. We put it on the stove and when it came time to eat, Chris bowed his head and said a prayer.

"Like the Sioux honor the buffalo, so we honor you, Great Superfish," he prayed. "We thank you for your sacrifice." No one laughed.

The fish tasted like rubber, with overdeveloped muscles too tough to taste any good. But Chris insisted we finish every bite. He felt an order in things and by that order you ate your monkey when offered, you ate every piece of a fish that wouldn't die, and if it wasn't your time, it wasn't your time. This must be how the people in the villages of Africa survive the insatiable plagues of their continent, by knowing the order of things. Still—"I'm bringing Helen and my son home in a Peace Corps car," Chris said the next day, boarding the bus for Lusaka, "not a damn bus."

As for me: I was still looking for an order I could understand. Back in Mununga, Jere took one look at me and dragged me to the bar where we had, almost a year ago, hashed out strategy during the trial over Alice's virginity. Now he showed me how to add little shot baggies of grain alcohol into bottles of Mosi for an extra powerful kick. He handed me one. He didn't mention the clinic or anything.

"What's this called?" I asked him.

"Medicine."

"But I'm not sick."

He brought the bottle forward on the table so that it was right under my chin, then put his warm hand on mine. There was music playing and drunks dozing on the floor and the Coca-Cola poster of happy white people still hung on the wall. Jere's other hand came to rest lightly on the back of my neck.

"Drink, Josh," he said, and I knew that he was my friend.

Gomorrah

Mununga had changed.

It had been changing all along, for the year and a half I'd been there, but only now did it all of a sudden seem a different place. To start with, there were many more people. They arrived in Mununga from every direction, mostly from the west and north, where the diamond provinces of Zaire were. Zaire was just then beginning what would become a decadelong disintegration, a spectacular self-immolation that would leave it a country with no government, no hope, home to a conflict that would end only when every last man had fled or died. Understandably, people were leaving in droves. Many other people came to Mununga from the south. Zambia's big mining cities had suffered hard times since the copper market crashed. They were lured by stories of a river and a lake that never ran low on fish. But the river and lake were running low; some of the bass Chiluba bought for lunch were not half the size of the ones she'd bought a year before—and still people continued to arrive.

With this influx of newcomers, the market doubled in size, the river's bathing areas were packed like rush-hour subway cars, and baby weighing was upped to three mornings a week from two. My first year in Mununga, I had not once seen a bus venture up the cratered, axle-destroying dirt road from Kashikishi; now there were several a day. With them came more gangs of toutboys, drinking, howling, and bullying.

The town had changed in another respect. The dragging death and dismemberment of Chitondo had opened a box of possibilities that could never be put away. Despite Mununga's fearsome reputation, nothing like a village-wide mass lynching had ever happened before. What would stop it from happening again? Old-timers blamed the newcomers, called it "the Zairian influence." A man in a fishing camp was found holding another man's wife and was stoned to death on the spot—the Zairian influence. Other men blamed the national government for having ignored Mununga for so long. And Mununga *was* ignored: the biggest bush town in Zambia by far, it still didn't have a single volt of electricity, a single phone. No hospital, no paved roads, no flush toilets, no foreign aid and no foreign volunteers save for the deaf white man who stayed in his hut, coming out only to work at the clinic, swim in the river, play chess and drink.

The clinic, as an extension of the government, had become a focus of the villagers' fears and distrust. That brother of Alice who had died, and whose funeral I had attended shortly after the bus crash—it turned out that the day before he passed, he had gone to the clinic for treatment. Mulwanda, the old and sleepy inpatient clinician, took his temperature and blood pressure. Finding nothing out of the ordinary, he sent him home and told him to rest. The next day the young man died. It happened like that sometimes. Ordinarily, people would chalk it up to the juju of a spurned lover and bury their grief after the funeral ended, but this time a crowd gathered in the clinic hallway yelling accusations of murder at Jere and Mulwanda. Where before they saw fate, they now saw villains who deserved punishment.

Bigger, angrier, more distrustful than ever: this wasn't the village I knew.

Then it turned on Jere and me.

AFTER OUR CONFRONTATION OVER THE CLINIC PROJECT AND THE sewing machine, Boniface bad-mouthed me throughout the town. Not to everyone, but to enough people, well-chosen people— aggressive toutboys, powerful headmen, and the chief, a distant relative—that my presence in Mununga was questioned in a way it hadn't been before. This time the suspicions ran deep, far more serious than the earlier spurious claims of my CIA connection. What *was* the white man doing here? I had only deepened a single well, I'd slept with a daughter of the village and caused her father's death, I'd been in a bus that crashed and, suspiciously, had been about the only person on board unharmed. Had I really come all the way from America just to weigh babies and bandage worm sores? People began to doubt my story. Some had always been wary of me because I was of the race that made planes and trucks and guns and that had treated Africa like it was a stray mutt for centuries, and Boniface's rumors just confirmed their suspicions.

At first, I wasn't aware of how damaged my status had become. Numbed from the accident, I stayed in my hut when I wasn't working. And when I was outside, I often had my hearing aids off. Silence never judged, never called me to task for making the boy switch. Silence gave the bustling market the same feel as an empty church, like a carnival stuffed in a snow globe, just like that. But removing my aids so much may have made matters worse. After a year and a half in Mununga, people still didn't understand that I was deaf, didn't understand that the caterpillar-size thing on my ear was what made our interactions possible. I passed through the village oblivious to their greetings.

Malama tried to warn me of the situation but I didn't take him seriously.

"People say you have become rude," he said.

"I'm not rude," I replied.

"They say you don't like black people."

"Malama, how can I not like black people?"

"Be careful," Chiluba took to saying as I left my hut for the clinic each morning.

"I'm just going to the clinic. I know the way with my eyes closed."

"I know," she said. "Be careful."

The rainy season arrived. The first rains of the year always brought disease, as bacteria and viruses that had slept in the dust through the dry season were suddenly reborn in mud puddles and streams and carried forth by fresh generations of mosquitoes. This year was especially bad. Cerebral malaria and dysentery hit the fishing camps at the lake back-to-back; they were burying a body a day down there. And other deaths: two toutboys drinking home-brewed spirits were found stone dead one morning on the steps of the market bar Jere and I often drank at, and a fourteen-year-old boy washed up under the bridge missing his heart. This last death led to a rash of reports of ndoshi theft: young children having theirs souls stolen as they slept. They woke up unwilling to live. Mothers carried the blank-eyed, dry-mouthed, and diarrheal babies to the clinic; immediately we put them on rehydrating solution—it was cholera, a fierce strain brought on by the rains.

"If we finish the new clinic ward," Jere said, "we could quarantine all the cholera patients there and the outbreak would pass in a couple of days."

"You sure?" I said.

"Yes. I am."

But how could we do it? Boniface was in charge, there was no money to pay workers even if he weren't, and at least half the supplies were gone. No one besides Jere even thought about the project anymore.

"Don't do it," Chiluba said as we ate dinner on the porch with

Malama. "You should just do like you are doing. Babies. Bamayos. Have meetings. That is plenty."

"Why is that plenty?"

She nervously touched her hair. "Mununga is dangerous."

I looked at her. Tall, broad-shouldered, and strong, she had recently become fearful and withdrawn. Moses Kapela, a market toutboy, had offered Chiluba's bamayo forty thousand kwacha for her hand. A fair offer, as she was already twenty-two, old for a virgin, but rumor had it that Moses had killed his father during an argument by striking him in the stomach with a heavy tree branch—she was not looking forward to this next chapter of her life.

"Chiluba, what do you hear?" I asked. "What is dangerous?"

This is when I learned about Boniface's campaign against me and about how the major topic in the village now was my poor character. The news was a surprise, though it probably shouldn't have been.

"People say you are here to steal money," Chiluba said, "and live big with your books and motorcycle and drinking."

"What should I do?" I asked her.

She didn't really answer. "Mununga is dangerous," she repeated.

"People are saying things about me," I said to Jere that night over chess.

"They are?" he responded. "What do they say?"

"You mean you haven't heard anything?"

He moved a pawn. "No. Nothing."

That made me more nervous than anything. For once this man who had his finger on nearly every pulse in Mununga—literally and figuratively—didn't know what was being said. Jere's knowledge had been my protection and now we were exposed.

Hidden in a grove of banana trees down near the river, Boniface's hut had gotten a radical makeover and was now the nicest one in town. It had a shiny new tin roof and a fresh coat of cement painted tan and rose was plastered on the walls. The whole house gleamed in the sunlight like a wet stone. It was obvious where the materials for this renovation had come from. Work on the clinic project had petered out a couple months ago, not a single brick had been laid or even made, yet building supplies kept dwindling. No one dared to say anything about it.

Was Boniface really ndoshi? To this day I don't know. Every death in Mununga had a nefarious explanation behind it, even a child's—the mother had angered an aunt, provoked a brother-in-law. Those two toutboys who drank themselves to death in the market—it wasn't because of bad homebrew—they had lusted after another man's wife. Ndoshi tales were everywhere, woven into the story of the town's creation. The very first settlers of Mununga had conquered the elephants, hyenas, and lions in the nearby forests with their shape-shifting magic. When the Christian missionaries arrived with stories of their God—seas parting, men living for centuries, angels riding flaming chariots, waters running red with blood and later turning into wine—the tales were proof that God was the most powerful ndoshi of all. What else could hold the universe in check? Belief carries its own power.

But was Boniface really using magic against me? Chiluba and Malama thought so. But consider: Bwalya had blackmailed me, but paid for it with his life. I had caught malaria, but I hadn't been taking the antimalarial medicine. The bus had crashed, but I lived. If all this was Boniface's doing, he wasn't quite finishing the job.

"Jesus is white and you are white," explained Malama. "And you hear with a machine. You have strong magic."

"What if I'm more of a Buddhist?" I asked, which tripped him up.

"Be careful," said Chiluba again, disapproving of any jokes on the matter.

"I will be. Stop saying that."

Alice's family remained angry about the death of her brother. They continued to accuse Mulwanda of poisoning him, and harassed him as he ate his meals. Uneasy, Mulwanda went to stay at the chief's palace for a few days. I paid him a visit and found him exhausted and resting heavily against a wall. Jere blamed Mulwanda's constant sleepiness on his having a young wife and an ulcer, but in fact he was dying of AIDS. He had put in at district headquarters for a transfer to get away from Mununga and would soon get one, to an island in the swamps where the mosquitoes descended like rain.

"What did you do?" I asked him at the palace, because I couldn't understand. People died all the time here—why was Alice's family so upset?

"Nothing," Mulwanda said. "I did nothing."

"Are you sure?"

He leaned back against the wall, closed his eyes. He didn't smile much anymore. "These people," he said, "they only know this place. They have never left. You and myself, we have seen some of the country, other provinces, the Copperbelt. Here, they only know this place. They are afraid. They don't understand what they do not know."

He was a good man caught up in events that really had little to do with him. A few days later an ambulance came for him and he left with his family for the swamp.

The district couldn't find a replacement right away, which meant Jere's workload doubled. But still he agitated for the clinic project. Again and again he described to me how it was Mununga's last chance—it was *his* last chance. In the end, that's why I finally agreed to do it. Not for Peace Corps, not for this town I no longer trusted, not for myself, not even for the opportunity to give Boniface a big metaphorical finger (okay, maybe a little), but for Augustine Jere.

I remember the moment I decided. I was in a treatment room,

counting out vitamin pills for the mother of a five-pound two-year-old baby. I stood up and went into Jere's office.

"You win," I said to him. "Let's build the ward."

He was holding a stethoscope to a boy seated on his desk. "Wonderful," he said. "Can I finish this exam first?"

"We have to really do it," I said. "You can't change your mind if things get rough."

"I won't."

"Even if there's juju, Jere. Promise me."

"I promise."

"Ai, ai, ai," said Chiluba, back at the hut. "Be careful."

We set to work immediately. Together Jere and I rode down to Kashikishi. There we called Zev from the house of Lars, the medical volunteer from the Netherlands (Jere talking for me on the phone, relaying my requests and my brother's insults). Zev came through with a wire transfer for four hundred dollars; where he got the money, I have no idea. From there, I went south to Mansa, picked up the cash, and hit the hardware stores for a few more supplies. Meanwhile, back in Mununga, Jere organized the construction of a massive brick kiln in the bomb crater behind the clinic. The brick cooked for a week until the fire burned out. After it was ready, the actual building began with a handful of workers Jere had hired to help us. Mostly refugees right off the boat from Zaire, they were desperate for money and didn't know what we were up against.

We worked so hard. My hands bled from the rough shovel grips. Jere skipped his weeding and let his maize fields go fallow in order to work. Dressed in his gas station jumpsuit named Mike, with a heavy look around his eyes, he approached the construction with the focus of a man going to battle, and I saw that he, too, had changed. He was a different person from the man who had offered me a chess lesson and a woman on my first day. I still ran the baby weighings but otherwise spent my days mixing concrete while Jere lay brick. We worked as long as we could stand it, then evenings we drank in Jere's insaka while Beauty and Palije played at our feet. Occasionally I awoke in the insaka in the middle of the night, passed out from exhaustion and wine, startled awake by dreams of falling, surrounded by the sleeping village, the clean smell of the river, the stars waving like grass in a field. Mununga was so peaceful then, not a soul was awake, and I remembered how it was the only place I'd ever lived where my deafness never mattered.

How I loved that town! Even as it cursed my name, even when it wanted me gone, I loved it. It wanted me dead; I love it still.

Patrick was the next to go. He had become an ephemeral presence at the clinic, appearing and disappearing at odd moments, diagnosing a few patients, taking the temperature of a child or two, abruptly pushing away from his desk, and going home. Finally he stopped coming to the clinic altogether and Jere and I took turns visiting him at his rooms, bearing rice gruel and attempting light conversation. But Patrick didn't really want to eat or to talk to us—his sickness exacerbated his shy, withdrawn nature. He wanted us to pretend nothing was wrong with him. So we did. I pretended not to notice when I walked in on him sitting in the pharmacy using a brand-new scalpel to cut extra holes in his belt to cinch it tighter on his wasted frame. Nor did Jere say anything when two rows of crusted razor-blade slashes appeared along Patrick's hairline—a traditional ndoshi treatment for AIDS, it had a success rate of zero.

We gave Patrick money to travel to his mother in Northern Province and walked with him to the bus stand. He'd given us all of his stuff save for what he wore or carried in a single plastic shopping bag. As we waited for the pickup to fill with enough passengers, Jere spoke to his young colleague in a low Bemba I couldn't follow. Patrick stared at the ground and nodded. What could Jere be saying? What do you say at such a time? *The sky is so clear today. Do you need to pee before leaving?* A group of young boys surrounded me. "How are you? How are you? How are you?" they sang until I chased them away.

Patrick turned to me. "Someday you will take me to America," he said.

"Definitely," I agreed, channeling Zev. "Good medicine and happy people."

"Yes," he smiled.

"Two months," Jere said, after Patrick's pickup pulled away.

"At least he'll be with his mother," I said.

"His mother's dead."

Dead? I didn't ask what he meant. Maybe I had misheard something. Or maybe Patrick, who worried to the last about being a burden, had left us because he wanted to die alone. I like to think he got his wish, on a bamboo mat underneath a mango tree somewhere, the warm sun shining on him, his thoughts trained to the last breath on a beautiful country of happiness.

Jere and I went right from the station to the clinic and back to work. Once the new building's walls had been laid and the mortar had dried, we plastered the walls inside and out with a skin of cement. Boniface appeared every morning to watch the construction. Still nominally the head of the project committee, he now and again proffered suggestions, but I barely pretended to listen to him before returning to whatever task was at hand and Jere, if he saw Boniface, immediately went to his office and shut the door.

"There should be a window here," Boniface would say to me.

"That's a storage room," I'd answer.

"There should be stairs here."

"That's a window."

Short of telling him to take a running leap off the bridge, I did everything possible to make it clear to Boniface that his presence was unnecessary. Then one morning I opened Jere's office to find five bags of cement, when the night before we had eight. I stormed down to Boniface's place.

I pounded on his door. He opened it after a while.

"I know what you did," I said.

"I don't know what you are talking about," Boniface replied.

"I will use my magic," I said, pointing my fingers in his face. "Don't mess with me. Haven't you seen I am unkillable? Return those bags or I will take you down."

The chief called me to his palace after this run-in. "Mr. Joshua," he said, "are you working for my people? Your friend Mr. Jere is not one of us. Make sure you know who you are working for."

Chiluba, again, every morning: "Be careful."

And suddenly Beauty died.

She was four. Almost past those dicey first five years of life when a third of the village children passed away. Out of the blue, two months into rainy season, her temperature shot up and her liver began to fail and her soulful eyes turned mustard yellow: cerebral malaria. Jere gave her extra doses of quinine, glass after glass of rehydrating solution, and all the rides on his leg she wanted, but she kept getting weaker. He took her to the district hospital in Kashikishi and there Beauty was hooked up to an IV and the worst seemed to have passed when suddenly she died.

Jere carried his daughter's body home on his lap in the ambulance, her head against his shoulder, like she had been lulled asleep by the rattling vehicle and was dreaming in his arms, and then he buried her in a field upriver in a shallow unmarked grave, one shallow brown mound in a clearing full of them, a few hundred yards past Museka village. As we dug her grave it rained, a light drizzle you could barely feel, evaporating as soon as it arrived. Just like her life. I was struck by how small all the mounds in that field were, how close they were. It was a burial field for children.

At home, Jere blacked out the windows, stacked his living room furniture in the corner, and covered the floor with bamboo mats. In the courtyard outside, his wife grieved by cooking and pounding maize meal nonstop and mourners squatted around a small fire talking in low voices. Inside, Jere sat on the mats for three days straight.

He belonged to a church on the other side of the river and on the first day male congregants from the church came to his house en masse, single-filing into the dark room and kneeling around Jere. In hushed voices, they assured him that his daughter was in a better place. These men had all buried children of their own, two, three, four children, and they spoke from experience. I sat in the corner and watched them, not hearing a word (Jere, as always, explaining later what I missed), but picking up their meanings from how they knelt, how they paused between words, and how they held Jere's hand with intent gentleness. God had taken her to heaven, they said, to run and play with the other child angels.

"I want no part of such a God!" Jere spat at them. "I wanted her here!"

They left, promising over their shoulders to pray for Jere.

"Pray for yourselves," he told them. "I don't want it."

I was sitting cross-legged watching all this.

"They have no minds," he said to me after the men had left, recounting their promises and homilies. "They can't think for themselves. Explain this to me. God wants to be close to her so He needs to take her away? But this world is God's, right? He made the whole thing—why can't He be close to her here?"

It was evening. A single kerosene lamp dimly lit the blacked-out room.

"Jere, I'm not the right person to explain that," I said. "I've got my own problems with that school of thought."

"It's your religion. You white men made it up and brought it here."

"Not me personally."

He eyed me suspiciously. "A Bible in one hand and a gun in the other," he said.

"What?"

"That's an expression. The white men, the missionaries, came to Africa with a Bible in one hand and a gun in the other hand and said, 'Take your pick.'"

It wasn't really a choice, I concurred. "Well, we do things very differently now," I said.

Jere snorted. "You can't be serious."

"I'm not."

He stared at me, then almost against his will he cracked his first smile all week. But it disappeared fast. "No," he cried, "don't make me laugh."

So I didn't. Instead, for three days we played long games of chess and talked of how Beauty held Jere's legs and walked on his shoes, and of the way she watched him protectively while he ate, like she was the parent and Jere the child.

Outside Jere's house, I ran into Boniface. "What are you doing here?" I asked him. He ignored me, ducked inside. All of us outside—mourners, strangers, Jere's wife—stopped what we were doing and watched the door. Five minutes later Boniface came out with his head down, walked right past everyone. I went inside and Jere was rolling up the mats, his face a grim line. "We must finish the clinic," he said. He never would tell me what had passed between them.

A week or so later Jere found me in a clinic treatment room. "I wrote a poem for my daughter," he said. "Would you like to hear it?"

"Yes, but let me read it. So I won't miss anything."

He pulled a piece of paper from his pocket, unfolded it, and handed it to me. It read:

In an unmarked grave in Museka,
My daughter lies.
Who will visit her besides the crows?

"You like?" he asked, taking the paper back, folding it neatly, and returning it to his pocket. "I couldn't think of what else to say."

"You are the best man I ever met," I told him.

He bent his head low. "Thank you."

When I went home, I sat down and cried on my couch. Everything was rushing to bad ends, I didn't know what, I didn't know why. My tears frightened Malama and Chiluba and they waited outside on the porch. Boniface walked by three times in an hour.

And in the village it was said that ndoshi took Beauty's life; that ndoshi fought everything Jere and I worked for and that they had cast the young clinic worker and the old one now living on the island in the swamp out of Mununga. But I still think it was just bad luck, bad luck and selfishness.

The new ward was nearly done. Rafters were laid on top of the walls, roofing sheets were laid on the rafters, and a ridge guard was set on the peak. The floor was cemented and smoothed flat with trowels and a ten-foot two-by-four. We still had to paint the walls and fit the windows and doors, but the second the floor had set, patients and their families moved into the structure, unrolling bamboo mats, unloading dishes, clothes, and small children in their hastily claimed rooms. It was a sweet, if disorganized, moment.

Jere and I traveled to Mansa for a special four-day Peace Corps conference for volunteers and their village counterparts. There, again, was the second group of volunteers to Zambia, twenty-three unforgivably enthusiastic young men and women. Their bright-eyed idealism, cheeriness, and thirst for adventures, while somewhat calmer since they'd been in their villages for six months—I still couldn't bear it. And I had nothing to say to them about what we were doing in Mununga because every last part of the project was against the rules. There were nightly gatherings at the Mansa Club, but I wasn't up for socializing, for the deaf man's forced solitude in noisy groups. I stayed in my room; Jere, deeply depressed, blew all the travel money Peace Corps gave him on overpriced beers; Chris, preoccupied with his wife and child, kept uncharacteristically silent; and the new Peace Corps nurse, an older man with owlish glasses, persisted in scolding me for not boiling my drinking water and taking better care of myself—so I ditched the conference early and went back home, dragging Jere with me. We reached Mununga just before dusk and went to our huts. Ten minutes later, while Chiluba boiled cassava for a quick meal and I sat shirtless on my couch answering Malama's questions about my trip, Jere burst in.

"Ai!" I heard him yell.

"What?" I jumped up, startled. "Say it again."

"Lye!"

"What?"

"Lye!" he screamed. "They painted the new ward with lye! Boniface. Men working for him. He waited until we were gone and painted the whole ward with lye. Lye in an hospital ward? It's poison. It'll kill all the patients!" He thrust up two fingers. "Two are already dead!" He pounded the table. A candle clattered to the floor. "He did it again! Our work is ruined. Ruined! The clinic is ruined. That's it!" He ran out.

Malama looked at me with wide nervous eyes. "What lye?" he said. I didn't really know. He handed me my shirt. We ran after Jere.

How could a paint job ruin everything? But this is how it would end. I felt it before it happened; felt the energy before I saw the crowd. Maybe I even wished for it.

First, we ran past the ward: a new coat of gritty white paint giving off the odor of dishwashing soap. Then, at the clinic: the large crowd where I knew it would be, crammed around the door of Jere's office, thrumming like a disturbed hive. I pushed Malama back, shouted at him to go home, and forced my way through the throng; inside the office, Jere and Boniface stood on opposite sides of the desk, glaring, yelling, throwing their hands the way furious men do. The crowd screamed, the sunlight died. Sweat plastered ragged shirts, filled the air with a loaded, dirty thickness. I stepped to the front of the crowd, dead center in the swirling energy, surrounded by all these people whom I could not reach, the wrong place at the wrong time, every cell in my body blasting, visions of torturous death running through my mind, and no idea what to do. Then Boniface kicked a chair, pointed an angry finger in my face, and bulled through the people outside.

I shut the door to the office. Jere and I were alone in the room.

"What just happened?" I gasped.

My friend's face hung slack, as if his jaw was broken.

"What's going on, Jere? What is he doing?"

"He's getting"—Jere stammered—"his people."

My heart dropped. I had an idea what that meant. I looked around. The small office had one window, with thick iron grilles covering it. Papers on the table and a chair on the floor completed the scene. There was only one way out.

"What do we do?" I asked.

Jere didn't answer my question. "I hate this place," he said. "This clinic, this ward, this village. I hate medical work. I never should have left Lusaka. I could have gone to work there. I could have been an actuary." He fell into a chair.

"What do we do?" I asked again, louder.

More yelling outside and someone pounded on the door. Both of us stared at it.

"Don't open that," Jere said.

"I'm not planning to," I responded.

But the doorknob twisted and someone pushed the door in. I had forgotten to lock it. Boniface, chin up high, glowered in the doorway. Behind him, the crowd was now enormous; it spilled off the porch into the darkness like lava carving its way down a hill and I couldn't see the end of it. In front were the drunkest, toughest-looking men from the market. They stunk of wine.

"Mr. Joshua from the American Peace Corps," Boniface said, in an even, measured tone that belied the fury in his bloodshot stare, "let me express our gratitude that you have come to our village to help us. But it is time for you to leave. Go home."

"I'm not leaving," I said.

He dropped any pretense of civility then. "You are warned!" he yelled. He turned to Jere: "Come out here!" he yelled, then he switched over to Bemba, angry words that I couldn't understand, but that incited the crowd further. Men shouted their own accusations and flailed their arms angrily at Jere and me.

Jere had gone ghastly gray. He had no response to whatever Boniface was saying. At the door, a hugely muscled man pushed his way inside and stood next to Boniface, bellowing at Jere. The shouting got louder and louder, overpowering my hearing aids and melding into one solid sound. I knew then that I was the only thing keeping them from ripping Jere limb from limb. And I knew, for the first time, how much they must have hated me. I knew I was afraid. And I knew I couldn't let them kill my friend.

I lifted my trembling hands up and over my ears, then down the back of them, switching off each hearing aid. Instantly, it was perfectly quiet. I put my hand on the chests of Boniface and the muscular man next to him and I could feel their hearts pounding under my palms.

"We need some room," I said, speaking into the silence, words my ears couldn't confirm.

Boniface's mouth made grotesque shapes. His hands moved like flames. Spit gathered at the corners of his mouth and spewed forth as he spoke. I smelled sweat and wine. I didn't see the rock until it hit my jaw.

WAITING. SITTING ON THE FLOOR OF JERE'S LIVING ROOM IN THE dark. Waiting for the men to come. Breath coming in gasps, a barricaded door, angry sounds I couldn't make out. In our hands, our handmade weapons—rakes Jere had made for hoeing his fields, two-by-fours fastened to each other in the shape of a T. Knowing that it ended here, one way or another.

The rock had been our saving grace. After it hit my face and knocked me off my feet (it was the size of a baseball), the crowd could have gone one of two ways: forward or back. The choice was theirs. They went back. From the ground, I felt their shock, their collective intake of breath. Jere pulled me up and took my hand and led me past Boniface and out of the office and through the baby-weighing area, the men parting guiltily. My jaw ached, but I'd taken worse shots playing basketball—I pretended to be more hurt than I was. Why the crowd didn't press forward and finish us off when they had the chance has never been clear to me, but I suppose for that moment they were just as afraid as we were. I kept my hearing aids off until we were halfway to Jere's.

After we reached his living room and had barricaded the door, Jere explained to me the whole lye business. Lye was cheaper than paint, and Boniface had probably rushed to paint the ward with it while we were gone so he could claim credit for the whole project. He'd stolen everything else, so why not that? But the lye ruined the ward—it was extremely toxic. It was just a stupid, stupid mistake. Patients were already dying from the fumes. And it had bonded with the cement, becoming unremovable. The ward would have to be destroyed.

But we couldn't think about that right then.

"If they try to force the door," Jere said, "the furniture will stall them, and if they try to come through the windows, we'll hit them with these." He held up his rake.

"We'll kill them," I said.

"You know what Boniface said to me just now? 'We don't want your kind here!'"

"We'll fucking kill them."

But I didn't like my chances with the rake I'd chosen. It seemed kind of flimsy. One year and seven months in the river town of Mununga, swimming, laughing, learning, playing chess, weighing babies, counseling bamayos, enduring accidents, malaria, dysentery, and a million other moments I will never forget, and it had come down to this: I wanted Jere's rake because it was bigger than mine.

"I'll give you five hundred kwacha for that," I said.

"Take it." He handed it over.

Jere's wife, thankfully, was not in Mununga; she had gone to Lusaka a few weeks earlier to tell their parents that Beauty had died. Palije, too young to grasp the intensity of the situation, slept soundly on a bamboo mat next to his father. I didn't know where Malama and Chiluba were; I worried the mob might go after them in lieu of Jere and me, just like on Christmas when two of Chitondo's friends had been killed when the mob couldn't find him. But this was different. They knew where we were. At any moment men could charge through the door, ropes in hand.

We would fight, I swore. Like lions, we would fight—they would remember the day they came for the Nyanja and the white man. I gave my new rake several practice swings.

"Careful," said Jere.

"It's heavy." I regretted asking him to switch.

We gulped from a jug of Jere's home brew. He cocked an ear toward the door. I tried to listen, too, but that wasn't much use.

"I think we're safe," Jere said.

A few seconds later, a rock sailed through the window.

Glass shattered, bursting across the floor, and the rock clattered into a corner. In rushed cool air and the noise of what had to be men shouting. We jumped up, flattened ourselves against the wall, and raised our weapons to ready position. Jere was closer to the door, and by exchanging glances we worked out that he'd get the first man in. For some reason, I started worrying then about my rake getting stuck in someone's back. I could picture it quite clearly. Palije woke up, looked at the broken window, looked at us with a perplexed expression, and started stacking pieces of glass.

"Palije!" His father hissed a warning to stay still. The kid was autistic, it finally occurred to me.

I tightened my grip on the rake. It was giving me splinters.

"Watch the window," said Jere.

"I'm watching it."

"They might come in the window, not the door."

"I'm aware of that."

Jere nodded, short quick jabs of his head. "All right, I'm nervous." His forehead dripped with sweat and he didn't have his handkerchief. "Get more ah."

I didn't hear him right. "Get more what?"

"More rah."

"More rocks?"

"Get mor ah!" he yelled.

"More what, dammit? Speak English!"

"Ahh!" Jere groaned and reached down for the bottle of banana wine. I pushed it away from him with my foot, thinking for a minute until I figured out what he had been saying.

"Sodom," I said.

Jere put his head down and started groaning—only no, he was laughing. It started as a silent chuckle, but then he dropped his rake and slid down the wall, holding his sides.

The minutes crept past and then the hours and at some point we knew we would live till morning. Mob or no mob, people in the village went to bed early and rose with the sun. In the morning we would deal with the morning, things would be different, but we were alive. We swept up the glass shards, put on extra shirts from Jere's wardrobe as it got colder, talked of what had happened, neither of us able to sleep.

That night I was in love with the sunrise before it came. Nothing was lacking. When you've been waiting for death to ram through the door, every additional minute feels more precious than all the diamonds in Zaire. It struck me that maybe this was what I had come to Africa to learn: not to save lives, not to exchange cultures, not to understand deafness or escape deafness or embrace deafness—just to be grateful for each moment. I saw that even the horror, the complete horror of Africa, spreading over the continent, hacking off limbs and heads, has an opposite and that opposite is a grace so profound that I still, many years later, have no words for it.

Jere felt it too—the terrific gratefulness that blanketed everything once our fear was lifted. All that seeking and striving and working and fighting and then this: the first cock crow of morning.

He had taken his son, sound asleep again, into his arms. Jere looked down at him now. "It would be a shame if they killed us," he said.

Another hour passed. My eyes ached with fatigue. As dawn lit up the room, the midnight feeling of everything being exactly where it needed to be began to fade. We were just two tired men sitting on a floor. And then Jere's cheeks were covered in tears.

"I'm sorry she died," I said.

"Did you see how she used to dance?"

I took his hand in mine. "I did."

Departures

Shortly after dawn the next day, the sky out the broken window a pale morning gray, Jere and I moved the furniture away from the door, took a deep breath to steel ourselves, and went outside.

The lawn was empty. Other than a dried puddle of vomit, it held no sign of the shouting, angry men from the night before. On a nearby path, women walked to market with wares to sell on their heads and infants strapped to their backs. A man, a complete stranger, walked by carrying a washbasin full of dried chisense under one arm. "Good morning, Ba Joeshua!" he called, and his wife, trailing behind him, curtsied shyly. For them nothing had changed; they had to sell their fish.

When I got to my hut, I saw that a rock had gone through a window there as well, landing on the couch and coming to rest on the center cushion. I took a quick inventory and nothing seemed to be missing except for Scoopy, but she often disappeared for a few days at a time.

Our plan: I'd fuel my bike, fill a small backpack with irreplace-ables, pick up Jere and Palije, and drive us all to Kashikishi on my motorcycle. But instead I just stumbled around the hut in a daze, trying to do three things at once, getting nothing done.

A kapaso appeared at the door, startling me. He took off his cap. "The palace," he said. "Oh nine hundred. The chief wants to see you." Then he was gone.

Malama appeared next and I immediately sent him to ask Jere if he thought I should go see the chief. He came back with the news that Jere thought I should; the palace was safe, off-limits to violence, and we could leave Mununga right after.

I changed my shirt, lay down on the couch, got up, drank some water, changed again. I washed my face, threw some clothes in a duffel bag along with a handful of books, took out the books, put them back, took out some of the clothes. Like this, an hour passed. Malama and Chiluba tried to help but gave up and just watched me. They had both spent the night with their families.

"How do I look?" I said to them when it was finally time to leave. I had put on a tie for only the second time in two years—Chris's wedding was the first.

"Very good," Chiluba said. She wrung her hands. "Isabi or inkoko today?"

"Malama's choice."

"Five hundred kwacha," she said, and I gave her the money even though we both knew I wouldn't be there for lunch. "Be careful," she added.

"Thank you," I said.

I parked my motorcycle outside the palace gate. A kapaso was waiting for me and he led me through the high thatch fence. I followed him in expecting that, having been called on such short notice, the meeting with the chief would be an intimate one, a quick face-to-face. Instead, a hundred men were gathered in and around the chief's insaka, the largest crowd I'd seen there since that first meeting after the inauguration ceremony, when the chief had yelled at the district government representatives and filled us all with hope. Every face turned toward me.

The kapaso directed me to a seat on the floor of the insaka.

The chief was already seated on his throne. Boniface, I noticed, sat two spaces to his right. After I was seated, the chief began to speak in English, thanking everyone for coming and for the help they had given him in his first year in Mununga. Then he sidetracked into a rambling denouncement of a Mansa fish company that was buying fish directly from his people without paying him his proper tribute. This was not acceptable—it was his lake, his river, his fish.

"*Ee mukwai,*" the men assented.

Finally he got down to it. "Hello, Mr. Joshua," he said, turning to me.

"Hello, Chief," I said.

He wagged a finger. "I hear you are causing problems."

"Excuse me?"

"You are causing problems," he repeated. "Why are you doing that? My people have been waiting for you to bring water for many months now. Instead you bring them trouble. Why?"

I didn't answer. Maybe things had sort of worked out like that, but I didn't think it was totally accurate.

"Why do you cause problems with my people?" he said again.

"The clinic was painted with poison," I said.

He glared down. "No. You lie."

The crowd watched us nervously. Those who knew English translated for the others. Boniface smiled from behind his gargantuan bone structure in his seat near the chief. Seeing that smile, I realized that I didn't have it in me to play snake-in-the-grass, not even with the chief. Not after last night.

"Chief, I am not a liar," I said. "I don't think you should say that."

The chief leapt from his seat. "Yes, you are a liar! And a thief!" he shouted. "Your friend Jere you follow like a monkey. He has poisoned you against my people. You steal from my people and you steal from my clinic."

"I am not a thief!" I yelled, rising to my feet.

"Sit down, umusungu!" he yelled back.

I should have just sat down, let his words roll off, and let him have this moment. Mununga's people needed a hero; they deserved a hero. The government ignored them; fishing companies took advantage of them; malaria, cholera, and the other diseases slaughtered them as efficiently as firing squads. The future was coming fast, pouring over the lake and up the road from the Copperbelt and it was unpredictable and dangerous. They needed their chief to be a hero, and to be a hero the chief needed an enemy. Enemy—that, after nineteen months, was my designated role in Mununga. But I wanted them to know that I had tried. And I just didn't know how to back off.

"Don't call me a thief," I said. "I'm not a liar. Jere is not a liar. We came here to help your people. I love Mununga. It is my home. I don't know where you get your facts, but you should check them out before you throw them in my face."

The crowd gasped. The chief rose to his feet shaking with rage, veins throbbing on his temples. His crown fell to the ground.

"Nobody yells at the Chief," he shouted. "Nobody points at the Chief! I am the Chief! Get out of here! Kapaso, take him away. Take this white man away!" But nobody moved. A chicken poked his head in the insaka and clucked through curiously. A man kicked it and it jumped away, screaming.

"Take him away," the chief repeated. "Kapaso?!"

Two thin young men in matching brown uniforms walked uncertainly toward me, they stopped with great relief when I turned and willingly started walking toward them. I took a last look around as I did. Many of the men in the crowd I knew—headman Museka, headman Kaseke, Ba Bule, and others, some I might have even called friends—but the eyes I caught quickly turned away. A hundred men averting their gaze all at once.

Jere ran over to my hut a few minutes after I got back.

"I just heard what happened," he said. "The ambulance is here. I've arranged for a ride. You go."

"You don't want me to wait for you?"

"No, go. It's best. We will meet at Kashikishi hospital."

"All right. Don't wait too long."

I put my duffel bag on the motorcycle carryall and lashed it down with rope. Malama and Chiluba watched as I got ready, Malama holding my helmet, Chiluba wiping away her tears.

"Don't cry," I said to her. "I will be fine. You will be fine."

"This is no good," she said. "Mununga is crazy. The chief is crazy. You stay far away from this place. Even me, I want to be away from this place."

I put my hand on her arm, one of the few times we ever touched. Men and women weren't supposed to touch unless they were married.

"No, it's a good place," I said. "I just made a mess of things."

I leaned down and kissed her cheek. She blushed deeply. Then she kissed me back, a shy peck.

"Go," said Jere.

I turned to Malama. Without being asked, he had wiped the dust off my helmet with his shirt. I took it from him, took off my tie and put it on his neck and told him to look after Chiluba and after Scoopy, whom I hadn't seen all morning.

"Anything inside the hut is yours," I said to him.

"Really?"

"Yes."

"Even the magazines?" he asked.

"Yes. Even them. All of them."

He thought about it for a few seconds then his head slumped down. "Ah, you keep," he said.

"Go," said Jere once more.

I was doing fifty miles an hour by the time I reached the bridge, leaning into the speed, the throttle fully open, the motorcycle's tiny engine shaking with the effort. I used the speed to slingshot up the far hill, past the turnoff to the palace and further, without stopping, right past the military checkpoint at the hilltop. The checkpoint soldiers gave me a half wave. I went another mile as fast as the bike could carry me before braking to a sharp stop beneath a jackfruit tree. There was no one on this stretch of road, not a hut in sight, and to the west you could see over the lake all the way to Zaire. Behind me, Mununga was hidden by a hill. Road dust hung in the air. I shut off the engine, took off my helmet, climbed off the bike, and screamed, until a boy appeared in the distance, walking down the side of the road toward town, leading a white goat on a leash. He stopped and turned back the way he came. Then I rode on.

JERE WAS TRANSFERRED BY THE MINISTRY OF HEALTH TO KAMBWALI, a small village seven miles south of Kashikishi, fifty miles south of Mununga. A week later I followed him there. Kambwali was a bedraggled cluster of shacks fanning across the paved Mansa-Kashikishi highway. Jere and I passed three months there, little of which was memorable. We played chess, drank wine. It was mango season and each morning I paid Palije a couple of sticks of Bazooka Joe to fill a bucket with them. He took forever, wandering from tree to tree, handling each mango like it was a new pet, turning it over and over, talking to it, tapping it against his head. When I would finally lose patience and take the bucket from him, he didn't really seem to notice. I ate the mangoes all day long, taking a bite from each and, if it wasn't top-notch, throwing it away. Then I caught a case of violent dysentery, which, if nothing else, kept me occupied for a week. When I was better I fueled up my motorcycle, tied five extra gallons of gasoline and a couple of adventurous village kids on the back, and rode straight out into the bush. There was a thin trail from the village that went through swamps and over hills, through tall woodlands and large meadows, by the sides of streams and in the middle of dry riverbeds canopied by purple-graped *musondo* trees, and into tiny primordial villages outside of time. For hours we just rode, the kids and I, further and further, to see where the trail went and to see what would get left behind.

Jere struggled to fill his days. He was used to constant activity and at Kambwali baby weighing took fifteen minutes, treating the morning line of patients a half hour. He organized the building of two new clinic latrines, the local chief saying, Great, I'll give you whatever you need, workers, tools, food—they were finished within a week. We were amazed how easy it was; we were bored to tears. Often there was nothing to do but sit and watch the road.

Chiluba and Malama arrived on a bus one morning. Chiluba looked uncomfortable; she had dressed in a beautiful blue wrap dress, one that she had bought with her first month's pay and that I had complimented her on many times, and I knew she had come to see if I would ask her to stay in Kambwali, which meant, to come inside my home and live as my wife. But I couldn't do that. We'd never had that kind of relationship, and I don't think it was what she really wanted either. And Chiluba saw that I couldn't and left after lunch and married Moses Kapela the very next day, the toutboy who had allegedly killed his father.

Malama stayed a little longer, but he was lonely for Mununga too, for his friends, for the river, the bustling market full of teenage girls. After a few nights he left as well. Before he did, he hesitantly told me in his honest way what had happened to Scoopy—she had been killed, kicked to death by the mob on that last long night.

About three weeks after evacuating from Mununga, I went back there one last time, in the company of Administration, four soldiers, two drivers, a Land Crusier, and a flatbed truck. Chris came along too, out of curiosity—my new village was only ten miles from his so we saw each other often and he knew about what had happened. First, we stopped by my old hut and loaded the pickup with my bed and mattress, my cooking utensils, and whatever clothes I'd left there. Then we went to the clinic to gather any materials left over from the project. I was sure all the supplies and tools would be gone, but strangely enough, nothing had been touched; in fact, there seemed to be more cement bags lined against the walls than when we had left. As we loaded the truck a kapaso approached and said that the chief would like to see me, so Administration and I left for the palace, taking two soldiers and leaving Chris to load the trucks.

At the palace, the chief was bashful and apologetic. They missed me, he said, they wanted me back—I had been so energetic! And friendly! Visiting all the villages!—And look, he added, I know it was Jere who filled your mind with poisonous ideas; now that Jere is gone, things will be better. You see? You must come back.

I kept quiet, letting Administration handle it. He listened amiably to the chief's explanations, flattered him for his hospitality, promised to think very seriously about his proposals. The chief was extremely encouraged by this response. For the first time since I'd arrived to Zambia, I was deeply impressed with Administration's skill.

"We're never putting another volunteer here," he said as we left. "That was a mistake."

On the way out of town we stopped by the post office so I could check for mail. There was nothing there for me save for the smiling postmaster. He was a friend, sad to see me go, and beneath the green national flag fluttering on the flagpole we ran through the greetings and salutations and good-byes. As we did, a couple of the soldiers, bored with nothing to do all day, fired their machine guns in the air. From the post office you could see across the valley and we watched as, across the river, hundreds of people ran panicked through the market, away from the crack of the gunshot. Their stampede kicked up a huge plume of dust that rose and hovered a hundred feet above the village like a final curtain. The soldiers cheered and high-fived. We climbed back into the

Land Cruiser and the last soldier to board took a stun grenade out of his shirt pocket, lit it, and placed it in the middle of the road. We drove slowly up the hill, our eyes on the grenade. It had a really long fuse and took a long, long time to burn, so long I thought it might be a dud. And then a bent-over old man wearing a red beret and dragging a walking stick crossed the road right where the grenade was, probably heading home as the day was getting on; he made it halfway across the road and the grenade blew. It threw him backward, flat out across the road. The soldiers laughed uproariously. Chris and I stared at each other in total disbelief. The Land Cruiser zoomed through the checkpoint. I never saw Mununga again.

WHEN ADMINISTRATION SUGGESTED I SPEND MY LAST THREE MONTHS of service in Kabwe, teaching the class of deaf children full-time, I thought, why not. A car came and I loaded up my stuff, leaving my cookware and my bed, the most beautiful thing I owned in Africa, for Jere.

This was good-bye. We stood on a dirt field between the Kambwali clinic and the road, the bright sun shining down on us, not knowing what to say to each other. A Peace Corps Land Cruiser with a driver and several other volunteers had come to gather me; their arrival attracted a crowd and Jere and I felt uncomfortable with our private feelings among all these people.

"Remember me," Jere said.

Remember? How could I ever forget? I will meet other men, remarkable men in this life, but you, there will never be anyone like you. Do you know how much you are? . . . but I didn't say this. I was there in the field saying good-bye, but I was being played by someone else.

"Give me your address in America," Jere said.

That scared me; it was too final, and America—I couldn't imagine it, couldn't believe I'd ever return or that it would have me. "No need to, Jere," I said. "I'll come visit next month and you'll get it then."

But I didn't come; I got malaria again. I was tired. The journey was too long. There was work. I got lost. I made a mistake.

Behind him a dozen barefoot children milled about, staring at the car. Kambwali children, they were largely unfamiliar, and for a second, I thought I saw Beauty in their midst, running just to run as village children like to do. But it was only another child. Jere's eyes teared up; I looked away, my own tears buried deep inside.

I've tried to find Jere. In the years since I saw him last, the disintegration of Africa has accelerated in ways neither of us foresaw. Wars, plagues, corruption, genocide; millions of people have been killed, millions more have been displaced. I've sent letters, placed newspaper ads. Last I heard Jere finally did leave the village and moved to Lusaka and there, idealistic and brave as ever, he got involved in organizing labor unions. Dangerous work. I hope he is still alive.

I LAST SAW CHRIS ABOUT FIVE YEARS LATER; WE HAD LUNCH AT AN ALL-you-can-eat buffet in Cape Cod. It was early fall and Chris was catching the ferry to Nantucket Island where he worked as a carpenter and Helen worked at a Stop-N-Shop and I was drifting through the area, in an old gray Taurus that had no windshield wipers. Helen, pregnant with their third child, was already on the island so it was just Chris and me.

Chris told me that after months of searching he had tracked down his birth mother in northern Kentucky. She had been in her forties and unmarried when she had Chris and for many difficult reasons decided to put him up for adoption. Their reunion was powerful. For twenty minutes, neither of them could speak they were so overcome, then they started a conversation that's continued to this day.

I walked Chris to his ferry and we shook hands. The salty ocean air whipped across our faces, making a *whup-whup* sound in my hearing aids. We had moved on to other lives and the one we had shared together seemed unbelievable. I had one more question.

"Do you ever think about—"

"Every day," Chris said.

The three months in Kabwe passed in a blur. I had an apartment near the mine and Kennedy, my questioning student, moved in, along with Rave, my old basketball-playing buddy from the Teachers College. At Broadway School, not much had changed: I fought with the headmaster, the teacher Mr. Mwelva took beer naps, Maba stole pencils, Miriam still planned her movie career, and Kennedy still wanted explanations for why his life wasn't more like mine. The whole thing made me tired.

Then there was an exit interview, a physical, a check-up with a dentist, and another round of good-byes with the deaf unit. Miriam handed me a note at my last class that she had written and had the class sign. It read:

Your love comforts my heart.
I will see Margaret Monday
I have snaps will bring and deaf
My friend, I have Broadway School.

Then I was at the airport, boarding a plane. It was windy. The plane sat in the middle of the tarmac, far from the terminal, and we drove the Peace Corps Land Cruiser right up to the rollaway stairs and sat waiting on the hood until the last possible moment.

And then I was gone.

I reappeared in Frankfurt for an hour, then at JFK. My three brothers picked me up and we fought the Van Wyck traffic to get to my aunt's in time for dinner. I don't remember what we talked about in the car. I do remember, at dinner, being speechless at the size of the portions and at the amount of food that went uneaten.

The meat on my plate spilled off the edges. Next to it were piled mixed vegetables and mashed potatoes scooped hollow and filled with brown gravy. A carrot floated in the gravy like a boat on a lake. I nudged it in little circles. Conversations flew around the table like punctured balloons, faster than I had remembered, way too fast for my ears to follow: politics, filial disputes, the stock market, a joke about pianists, a series of toasts I couldn't follow. Everyone had a lot to say. The women wore makeup. The silverware gleamed. There were eight different lamps in the dining room alone.

The Rain

I take the boy from the bus with me. He visits me at night, in dreams that are like slow-motion explosions of light. *How is this?* I say to him at each stop in my travels. *Did you see that eagle? Can you taste this cool water? Thank you for this. Thank you for this.* To others, I complained about my circumstances often enough; about the injuries I racked up, about being broke, about my hearing, which worsened and worsened for years. But from another perspective these challenges were treasures to savor. *Thank you for this.*

Way back before I joined Peace Corps, when I was at Gallaudet learning sign, I made the acquaintance of a deaf-blind man. Evenings there, I ran around the school's cinder track and often met this man who walked laps at the same time. He was about fifty, with a heavy pear-shaped body and a big head perpetually cocked smiling toward the sky. He held his hands on mine when I signed in order to understand me. He may have been a Ph.D. student for all I knew. I didn't have much to say, but he liked the company. He couldn't hear and couldn't see and just pumped away in endless circles and was happy. When a thunderstorm vibrated in the distance and the warm summer rain fell, he was even happier. He would pump along for hours then, head tilted up even farther, catching the rain with his face.

The point is: the rain, the face.

I've tried not to get upset about unimportant things. I wouldn't want the boy to feel cheated. He continues to travel with me. He sees me doing all the thinking things through and figuring things out—and he says slow down. He says: It's just a dream, a gift. It's not who you are. I tell him: But this world is burning itself in the flames of its own selfishness and men kill other men and back in Africa they are rounding up the children and taking them to the woods.

I know, he says. I know. But feel the rain on your face.

acknowledgments

Thanks to my generous, brave, and amazing parents and to my three brothers, the greatest brothers anyone could possibly ask for.

Thanks to Anna Jane for everything.

Dante Paradiso, Chris Boerboom, Carl Voss, Amy Meckler, Cat Onder, and Jennifer Ivers helped tremendously by reading drafts, making suggestions, and just being the phenomenal people they are. Gary and Deana Gurney took me in for a summer so I could start this; later, Vicki Morgan and Ralph Erenzo also gave me a place to write. Deborah Emin provided encouragement, and David and Marcia Radin, as always, provided perspective and green tea. Thank you.

Thanks to the United States Peace Corps for the opportunity. I was lucky to serve as a volunteer with Chris Haydon, Sarina Ochoa, and Roslyn Docktor (who helped immeasurably with this book) and am a better person for knowing them.

Thanks to my agent Heather Schroder at ICM and Margot Meyers, for taking a chance on me. Thanks to Supurna Banerjee, my editor at Henry Holt. Her dedication and skill are extraordinary and made this book what it is.

And to Jere, Chiluba, and Malama, for all we did and shared together, this book is my thanks.

Pano nkwanke; ni pa kuboko.
Let yourself drop, I will catch you in my arm.

Augustine Jere and Josh Swiller, May 1994

about the author

Josh Swiller was born with moderate hearing loss and was deaf by age four. A graduate of Yale University, he has had a wide variety of careers: forest ranger, carpenter, slipper salesman, raw food chef, Zen noviate, journalist, and teacher among other things. In August 2005, he had successful surgery for a cochlear implant and partially recovered his hearing. Swiller now speaks often on issues facing mainstreamed deaf individuals, and currently works at a hospice in Brooklyn, New York. Visit his Web site at www .joshswiller.com.